THE
1991 YEARBOOK
OF THE
NCAA
BASKETBALL
TOURNAMENT

Also by Jim Savage:

THE ENCYCLOPEDIA OF
THE NCAA BASKETBALL TOURNAMENT:
The Complete Independent Guide to College Basketball's
Championship Event

THE
1991 YEARBOOK
OF THE
NCAA
BASKETBALL
TOURNAMENT

JIM SAVAGE

A DELL TRADE PAPERBACK

A DELL TRADE PAPERBACK

Published by
Dell Publishing
a division of
Bantam Doubleday Dell Publishing Group, Inc.
666 Fifth Avenue
New York, New York 10103

The trademark Dell® is registered in the U.S. Patent and Trademark Office.

ISBN: 0-440-50425-2

Printed in the United States of America

Published simultaneously in Canada

November 1991

10 9 8 7 6 5 4 3 2 1

RRH

ACKNOWLEDGMENTS

To all those who helped me fast break this book into reality:

My wife, Nancy, who edited, critiqued, and supported me through every turn in the road.

Joe Sklarin, who tirelessly tinkered to turn the book into a smooth running machine.

Leslie Schnur, Jill Lamar, John Mooney, Richard Hunt, Barry Porter, and the rest of the good people at Dell whose continuing enthusiasm and encouragement is invaluable to my state of mind.

The many helpful people at the NCAA, most especially statman Gary Johnson, who went the extra mile to help me get it right.

The sports information directors who helped me fill in the blanks and make the book whole.

The players and coaches who made the tournament memorable, and most especially those whose honesty and willingness to talk were a breath of fresh air.

To my friend John Krasnow,
whose beautiful music fell silent
much too soon.

TABLE OF CONTENTS

PART 1

The 1991 Tournament

PART 2

The Conferences

PART 3

All-Time Tournament Records

THE
1991 YEARBOOK
OF THE
NCAA
BASKETBALL
TOURNAMENT

✪ 53 YEARS OF NCAA CHAMPIONSHIP ✪
GAME RESULTS

YEAR	CHAMPION	SCORE	RUNNER-UP	SITE	ATTENDANCE
1991	DUKE	72–65	KANSAS	INDIANAPOLIS, IN	47,100
1990	UNLV	103–73	DUKE	DENVER, CO	17,765
1989	MICHIGAN	80–79*	SETON HALL	SEATTLE, WA	39,187
1988	KANSAS	83–79	OKLAHOMA	KANSAS CITY, MO	16,392
1987	INDIANA	74–73	SYRACUSE	NEW ORLEANS, LA	64,959
1986	LOUISVILLE	72–69	DUKE	DALLAS, TX	16,493
1985	VILLANOVA	66–64	GEORGETOWN	LEXINGTON, KY	23,124
1984	GEORGETOWN	84–75	HOUSTON	SEATTLE, WA	38,471
1983	N.C. STATE	54–52	HOUSTON	ALBUQUERQUE, NM	17,327
1982	N. CAROLINA	63–62	GEORGETOWN	NEW ORLEANS, LA	61,612
1981	INDIANA	63–50	N. CAROLINA	PHILADELPHIA, PA	18,276
1980	LOUISVILLE	59–54	UCLA	INDIANAPOLIS, IN	16,637
1979	MICHIGAN ST.	75–64	INDIANA ST.	SALT LAKE CITY, UT	15,410
1978	KENTUCKY	94–88	DUKE	ST. LOUIS, MO	18,721
1977	MARQUETTE	67–59	N. CAROLINA	ATLANTA, GA	16,086
1976	INDIANA	86–68	MICHIGAN	PHILADELPHIA, PA	17,540
1975	UCLA	92–85	KENTUCKY	SAN DIEGO, CA	15,151
1974	N.C. STATE	76–64	MARQUETTE	GREENSBORO, NC	15,742
1973	UCLA	87–66	MEMPHIS ST.	ST. LOUIS, MO	19,301
1972	UCLA	81–76	FLORIDA ST.	LOS ANGELES, CA	15,063
1971	UCLA	68–62	VILLANOVA	HOUSTON, TX	31,765
1970	UCLA	80–69	JACKSONVILLE	COLLEGE PARK, MD	14,380
1969	UCLA	92–72	PURDUE	LOUISVILLE, KY	18,669
1968	UCLA	78–55	N. CAROLINA	LOS ANGELES, CA	14,438
1967	UCLA	79–64	DAYTON	LOUISVILLE, KY	18,892
1966	TEXAS WESTERN	72–65	KENTUCKY	COLLEGE PARK, MD	14,253
1965	UCLA	91–80	MICHIGAN	PORTLAND, OR	13,204
1964	UCLA	98–83	DUKE	KANSAS CITY, MO	10,864
1963	LOYOLA-CHICAGO	60–58*	CINCINNATI	LOUISVILLE, KY	19,153
1962	CINCINNATI	71–59	OHIO STATE	LOUISVILLE, KY	18,469
1961	CINCINNATI	70–65*	OHIO STATE	KANSAS CITY, MO	10,700
1960	OHIO STATE	75–55	CALIFORNIA	SAN FRANCISCO, CA	14,500
1959	CALIFORNIA	71–70	WEST VIRGINIA	LOUISVILLE, KY	18,498
1958	KENTUCKY	84–72	SEATTLE	LOUISVILLE, KY	18,803
1957	N. CAROLINA	54–53#	KANSAS	KANSAS CITY, MO	10,500
1956	SAN FRANCISCO	83–71	IOWA	EVANSTON, IL	10,600
1955	SAN FRANCISCO	77–63	LA SALLE	KANSAS CITY, MO	10,500
1954	LA SALLE	92–76	BRADLEY	KANSAS CITY, MO	10,500
1953	INDIANA	69–68	KANSAS	KANSAS CITY, MO	10,500
1952	KANSAS	80–63	ST. JOHN'S	SEATTLE, WA	10,700
1951	KENTUCKY	68–58	KANSAS ST.	MINNEAPOLIS, MN	15,348
1950	CCNY	71–68	BRADLEY	NEW YORK, NY	18,142
1949	KENTUCKY	46–36	OKLAHOMA A&M	SEATTLE, WA	10,600
1948	KENTUCKY	58–42	BAYLOR	NEW YORK, NY	16,174
1947	HOLY CROSS	58–47	OKLAHOMA	NEW YORK, NY	18,445
1946	OKLAHOMA A&M	43–40	N. CAROLINA	NEW YORK, NY	18,479
1945	OKLAHOMA A&M	49–45	NYU	NEW YORK, NY	18,035
1944	UTAH	42–40*	DARTMOUTH	NEW YORK, NY	15,000
1943	WYOMING	46–34	GEORGETOWN	NEW YORK, NY	13,300
1942	STANFORD	53–38	DARTMOUTH	KANSAS CITY, MO	6,500
1941	WISCONSIN	39–34	WASHINGTON ST.	KANSAS CITY, MO	7,219
1940	INDIANA	60–42	KANSAS	KANSAS CITY, MO	10,000
1939	OREGON	46–33	OHIO STATE	EVANSTON, IL	5,500

* Overtime   # Triple Overtime

PART I

The 1991 Tournament

1991 TOURNAMENT HIGHLIGHTS

The crowd at Cameron Indoor Stadium went stone-cold crazy. A thousand miles away, in Indianapolis' Hoosier Dome, their beloved Duke Blue Devils had just overcome the evil monster from UNLV, and the clean-cut spirit of young America could once again sleep soundly, except of course for the hangover that would come tomorrow from all the beer consumed tonight.

Fifty-two NCAA tournaments were played before March 1991. Duke had come close many times, but had never before brought home the bragging rights to American college hoops. While the Blue Devils held the dubious record of most Final Four appearances without a championship—eight—what was particularly galling was that North Carolina, the hated Tar Heels from down the road in Chapel Hill, and the upstart Wolfpack from North Carolina State had each won the whole shebang not once, but twice.

Now, though, on March 29, 1991, all the dreams of Blue Devils past and present were focused on Christian Laettner, Bobby Hurley, the Hill boys (Grant and Thomas), and their teammates. The evening's events had finally brought Coach Mike Krzyzewski's quiet dynasty into sharp focus—not since the days of UCLA's legendary John Wooden had a school reached the Final Four five times in six years.

Coach K's strategic gifts were recognized almost twenty-five years earlier, when he played point guard for Bob Knight at West Point. After serving out his military commitment as a coach, he resumed his apprenticeship under Knight as an Indiana graduate assistant in 1975. He then returned to Army as head coach, and five years later moved on to Duke. Since 1986, his program had been one of the most successful in the nation, with an average of over 29 wins a year. He had only one thing left to accomplish: to be placed on the same level as Knight and his peers, he still had to lead his Blue Devils to the brass ring.

Coach K, whose buttoned-down image was symbolized by a product endorsement portfolio including not only sneakers but also financial services, was about to be transformed in the light of victory into a genius of reserve, tenacity, cunning, and consistency. He calmed his players down, reminding them that despite their monumental victory over UNLV it was still too soon to celebrate. Meanwhile, back home, the Duke campus went wild.

The university in Durham, North Carolina, was known far and wide for its towering chapel and Gothic arches, its 55-acre manicured Sarah P.

Duke Gardens, its perennial Top 10 ranking—not just in basketball, but also in medicine, law, and business—and of course, Cameron Indoor and its "crazies." Since Cameron's inauguration in January 1940, just months after the first NCAA tournament, the Dukies had compiled a record of better than four victories in every five games at home in the arena described by Dick Vitale of ABC as "the greatest college basketball environment in the country" and by Al McGuire of NBC as "a zoo."

Now, just moments before Easter Sunday, Duke was one victory away from claiming its first national title. They had finally exorcised the UNLV demon that caused Bobby Hurley to dream of sharks the previous summer. To make the moment even sweeter, hated North Carolina had lost in the dome that evening, to Kansas. And the Tar Heels' venerable Dean Smith had been unceremoniously ejected from that semifinal game in its final seconds.

Before the tournament began, a Duke-Kansas finale seemed almost out of the question. Kansas had lost four of the five starters from its 1990 Top 10 team. After the school was placed on NCAA probation following their 1987 national title run, two of the Jayhawks' key 1988 recruits had backed out of their commitments and gone on to star elsewhere (Harold Miner at USC and Thomas Hill at Duke). And their top 1989 recruit, Chris Lindley, had lost a foot in an accident before he even arrived in Lawrence. Despite it all, the Jayhawks clawed their way through a surprisingly successful 1990–91 regular season, finishing in a tie for the Big Eight lead and just outside the nation's Top 10. But in mid-March they still looked eminently beatable, having had a tough time against Colorado before losing to Nebraska in the second round of the postseason Big Eight tournament.

Come NCAA tournament time, Kansas found itself in the tough Southeast regional, where Nolan Richardson's Arkansas Razorbacks were expected to fight it out for a Final Four spot with Bob Knight's Indiana Hoosiers. Despite a home loss to UNLV, the Razorbacks were still considered the deepest and most talented team in the country, outside of Nevada. Richardson's squad played a scorching, full-court game—"forty minutes of hell"—that wore down their opponents. If they had a weakness, it was an inclination to get rattled and lose their concentration in close games, along with the tendency of their only quality big man—soft-handed, hotheaded, 275-pound Oliver Miller—to get into foul trouble.

Professor Bob Knight's No. 2–seeded Hoosiers, despite having only one senior on the entire squad, had lost just four games all season, and only one—to Ohio State at home—by more than three points. When the draw was announced, pundits all across America overwhelmingly predicted that the Arkansas-Indiana winner would be the most likely candidate to dethrone UNLV. If Arkansas prevailed, it would set up a rematch of the midseason rumble in Fayetteville (where the Rebels blew by the home team in the opening minutes of the second half), only this time Arkansas was determined to change the outcome. If Indiana won, it would be a storybook Hoosier victory, with Bob Knight bringing his young team to its peak at just the right moment, using his master's discipline and guile to outlast the powerful Razorbacks and emerge— back home again in Indiana—before 40,000 fanatics for the Final Four. For America, for Hoosiers, and especially for CBS (which had forked over a cool billion to the NCAA for seven years of tournament telecasts), the anticipated final confrontation between Knight's Hoosiers and Tarkanian's Runnin' Rebels would be a dream come true.

After Arkansas and Indiana, Kansas was an afterthought. They were the region's No. 3 seed, so they couldn't be dismissed out of hand. Still, the perception remained that they were nothing more than a good, solid Round of Sixteen team. They didn't have enough size, athletic ability, or fire in the belly to go further. Coached by forty-year-old native North Carolinian Roy Williams, they were a team built in the mold of their coach's own mentor, North Carolina's living legend, Dean Smith. After ten years as a Smith assistant, Williams had taken over a program that was both highly successful (the defending national champions) and in deep trouble (under NCAA probation). Though he was in just his third year at Kansas, he'd already made his mark by maintaining the program's competitiveness in his first season and leading them to a No. 1 ranking through much of his second. Despite their lack of team size and speed, Coach Williams had instilled in his 1991 squad a strong work ethic and team concept—his players invariably made the extra pass on offense and helped out on defense—that carried them into the tournament.

In the first round, the Jayhawks had trouble getting by New Orleans, but the Privateers, led by center Ervin Johnson, ran out of magic at crunch time; next Kansas needed a strong second half to put away Pitt— which brought them to Charlotte and a confrontation with Professor Knight and his Hoosiers.

It wasn't really much of a confrontation. From the opening tip the Jayhawks dominated. They dove for loose balls, crashed the boards, and attacked favored Indiana on both ends of the court. After seven and a half minutes the score was 26–6 and the game was all but over. "Kansas came out and played like you really want a team to play," said Knight as he graciously bowed out after his worst tournament defeat ever.

Arkansas center Oliver Miller was disappointed with his team's next opponent. "I wanted to go out and brutally beat Indiana, Arkansas-style," he said without a trace of doubt. Now, he continued, Kansas would "have to take the brutal beating Indiana was going to take."

At the start of the regional final, Miller's forecast seemed right on the mark. Arkansas jumped into a quick 17–6 lead and seemed headed for an early knockout. But the Jayhawks hung tough, fought back, and even took a momentary 29–27 lead with six minutes left in the half. Then Arkansas, led by a turbocharged Todd Day, counterattacked with 15 straight points. The score was 47–35 at the half.

But the Jayhawks wouldn't give up. "It's not going to be forty minutes of hell," Williams had told his players in a pregame speech, "it's going to be eighty, because that's the way we're going to go right back at them." At halftime the usually laconic coach was not so laid back. "I didn't throw any chairs or cuss anyone out," he said, "but I was upset."

Kansas came out with a vengeance, opening the second half with an eight-point burst and tying the score at 51 before four minutes had passed. Arkansas regrouped, with Day scoring his first points of the second half to give the Razorbacks a 62–57 lead. With the score 62–61 and 9:10 left, Kansas coach Williams took Terry Brown and Mark Randall out of the game with four fouls each.

Despite having their two top scorers on the bench, the Jayhawks proceeded to make the trash-talking Razorbacks eat their words. Led by Alonzo Jamison, who went over and around Miller time and again for seven of his game-high 26 points, Kansas destroyed the disoriented Southwest Conference champs by scoring 26 of the next 37 points. When it was over, still another Kansas role player, future law student Mike Maddox, pronounced the game "forty minutes of heaven." The badly beaten Razorbacks were on their way home to Fayetteville and the Jayhawks were on their way to Indianapolis.

On the surface, the road to the Final Four looked much smoother for Roy Williams' mentor and his North Carolina Tar Heels. In fact, the Eastern regional became known as the Dean Smith Invitational after five of the top eight seeds (including No. 2 Syracuse) were knocked out in the first round. The Tar Heels were hot (they'd massacred Duke 96–74 for the ACC championship), deep (their five blue-chip freshmen, touted in the press as the greatest recruiting class ever, sat on the bench as they learned Smith's system), smart, and disciplined. Everyone thought Carolina would breeze through to Indy. They had no problems with Northeastern and Villanova, and used their full ten-man rotation to wear down stubborn Eastern Michigan in the regional semis. With an average 25-point victory margin, everything was going exactly as planned. Except that they didn't count on Temple.

John Chaney's Owls had struggled to make the tournament, and were generally expected to go quietly back to Philly after an early loss. Three years earlier, the expectations had been much greater. Back then they were ranked No. 1 and a contender for the national title. But their freshman phenom, Mark Macon, had self-destructed against Duke in the regional final, burying himself and his team in the Jersey swamp with pitiful 6-for-29 shooting. Still, Chaney never lost faith, and in 1991 Macon paid him back.

The Owls blew by favored Purdue in their opener (with Macon in a supporting role), and then played Richmond. Dick Tarrant's Spiders, the lowest-seeded non-play-in team in the field of 64, had worked their butts off to become the first fifteen-seed ever to win a tournament game. Their startling victory over Big East regular-season champ Syracuse shouldn't have been such a surprise, though. It was their third major tournament upset since 1984, more proof (if any was needed) that their coach is one of the game's genuine masters.

Against Temple, the wily Tarrant created a new offense to attack the Owls' heralded match-up zone defense: he unleashed his secret weapon, the season-long nonscoring threat Chris Fleming, for seven three-pointers. Finally, Chaney started yelling at his players to put the clamps on the Spiders' bomber. "But Coach," they said, "you told us not to worry about him." Chaney responded, "Don't listen to me. Just get him."

After taking Richmond, the Philadelphians returned to the scene of their 1988 massacre, the Meadowlands, for a game against Eddie Sutton's big, bad Big Eight powerhouse from Oklahoma State. Macon was the difference; every time the Owls needed him to come through, he did. Finally, with the game deadlocked at the end of regulation, he scored his team's first six overtime points on the way to a 72–63 Temple victory.

With each game Macon grew more confident, more mature, and more of a leader. In the regional final, after North Carolina raced out to a 10–0 lead, Macon took over, bagging 15 of his team's first 16 points to bring Temple back into the game. In the second half, when the Tar Heels built their lead back to double figures, it was again Macon who led the Owls back, finally hitting a trey with 9.5 seconds left to bring his team to within 1. After Carolina's King Rice converted a one-and-one, Temple raced downcourt. With a little over a second left, Macon put it up from deep. "Good!" he cried, but the ball bounced off the rim, just short.

A week later Chaney, a spectator at the Final Four, was still basking in the afterglow of his team's unexpected success. His face lit up as he spoke about his star pupil. "Macon's a rare kid," he said, smiling, "who listens to old folks."

Dean Smith was happy too. For, unlike Chaney's Owls and 59 other teams, his Heels were still alive.

Kansas may have looked like a bit of a gate-crasher, but neither they nor the other three invitees to the hoedown at the Hoosier Dome even remotely resembled Cinderella. Since the NCAA inaugurated its big dance with eight teams in 1939, Kansas, North Carolina, Duke, and UNLV had been invited a total of 69 times, compiling a combined won-lost record of 141–74 with 28 Final Four appearances and five titles (only Duke had never been national champs).

There was nobody in Indy like tournament first timers St. Francis of

Pennsylvania, Georgia State, Coastal Carolina, or Wisconsin–Green Bay. The St. Francis Red Flash, led by Altoona's 5–10 Academic All-American Mike Iuzzolino, had the steam to stay with nationally ranked Arizona, but the lack of a pep band (they had to borrow Seton Hall's) and blue-chip talent did them in in the end. Georgia State's Crimson Panthers were ranked No. 235 (out of 296) in the computer ratings before they won the Trans-America tournament and an automatic bid. And after a break from the NCAA allowed their star, Chris Collier, to play in the first round (his religious beliefs forbid physical activity from sundown Friday to sundown Saturday), they were beating Arkansas 15–6. But once the Razorbacks realized the game had started, they outscored the Panthers by 50 points.

In other long-shot action, miraculous shooting by Brian Penny of the Coastal Carolina Chanticleers (named after a rooster in Chaucer's *Canterbury Tales*) led his team from 18 back to within 3 against Indiana, before the Big Ten powerhouse pulled away in the final minutes.

Another Big Ten power, Michigan State, survived an even bigger scare in their game against Wisconsin–Green Bay. The Fighting Phoenix, led by Coach Dick Bennett's son Tony and a bunch of kids the Big Ten didn't want, held a 56–52 lead with four minutes left. But Spartan All-American Steve Smith scored his team's last nine points, including a buzzer-beating 21-foot jumper, to escape with a 61–58 victory.

All in all, despite a few nail-biters, an upset here and there, and a couple of great matchups (notably CBS's prime-time Friday night first-round chess match between two wily old masters, Pete Carril of Princeton and Rollie Massimino of Villanova), the early rounds went much as expected, with thirteen of the sixteen top-seeded teams making it to the regionals and the four tournament perennials moving on to Indianapolis.

The first semifinal, a contest Kansas alumnus Dean Smith self-deprecatingly called the "preliminary" game, featured one of the most talked-about matchups of the entire tournament, with the teacher (El Deano) and student (just plain Roy) going head to head. The two coaches' systems were almost mirror images; each employed a motion offense that stressed hitting the open man, a variety of defenses that started with a pressure man-to-man, and a philosophy that revolved around teamwork, selflessness, and responsibility. Despite his respect for Coach Smith, however, Williams conceded nothing. His team came to play.

At first it looked like the bigger, stronger Tar Heels would have an easy time of it, as they took a 24–15 lead midway through the first half. Rick Fox had 7 points, and freshman Eric Montross, coming in off the bench, was a dominating force under the boards.

After Williams reminded his players how they'd gotten so far, the Jayhawks regrouped and brought their intensity up a notch. They became more aggressive on defense, with Adonis Jordan picking up North Carolina point guard King Rice at halfcourt, and they began to force the Tar Heels into taking bad shots. On the offensive end Kansas became more patient, moving without the ball, waiting for the good shot. Carolina, caught off-guard by the Jayhawks' quickness and aggressiveness, were forced into turnovers. And despite their size advantage, they also found themselves outhustled and beaten under the boards. They lost their poise, and then the lead. Finally a frustrated Coach Smith, incensed at a foul call on Pete Chilcutt, was whistled for a technical by referee Pete Pavia. By halftime, Kansas had run off 24 of the last 33 points and was up by 9.

In the second half, Carolina pulled to within a point with 8:30 left to play, but they couldn't get over the top. With their season high scorer, Rick Fox, throwing up bricks from all over the court, they missed three straight chances to take the lead and didn't score for almost four minutes. By then Kansas was firmly back in control. Finally, with 35 seconds left and the Jayhawks holding a 5-point lead, Fox fouled out. As the Jayhawks' fans (joined by Duke's Carolina-haters) waved good-bye to Fox, Smith sauntered out of the coaches' box and walked toward the scorers' table with Fox's replacement. "How much time do I have," he asked referee Pavia once, twice, then a third time, in an attempt to stall his substitution and ice the foul shooter. Pavia's response was to turn around and hit Smith with a second technical. In Dean's 926th game as North Carolina's coach, he was thrown out for the third time!

The Tar Heel coach walked over to the Jayhawk bench, shook hands with Williams and all the Kansas players, and left the court. Seconds later the game was over, and the brilliant, gutty defensive performance of the Jayhawks (holding a team that had been shooting better than 52 percent for the tournament to 38 percent) was all but forgotten. In the runway to the locker room, a screaming Carolina assistant, Bill Guthridge, raced after Pavia and was slammed against the wall by the Indianapolis police. Several Tar Heel players, in an attempt to protect Guthridge, joined in the fray.

Later, after Smith told his side of the story and Kansas coach Williams called the referee's action "ridiculous," NCAA officials announced that Pavia was simply enforcing a rule (almost universally ignored in recent years) prohibiting coaches from leaving the coaching box. They then refused to allow the ref to tell his version to the press.

North Carolina's season was over. In three games, Kansas had chopped down three of the five top-rated teams in the country. The Jayhawks' brilliant play, which had already been upstaged by the inexplicable ejection of the dean of college coaches, was about to be upstaged again—this time by the one truly miraculous event of the entire tournament. Duke, which had been humbled by the Tar Heels in the ACC tournament final but had recovered quickly enough to sail through the Midwest regional with four consecutive double-digit victories, was about to face the undefeated, virtually untested, UNLV Runnin' Rebels.

Vegas had been touted all season long as one of the greatest teams in history. Quinn Buckner, a key member of major college basketball's last undefeated national champion, the 1976 Indiana Hoosiers, declared unequivocally that the Runnin' Rebels were the "best group I've ever seen to come out of college basketball, bar none." But there were dissenting voices too. The legendary UCLA coach, John Wooden, whose team won seven consecutive titles between 1967 and 1973, took a wait-and-see position, remarking as to how lots of teams had won one in a row. And besides, opposing fans in Tucson, Seattle, and Indianapolis muttered, even if the Rebels were that good it was only because they were "the best team money can buy."

Playing UNLV, it was widely believed, was like being a Christian fed to the lions. In the 1990 final, Vegas had handed Duke the most humiliating defeat in the history of the championship game. And in their 34 wins since, they hadn't been seriously threatened even once.

But the question persisted: Who were really the Christians, and who were the lions? For an entire year, the pressure on the UNLV players had been unrelenting. It wasn't just that they were expected to repeat and go down in history as one of the all-time great teams. Even more, it was the constant need to defend themselves against the outside world. For the Runnin' Rebels, the presumption of innocence did not hold; as a team, their collective reputation was awash in innuendo and unfounded charges.

All the top players on the UNLV team were kids from the inner city who grew up with few of the advantages most of their college-student peers took for granted. On top of that, their coach was a known rebel with a not-undeserved reputation for recruiting the most marginal of students at UNLV. They were, as a result, not only the biggest tournament favorites in over a decade, but also, as jazz great Charles Mingus would say, "beneath the underdog"—they couldn't win no matter what they did.

Rebel point guard Greg Anthony knew, despite the portrayal of his squad as one that got by on superior natural athleticism, that their success was grounded elsewhere. "We don't rely on our athletic ability," he said. "If we did, we wouldn't work on our fundamentals so much." As his team was about to board the charter plane that took them back from the regionals in Seattle to Las Vegas, he added, "We've all succeeded because of our individual talents being in communion with each other. We realize that the only way you're ever truly successful is making others around you successful."

When asked about UNLV's reputation for aggressive, physical, intimidating, and taunting play, he responded softly, "You have to realize the situation we've been in the last couple of years—as the ones who've been hunted. Teams are always going to try to get you out of the right frame of mind, the mental focus that's made you successful." As he left to join his teammates on the plane, Anthony concluded, "It's not fair, but we really can't control the perceptions others have of us. We've learned to not allow that to affect us individually or as a team. We've basically relied on each other."

Under the constant scrutiny of both the NCAA and the press, the Rebels responded with aloofness, even unapproachability, and a defensiveness that appeared arrogant. All of which made them seem even more suspect to their detractors.

The controversy that combined with their winning streak to define the Rebels' season was set off long before a single player on the 1991 squad completed grade school. Back in 1977, the NCAA placed UNLV on probation for a series of violations; the enforcement committee also recommended that Coach Tarkanian be relieved of his athletic-department duties during the probationary period. When then-university president Dr. Donald Baepler suspended Tarkanian, the coach responded with a lawsuit, and obtained a temporary restraining order barring the university action. In his suit, he asserted that his constitutional right to due process had been denied, and that his suspension would prevent him from making a living. For the next eleven years, Tarkanian and the NCAA slugged it out in court, with Tark winning every round until the very end. But in the final round the big boys from Mission, Kansas, won a split decision, as the U.S. Supreme Court decided 5–4 that the NCAA, as a private organization, is not required to give due process. The NCAA had a legal green light to punish Tark once again. On July 20, 1990, less than four months after the Rebels' historic blowout of Duke for the national championship, UNLV was barred by the NCAA from defending its title, because the school had never carried out the NCAA-ordered suspension of Jerry Tarkanian.

By then, Rebel stars Larry Johnson, Stacey Augmon, and Greg Anthony were committed to returning to school for their senior year. They were aware that the NCAA ax might fall when they made their decisions, yet they returned, passing up (at least for a year) the NBA's millions. "I weighed the options," said Johnson, "and came back for my team, my university, my family, my degree." When asked what he felt when the team was placed on probation, Anthony said, "I knew we'd all made the right decision. . . . We all matured and became more responsible because of that experience."

At a preseason practice, Tark spoke of appealing the ban, of reluctantly accepting the NCAA's guilty verdict if it meant giving his team the chance to repeat as national champions. Tarkanian, his players, and supporters were already applying every sort of pressure they could in order to get back into the tournament. After a series of legal and extralegal maneuvers, including the threat of a lawsuit by All-Americans Johnson and Augmon against the NCAA and the introduction of bills in several state legislatures that would require the NCAA to give due process guarantees, Tark proposed a unique multiple-choice plea bargain to the NCAA:

A. Let us sit out next year instead;
B. Let the kids play but don't let me coach;
C. Don't let me collect my tournament bonus (he made over $100,000 *extra* for winning the 1990 NCAA championship);
D. Limit my scholarship allotment.

The only apparent advantages to the NCAA in accepting any of Tarkanian's proposals were that the players might not sue and the UNLV coach would finally be accepting NCAA enforcement authority and the guilty verdict. Of course, that would also mean no more talk from Tark about due process.

Lost in this endless controversy was the question of how good the team really was.

In a preseason encounter, Tark bemoaned his squad's lack of depth and suggested that the Rebels were not as good as everyone thought. But Tark seemed to carry impending doom along with him wherever he went, so how could you take him seriously when he spoke of his team's weakness outside the starting five, when he wondered aloud what would happen if one of his stars had an off day or an injury? Early in the season, the Rebels' performance made his words sound hollow; they blew opponents out with a regularity and intensity that was astonishing. The team, playing with fire, precision, and pride, looked like one of the best in history. The "us against them" attitude they carried seemed to motivate them, galvanize them into a glorious picture of basketball perfection.

Though their in-your-face flash and dash, smothering defensive pressure, physical intimidation, thunderous slam dunks, lightning fast breaks, and rainbow arching treys may have been somewhat lacking in subtlety, they were very effective. In December, the Rebels beat three consecutive tournament teams—Michigan State, Princeton, and Florida State—by an average of 29 points. Soon after the New Year, however, their play began to level off. They still seemed able to turn it on at will (as in their convincing victory over No. 2–ranked Arkansas in Fayetteville). And they always won. But it grew harder as the season progressed. Despite their cushy schedule (the Big West is no ACC), they continued to appear invincible. But beneath the surface, the constant stress began to wear them down.

As the tournament approached, and during their relatively easy West Regional, the players themselves began to express concern about what was happening. They talked about the need to maintain their intensity, and openly worried about their inability to dominate the opposition as they had all season long. The confidence that was so important in creating the Rebels' aura of invincibility began to erode.

UNLV breezed through their first tournament game against Montana, then struggled to beat Big East also-ran Georgetown by 62–54 to advance to the regionals. Still, hardly anyone outside their own inner circle seriously believed they could lose.

Their fans certainly thought they were a lock. And the Rebels, despite their outlaw reputation, do have their share of fans. Tarkanian put his team's appeal into perspective, saying, "All the truck drivers, beer drinkers, and inner-city people are Rebels fans. In Beverly Hills," he continued, "they're UCLA fans."

The Rebels are also the darlings of the city of Las Vegas, which, with no professional sports franchise to call its own, embraces Tark and his team with a unique passion. They belong as much to the city as to the college; everyone wants to get close to them, to get a taste of their magic, to be winners. In some way, it's almost as if the Rebels' success proves their city is not a mirage.

In the West regional playoff in Seattle, the Vegas fans were as confident as ever, even when overmatched Utah stayed with the Rebels for an entire half. Finally though, UNLV's superior size and quickness, aided by a coaching adjustment by Tarkanian, enabled them to put the Utes away by a convincing 83–66 margin.

Despite the win, Anthony admitted, "Right now we're a very average basketball team. I love all my teammates and know we're giving effort, but we're just not getting it done." Tark concurred, saying, "We've got to get it back, and we've got to get it back in a hurry."

Two nights later, against the tough Seton Hall Pirates, UNLV got their intensity back. For a period of 4 minutes and 14 seconds at the start of the second half, they were the blindingly fast, overwhelmingly aggressive Rebels again. "Their defensive intensity was unbelievable," said Pirate forward Jerry Walker after Greg Anthony's steals and assists and Larry Johnson's shooting led UNLV from a 3-point halftime lead to a 17-point bulge—all before the Pirates were able to score a single second-half point.

Although the Rebels knew they had played well (at least for a few minutes), their postgame locker room was filled more with relief than with excitement. Looking ahead to Indianapolis, Anthony's misgivings were apparent when he said, "To celebrate too much right now would not be a wise move."

In the week before the Final Four, Jerry Tarkanian worried. He knew his team hadn't played well since early in the Big West tournament. He looked at the matchups against Duke and saw no one equipped to handle Christian Laettner. After arriving in Indianapolis, he tried to minimize the pressure by shielding his squad from their fans and the media.

Meanwhile, Duke coach Mike Krzyzewski watched the tape of the 1990 championship debacle for the first time. What he saw amazed him. "After watching it," he said, "I became more confident that we could win. They were better than us, but not that much better." He showed selected portions of the tape to his players, and they began to realize that maybe they weren't in over their heads after all.

On Thursday, March 30, after Kansas beat North Carolina, Duke met UNLV in a semifinal rematch of the previous year's championship game. As they were introduced, the Blue Devils were noticeably pumped up. They were loose as a goose and had nothing to lose. The UNLV players, on the other hand, were subdued. The strain showed most clearly on Stacey Augmon's worried face, but even Larry Johnson, whose smile was often compared to Magic Johnson's, came out stone faced.

Looking at the two teams take the floor, it was hard to tell which was the favorite and which was the underdog.

Duke came out smoking. Before the game was two seconds old, Grant Hill raced in front of Greg Anthony to pick off the opening tip and speed ahead for a breakaway layup. Anthony came back quickly to feed Anderson Hunt, who buried a three-pointer. But Duke answered with a trey from Christian Laettner. The Duke defense sagged inside on Larry Johnson, leaving UNLV center George Ackles wide open at the top of the key. But Ackles missed, and Grant Hill came back for another lay-up. The tone was set. This time Duke would not be intimidated.

By the first TV time-out, Duke had established their game plan: on offense they were isolating Laettner, a natural forward, on the much slower Ackles; on defense they were double-teaming Johnson, denying him the ball in the hole, where his superior strength made him virtually unstoppable. The score was 15–8. "What are we doing?" Tarkanian asked his players. "We're playing like we're afraid of them."

Switching into their vaunted amoeba defense, UNLV stormed back, and in barely three minutes they tied the score at 18. The Rebels appeared to be on the verge of breaking the game open, but the Blue Devils held on. Johnson and UNLV reserve center Elmore Spencer both missed easy inside shots, and Thomas Hill, taking advantage of UNLV's all-out assault on the offensive board, came back with a transition basket. Augmon, the best finisher in the college game, missed on a fast break, and Anthony couldn't put in the follow. Augmon missed inside, awkwardly. Again Duke converted on the fly, with a beautiful two-on-one exclamation-point dunk by Grant Hill off a feed from Bobby Hurley.

With just under eight minutes left, Duke regained the lead when Hurley stripped a rebound out of Augmon's hands and coolly popped in a trey. By the time the half was over, the lead had changed hands seven more times. And although UNLV left the floor holding a two-point edge, it was obvious that the matchup and depth problems Tarkanian had talked about all week were real; while Laettner had an astonishing twenty points, the UNLV All-Americans, Johnson and Augmon, were virtually invisible on offense, scoring just half that number between them. Only the brilliant play of Greg Anthony at point guard had kept UNLV in the game.

Still, nearly everyone expected the Rebels to open the second half with the same sort of crushing surge that had overpowered Utah and Seton Hall in the regionals. Only this time it didn't happen. The half opened with a Duke bucket—Hurley to Laettner for a lay-up. Just under two minutes were gone when Ackles was called for his fourth foul. Twenty seconds later, Hurley drove the length of the court and scored, turning it into a three-point play when Anthony was called for a phantom foul. And Johnson and Augmon remained invisible.

With the score tied at 53, the Rebels were unable to convert a three-on-two. Anthony was hammered by Laettner, but the foul was called on the Vegas point guard. And Duke was growing increasingly confident and physical. Less than ten seconds later, Anderson Hunt flew downcourt and began his rise toward a patented Vegas slam dunk. Bill McCaffrey raced over to intercept him, hit him hard from below, and sent him crashing to the floor on his injured shoulder. An angry Hunt shook off the pain to hit the second of two shots. On Duke's next possession, Augmon, fighting through a screen, threw his elbow in the direction of McCaffrey. The whistle blew; the call, an intentional foul on Augmon, not only sent Duke's Brian Davis to the line for two shots, it also gave the Blue Devils possession.

By the time Larry Johnson came out with 13:31 remaining, the score was 56–54 Duke. Johnson had hardly touched the ball all half, UNLV had six team fouls, and Hunt had scored all eleven of his team's second-half points.

Less than a minute later, Laettner hit a sensational reverse lay-up off a feed from Hurley, extending the lead to four. Tarkanian rushed Johnson back into the game, and when Hunt was hit hard by Hurley to stop still another Vegas fast break, Johnson joined his teammate in arguing for an intentional foul and was whistled for a technical—two shots and possession for Duke.

With 11:10 left, Johnson finally scored his first second-half points, but on Duke's next possession, he lost his cool again, fouling Laettner as they fought for a rebound.

With 8:16 left, Anthony fouled Thomas Hill deep in 3-point territory. Hill's two shots put Duke back into the lead, and the foul sent Anthony to the bench.

But if there was one player Tark needed in the game, it was Anthony; he was back within a minute. With 3:51 remaining and Vegas holding a three-point lead, Anthony drove toward the hoop . . . and charged. He was gone.

It didn't happen right away, but without Greg Anthony, the Runnin' Rebels lost their way to a second national championship. After George Ackles tipped in his own miss for a 5-point lead, Bobby Hurley coolly came back for a three. With Anderson Hunt playing the point, Vegas was unable to move the ball. They forced it inside to a double-teamed Larry Johnson, but Christian Laettner got his hand on it and sent it out of bounds with just three seconds left on the shot clock. The ball was inbounded to Stacey Augmon, who heedlessly dribbled out the clock for the Rebels' first 45-second violation of the season. At the other end, Grant Hill fed Brian Davis for a lay-up, and Davis finished off the three-point play after being fouled by Johnson. Duke was back in the lead.

On UNLV's next possession, Augmon missed from in close, but Johnson, grabbing the rebound in the lane, was fouled. An 82 percent free-throw shooter all year, Johnson missed both shots, but converted a third chance after Thomas Hill stepped into the lane early. With the score tied, Duke held for the game winner. When Thomas Hill missed, an exhausted Christian Laettner grabbed a gigantic rebound and was fouled. UNLV Coach Tarkanian called a time-out in a desperate attempt to rattle the Duke star. But the Blue Devils had come so far and victory was so close—there was no way Laettner would miss.

The two shots hit nothing but net, and Duke had a two-point lead. After a time-out the ball come in to Johnson, who dribbled downcourt to the top of the key. Only Laettner stood between him and the basket. Instead of taking Laettner deep, he pulled up his dribble. Instead of taking the open three-pointer, he passed the ball to Hunt, who was double-teamed 24 feet from the hoop. As the seconds ticked off toward Easter Sunday, Hunt forced up a prayer. And as the ball bounced harmlessly off the board, Hurley turned his face toward heaven. Victory, blessed victory.

For Mike Krzyzewski and his Duke Blue Devils, the victory meant redemption. Last year was gone, expunged forever. They had come up big with heart and desire and an unquenchable will to win. They had beaten the unbeatable Runnin' Rebels.

But for Tark and his team there would be no next year, no second chance. The sixty-year-old coach, whose battles with the NCAA too often overshadowed his extraordinary achievements, would not go out in a blaze of glory. He would never get this close again. His players would move on, holding on to the memory of their 45-game winning streak, their extraordinary closeness and camaraderie, and their thoughts of what might have been. If they had won, they might have been called the greatest team in history. But now, on the floor of the Hoosier Dome, their dream was done.

"They played a great game," Greg Anthony told the press. "You can make excuses all day, but I credit Duke for outplaying us." Then, speaking as much to his teammates as to the world, he said, "I'd rather lose with this team than win with any other."

UNLV was gone, but the season wasn't over. Reminding his young Blue Devils that their job was not yet done, Duke's Coach K calmed them down and ordered them to refocus their energies on Monday night, when they would play Kansas for the national championship.

Duke had beaten Vegas and taken over the role of favorite. But as the fans filed into the Hoosier Dome on April 1, it was clear that the remnants of the Carolina and UNLV cheering sections solidly backed Kansas. "Roy Williams is a Carolina boy," one demure young Tar Heel told anyone who would listen. "Duke sucks."

Despite the divisions that separated the Duke and Kansas partisans, when the public-address announcer declared that the "Star-Spangled Banner" would be sung in honor of American troops in the Persian Gulf, 47,100 people rose as one.

It was almost unbelievable how much of a roller-coaster ride the national mood had been on in the previous few months. As the college basketball season heated up, the nation had been gripped by events taking place half a world away. Over half a million young Americans were digging trenches in Saudi Arabia, preparing to confront a dictator who had never hesitated to use any and all weapons at his disposal. Everywhere in the country, from Carolina to Connecticut, from Las Vegas to Tennessee, there was an outpouring of hope, sympathy, pride, and many more complex emotions about the developing conflict in the Persian Gulf. In early December, LSU coach Dale Brown read a letter to his team from Specialist Deacon Guidry, a member of the 101st Airborne Division serving in the Gulf, urging him to have his players wear American flags on their uniforms as a sign of support for American troops. The players unanimously agreed, and for the Tigers' next game (on December 7, the forty-ninth anniversary of Japan's attack on Pearl Harbor), the Louisiana State players wore flag patches.

Almost overnight, the flag appeared on basketball uniforms across the country. For some players, like East Tennessee State's star point guard Keith "Mister" Jennings and UNLV reserve forward Chris Jeter, it was a way of keeping the home fires burning for their own brothers who were stationed in the Gulf. For others it was a way of not repeating what had happened to our soldiers during Vietnam, of saying that whatever happens we will not blame the messengers for bad news. North Carolina coach Dean Smith wore a yellow ribbon on his own lapel, thus clearly communicating that his thoughts were with the safety of the troops. And many Americans felt that displaying the flag was a clear symbol of their support for the government's battle against a ruthless dictator.

But a few others went much further, disgracing the symbol of American freedom by branding dissenters of any kind, even those who merely had questions about administration policy, as traitors. Nebraska Coach Danny Nee, who'd served a hellish tour of duty in Vietnam twenty-five years earlier, told *Sports Illustrated*, "I pray every night that not one kid loses a drop of blood. I have a son who's thirteen, and the police would have to pull me off of him before I'd let him go through what I did." Soon after he made his statement, Nee, who as a helicopter crewman with the First Marine Air Wing had paid for his citizenship in blood, began to get angry letters, phone calls, and catcalls from detractors who questioned his patriotism. Seton Hall's reserve point guard Marco Lokar had it even worse when he refused to wear the flag. By the time the Pirates played St. John's in Madison Square Garden on February 2, Lokar, who had come to America from Italy one year earlier to study and play basketball, was booed every time he touched the ball. Soon he and his pregnant wife began getting threatening phone calls at their home. He withdrew from the university on the 13th, releasing a statement that read in part, "From a Christian standpoint, I cannot support any war, with no exception for the Persian Gulf war." Soon after, he returned home to Italy.

When the shooting started, players with relatives and friends in the Middle East were among the millions of Americans anxiously monitoring CNN, hoping that their loved ones were safe, that Saddam Hussein would not be able to use his chemical and biological weapons, that the war would soon be over with a favorable conclusion. The night the Scuds started to fall on his native Tel Aviv, U.Conn.'s Israeli point guard, Gilad Katz, had his concentration shattered. Although Katz had been a some-time starter and was expected to make a significant contribution to the Huskies' season, he never recovered from the experience. And just weeks before his team qualified for the tournament, Coastal Carolina's Eddie Lesaine, a Marine reserve, got his orders to report for active duty and prepared to leave for the Gulf.

And then, almost instantaneously, the war was over. The vaunted Iraqi army, fourth largest in the world, with stocks of poison gas, biological weapons, and a developing nuclear capacity, battle hardened in a decade of war with Iran, crumbled, exposing Saddam as a paper tiger. America celebrated. Less than two weeks after a cease-fire was announced, the NCAA tournament—the first major home-front event since the end of the war—began.

Seventeen days after the opening-round games (almost as long as it took to decide the war in the Gulf), the tournament was about to enter its final phase. As the Hoosier Dome crowd rose in their places to sing the national anthem, the players took the floor.

Just as they had against Vegas, Duke started out on fire, quickly dispelling any idea that they had peaked in their emotional Saturday night win. Senior forward Greg Koubek, the first player ever to appear in four Final Fours, almost matched his season average in the first two minutes as he scored the Blue Devils' first five points. With the score 5–1, Bobby Hurley raced downcourt and threw a pass in the direction of the rafters; Grant Hill leaped high above the rim and jammed it home. The spectacular soaring alley-oop slam was followed by another Hurley-to-Hill combination, and ten seconds later Coach K removed three starters, leaving only Hill and Hurley in the game. (Laettner and Koubek came back less than a minute later, after the first TV time-out.)

The pattern was soon set. Both teams were disciplined, deep, and well-schooled in fundamentals. Both coaches shuttled players in and out, resting their worn-out starters (all except Duke's indispensable point guard, Bobby Hurley) while looking for momentary matchup advantages. Hurley flawlessly and patiently ran the Blue Devils' varied offense, while Laettner, fighting his exhaustion, was automatic from the foul line, hitting ten straight in the first half alone. Kansas worked the ball inside, but they missed far too often from inside the paint. Despite their poor inside shooting, the Jayhawks' perimeter game and offensive boardwork kept them close.

Twelve seconds remained in the half when Krzyzewski put Thomas Hill back into the game. With time running down, Hurley fed him in the corner. He coolly popped in a jumper from downtown, and the Blue Devils left the court with an 8-point lead.

It was too much for the Jayhawks to overcome. In the second half, Duke answered everything Kansas put up, building their advantage to 14 on two Hurley free throws with 8:30 left. Still the Jayhawks fought back, closing to within 5 in the last minute. But it was too little, too late. A perfectly executed fast break, ending in a Brian Davis dunk, broke the Kansas defensive pressure and gave the Blue Devils a 72–65 lead, putting the game out of reach.

For Duke, it was finally time to celebrate.

"My father took me to the 1984 Final Four when I was in elementary school," recalled high-flying freshman Grant Hill. "From that point on I decided I wanted to be here . . . I wanted to play for the NCAA champs." Now he and his teammates—Jersey City's unlikely iron man, Bobby Hurley, who directed his team's offense for every minute of both Final Four games; bomber-off-the-bench Billy McCaffrey; solid Thomas Hill; senior Greg Koubek, cutting the nets in his last game; Christian Laettner, in the right place at the right time (as usual), and the rest—were going home to Durham, to join the celebration that was just beginning at Cameron Indoor. The Blue Devils had erased the memory of their shark-infested nightmare of the year before. They were the national champions. And Grant Hill smiled and said, "It's a dream come true."

1991 BOX SCORES

Following is a list of abbreviations used in box scores and other statistical material.

Min.	Minutes
FG	Field Goals
FGA	Field Goals Attempted
FT	Free Throws
FTA	Free Throws Attempted
Reb.	Rebounds
O/T	Offensive/Total
A	Assists
TO	Turnovers
PF	Personal Fouls
S	Steals
Blk.	Shots Blocked
TP	Total Points
Pct.	Percentage
PPM	Points Per Minute

FIRST ROUND EAST

N. Carolina (101)   Coach: Dean Smith   Season Record: 25-5

	Min.	Total FG/FGA	Pct.	3-Pt. FG/FGA	Pct.	FT/FTA	Pct.	Reb. O/T	A	TO	PF	S	Blk	TP	PPM
FOX, RICK	26	6/8	.750	2/2	1.000	2/2	1.000	3/6	3	4	0	4	0	16	.615
CHILCUTT, PETE	21	6/8	.750	0/0	.000	0/0	.000	0/4	0	2	0	0	0	12	.571
MONTROSS, ERIC	17	2/7	.286	0/0	.000	1/1	1.000	1/5	2	1	2	1	2	5	.294
DAVIS, HUBERT	21	5/9	.556	1/4	.250	5/5	1.000	1/1	5	1	1	1	1	16	.762
RICE, KING	23	3/5	.600	0/1	.000	2/2	1.000	0/1	6	6	1	1	0	8	.348
LYNCH, GEORGE	24	5/6	.833	0/0	.000	2/2	1.000	1/7	0	1	2	1	0	12	.500
RODL, HENRIK	16	2/2	1.000	0/0	.000	0/5	.000	1/2	3	3	1	0	0	4	.250
PHELPS, DERRICK	12	1/2	.500	0/0	.000	0/0	.000	1/3	5	0	0	0	0	2	.167
ROZIER, CLIFFORD	8	4/8	.500	0/0	.000	2/3	.667	2/4	0	1	2	0	2	10	1.250
REESE, BRIAN	8	3/5	.600	0/0	.000	0/1	.000	0/3	0	0	0	0	1	6	.750
SULLIVAN, PAT	8	0/1	.000	0/0	.000	0/0	.000	0/1	0	0	0	0	0	0	.000
HARRIS, KENNY	4	0/1	.000	0/0	.000	2/2	1.000	0/1	0	0	1	0	0	2	.500
CHERRY, SCOTT	4	0/0	.000	0/0	.000	0/0	.000	1/1	1	0	0	1	0	0	.000
SALVADORI, KEVIN	4	1/2	.500	0/0	.000	4/6	.667	0/0	0	1	0	0	1	6	1.500
WENSTROM, MATT	4	1/3	.333	0/0	.000	0/0	.000	2/2	0	0	2	0	0	2	.500
Totals	200	39/67	.582	3/7	.429	20/29	.690	13/41	25	20	12	9	7	101	.505

Northeastern (66)   Coach: Karl Fogel   Season Record: 22-10

	Min.	Total FG/FGA	Pct.	3-Pt. FG/FGA	Pct.	FT/FTA	Pct.	Reb. O/T	A	TO	PF	S	Blk	TP	PPM
ANDERSON, MARCELLUS	31	3/5	.600	0/0	.000	3/3	1.000	2/4	1	0	5	1	0	9	.290
LACY, RON	31	5/10	.500	0/1	.000	2/2	1.000	1/4	3	4	4	2	0	12	.387
CARNEY, STEVE	31	9/19	.474	0/0	.000	4/4	1.000	3/9	2	1	2	2	1	22	.710
ROBINSON, GEORGE	24	0/5	.000	0/3	.000	0/0	.000	1/3	8	3	2	2	0	0	.000
JENKINS, DEXTER	23	4/15	.267	1/2	.500	0/1	.000	1/3	3	5	3	3	0	9	.391
HARLEE, BEN	21	0/5	.000	0/3	.000	0/0	.000	0/1	0	1	4	1	0	0	.000
HODGE, LEROY	13	2/3	.667	0/0	.000	0/2	.000	0/0	0	2	3	0	0	4	.308
HOUGH, LAMONT	12	3/9	.333	2/6	.333	0/0	.000	1/2	0	3	2	1	0	8	.667
MCBRIDE, ANTHONY	1	0/0	.000	0/0	.000	0/0	.000	0/0	0	0	0	0	0	0	.000
CALLAHAN, DAN	6	0/0	.000	0/0	.000	0/0	.000	0/1	0	0	0	0	2	0	.000
BRIGHTHAUPT, MAURICE	2	1/1	1.000	0/0	.000	0/0	.000	0/1	0	0	0	1	0	2	1.000
BATTLE, VON	4	0/0	.000	0/0	.000	0/0	.000	0/0	0	2	0	0	0	0	.000
SPOKAS, ERIC	1	0/0	.000	0/0	.000	0/0	.000	0/0	0	0	0	0	0	0	.000
Totals	200	27/72	.375	3/15	.200	9/12	.750	9/28	17	21	25	13	3	66	.330

Team Rebounds: N. Carolina 6; Northeastern 4. Deadball Rebounds: N. Carolina 5; Northeastern 1. Disqualified: Northeastern—Anderson.

	1st Half	2nd Half	Final
N. Carolina	50	51	101
Northeastern	29	37	66

Princeton (48)   Coach: Pete Carril

Season Record: 24-2

	Min.	Total FG / FGA	Pct.	3–Pt. FG / FGA	Pct.	FT / FTA	Pct.	Reb. O / T	A	TO	PF	S	Blk	TP	PPM
EASTWICK, MATT	19	1/ 3	.333	0/ 0	.000	1/ 2	.500	1/ 1	1	1	1	1	0	3	.158
MOONEY, CHRIS	16	1/ 3	.333	1/ 1	1.000	0/ 0	.000	0/ 1	0	1	2	0	0	3	.188
MUELLER, KIT	40	5/13	.385	0/ 0	.000	4/ 6	.667	1/ 2	8	1	2	0	0	14	.350
BRENNAN, MIKE	27	3/ 5	.600	2/ 3	.667	1/ 1	1.000	0/ 1	1	0	4	2	0	9	.333
JACKSON, SEAN	40	3/ 7	.429	2/ 6	.333	0/ 0	.000	0/ 0	0	0	3	0	0	8	.200
HENSHON, MATT	24	1/ 2	.500	0/ 1	.000	2/ 2	1.000	0/ 1	2	2	1	0	0	4	.167
MARQUARDT, CHRIS	21	3/ 4	.750	1/ 2	.500	0/ 1	.000	0/ 3	3	1	1	0	0	7	.333
LEFTWICH, GEORGE	13	0/ 0	.000	0/ 0	.000	0/ 0	.000	0/ 0	1	1	2	1	0	0	.000
Totals	200	17/37	.459	6/13	.462	8/12	.667	2/ 9	16	7	16	4	0	48	.240

Villanova (50)   Coach: Rollie Massimino

Season Record: 16-14

	Min.	Total FG / FGA	Pct.	3–Pt. FG / FGA	Pct.	FT / FTA	Pct.	Reb. O / T	A	TO	PF	S	Blk	TP	PPM
BAIN, ARRON	31	3/ 7	.429	2/ 4	.500	4/ 4	1.000	0/ 7	0	4	4	0	1	12	.387
MILLER, LANCE	34	8/ 9	.889	0/ 0	.000	3/ 3	1.000	4/ 5	3	1	3	0	1	19	.559
DOWDELL, MARC	33	3/ 4	.750	0/ 0	.000	2/ 2	1.000	1/ 3	3	4	5	1	0	8	.242
WOODARD, GREG	34	2/ 4	.500	0/ 2	.000	2/ 3	.667	0/ 0	0	1	3	0	0	6	.176
WALKER, CHRIS	40	0/ 4	.000	0/ 2	.000	3/ 3	1.000	0/ 4	3	2	2	0	0	3	.075
BYRD, CALVIN	18	0/ 0	.000	0/ 0	.000	0/ 0	.000	0/ 5	0	1	0	0	1	0	.000
BRYSON, JAMES	8	1/ 1	1.000	0/ 0	.000	0/ 0	.000	0/ 2	0	2	1	0	0	2	.250
MUMFORD, LLOYD	1	0/ 0	.000	0/ 0	.000	0/ 0	.000	0/ 0	0	0	0	0	0	0	.000
MILLER, DAVID	1	0/ 0	.000	0/ 0	.000	0/ 0	.000	0/ 0	0	0	0	0	0	0	.000
Totals	200	17/29	.586	2/ 8	.250	14/15	.933	5/26	9	15	18	1	3	50	.250

Team Rebounds: Villanova 1; Princeton 1. Disqualified: Villanova—Dowdell. Technical Fouls: None.

	1st Half	2nd Half	Final
Princeton	30	18	48
Villanova	25	25	50

Mississippi State (56)   Coach: Richard Williams   Season Record: 20-8

	Min.	Total FG/FGA	Pct.	3–Pt. FG/FGA	Pct.	FT/FTA	Pct.	Reb. O/T	A	TO	PF	S	Blk	TP	PPM
CARTER, GREG	40	6/19	.316	1/ 5	.200	0/ 0	.000	3/ 6	3	2	3	2	0	13	.325
BURNS, CAMERON	34	8/18	.444	0/ 1	.000	6/ 8	.750	3/ 7	2	3	1	0	2	22	.647
NICHOLS, CARL	22	2/ 4	.500	0/ 0	.000	0/ 0	.000	2/ 6	1	1	3	3	1	4	.182
HARTSFIELD, DOUG	34	2/ 8	.250	1/ 3	.333	0/ 0	.000	1/ 2	4	2	3	1	0	5	.147
SMITH, BRAD	15	1/ 4	.250	0/ 0	.000	0/ 0	.000	0/ 4	3	1	2	0	1	2	.133
WATTS, TONY	28	3/ 7	.429	2/ 3	.667	2/ 2	1.000	2/ 3	2	2	3	3	0	10	.357
MORRIS, NATE	7	0/ 0	.000	0/ 0	.000	0/ 0	.000	0/ 0	0	0	1	0	0	0	.000
WATSON, ORIEN	2	0/ 0	.000	0/ 0	.000	0/ 0	.000	0/ 0	0	0	0	0	0	0	.000
HOOPER, KEITH	13	0/ 2	.000	0/ 1	.000	0/ 0	.000	1/ 1	1	1	4	0	0	0	.000
PETERSON, IRA	5	0/ 0	.000	0/ 0	.000	0/ 0	.000	0/ 0	0	0	1	1	0	0	.000
Totals	200	22/62	.355	4/13	.308	8/10	.800	12/29	16	12	21	10	4	56	.280

Eastern Mich. (76)   Coach: Ben Braun   Season Record: 24-6

	Min.	Total FG/FGA	Pct.	3–Pt. FG/FGA	Pct.	FT/FTA	Pct.	Reb. O/T	A	TO	PF	S	Blk	TP	PPM
HALLAS, KORY	32	4/ 6	.667	0/ 0	.000	1/ 1	1.000	1/ 6	3	5	4	2	0	9	.281
THOMAS, CARL	35	5/ 9	.556	4/ 7	.571	2/ 3	.667	0/ 3	2	3	1	0	0	16	.457
KENNEDY, MARCUS	35	9/13	.692	0/ 0	.000	4/ 6	.667	4/16	1	4	2	3	0	22	.629
THOMAS, CHARLES	33	2/ 6	.333	2/ 5	.400	3/ 4	.750	1/ 4	6	0	0	1	0	9	.273
NEELY, LORENZO	37	6/16	.375	0/ 0	.000	5/ 8	.625	1/ 7	5	3	0	0	0	17	.459
BOYKIN, MIKE	7	0/ 1	.000	0/ 0	.000	0/ 1	.000	0/ 0	0	0	3	0	0	0	.000
LEWIS, ROGER	16	0/ 1	.000	0/ 0	.000	1/ 2	.500	1/ 1	3	0	0	0	0	1	.063
FELDER, KAHLIL	3	0/ 1	.000	0/ 0	.000	0/ 0	.000	0/ 0	1	1	0	1	0	0	.000
FRASOR, JOE	1	1/ 1	1.000	0/ 0	.000	0/ 0	.000	1/ 1	0	0	0	0	0	2	2.000
PANGAS, PETE	1	0/ 0	.000	0/ 0	.000	0/ 0	.000	0/ 1	0	0	0	0	0	0	.000
Totals	200	27/54	.500	6/12	.500	16/25	.640	9/39	21	16	10	7	0	76	.380

Team Rebounds: Eastern Mich. 4; Mississippi St. 2. Deadball Rebounds: Eastern Mich. 4; Mississippi St. 0. Disqualified: None.

	1st Half	2nd Half	Final
Mississippi St.	28	28	56
Eastern Mich.	35	41	76

UCLA (69) Coach: Jim Harrick   Season Record: 23-8

	Min.	Total FG/FGA	Pct.	3–Pt. FG/FGA	Pct.	FT/FTA	Pct.	Reb. O/T	A	TO	PF	S	Blk	TP	PPM
MURRAY, TRACY	34	6/12	.500	1/ 6	.167	4/ 4	1.000	3/ 4	1	3	2	0	1	17	.500
BUTLER, MITCHELL	26	4/ 9	.444	0/ 0	.000	1/ 2	.500	3/ 6	4	3	3	1	0	9	.346
MACLEAN, DON	33	7/10	.700	0/ 0	.000	1/ 2	.500	0/ 1	1	2	4	0	0	15	.455
MARTIN, DARRICK	29	1/ 9	.111	0/ 3	.000	3/ 4	.750	0/ 3	5	4	4	1	0	5	.172
MADKINS, GERALD	36	5/ 7	.714	1/ 3	.333	0/ 0	.000	1/ 3	4	1	5	2	1	11	.306
TARVER, SHON	15	1/ 5	.200	0/ 0	.000	0/ 0	.000	1/ 1	0	2	0	0	0	2	.133
OWENS, KEITH	27	4/ 6	.667	0/ 0	.000	2/ 3	.667	5/14	1	0	2	2	3	10	.370
Totals	200	28/58	.483	2/12	.167	11/15	.733	13/32	16	15	20	6	5	69	.345

Penn State (74) Coach: Bruce Parkhill   Season Record: 20-10

	Min.	Total FG/FGA	Pct.	3–Pt. FG/FGA	Pct.	FT/FTA	Pct.	Reb. O/T	A	TO	PF	S	Blk	TP	PPM
BARNES, JAMES	33	6/10	.600	0/ 1	.000	7/ 8	.875	5/ 8	2	2	2	0	0	19	.576
HAYES, DERON	38	8/15	.533	0/ 0	.000	0/ 0	.000	1/ 4	3	0	3	0	0	16	.421
DEGITZ, DAVE	28	4/ 9	.444	0/ 0	.000	2/ 6	.333	4/ 5	1	2	2	1	0	10	.357
BARNES, FREDDIE	14	1/ 3	.333	0/ 1	.000	2/ 2	1.000	1/ 1	1	2	4	1	0	4	.286
BROWN, MONROE	38	3/ 6	.500	1/ 2	.500	3/ 6	.500	0/ 3	10	5	4	6	0	10	.263
JENNINGS, MICHAEL	26	4/ 8	.500	2/ 4	.500	0/ 0	.000	1/ 2	0	1	0	1	0	10	.385
JOHNSON, C.J.	13	1/ 3	.333	0/ 0	.000	1/ 1	1.000	2/ 3	3	3	0	0	0	3	.231
JOYNER, LEM	2	0/ 0	.000	0/ 0	.000	0/ 0	.000	0/ 0	0	0	0	0	0	0	.000
CARTER, ELTON	6	1/ 1	1.000	0/ 0	.000	0/ 0	.000	0/ 1	0	0	1	0	0	2	.333
DIETZ, JON	2	0/ 1	.000	0/ 0	.000	0/ 0	.000	0/ 1	0	0	0	0	0	0	.000
Totals	200	28/56	.500	3/ 8	.375	15/23	.652	14/28	20	15	16	9	0	74	.370

Team Rebounds: Penn State 3; UCLA 3. Deadball Rebounds: Penn State 3; UCLA 1. Disqualified: UCLA—Madkins.
Technical Fouls: None.

	1st Half	2nd Half	Final
UCLA	36	33	69
Penn State	32	42	74

N.C. State (114)   Coach: Les Robinson

	Min.	Total FG/FGA	Pct.	3-Pt. FG/FGA	Pct.	FT/FTA	Pct.	Reb. O/T	A	TO	PF	S	Blk	TP	PPM
GUGLIOTTA, TOM	36	5/12	.417	2/ 7	.286	4/ 4	1.000	5/11	4	1	0	2	1	16	.444
FEGGINS, BRYANT	23	7/12	.583	0/ 0	.000	1/ 2	.500	0/ 2	0	0	3	0	1	15	.652
THOMPSON, KEVIN	33	3/ 5	.600	0/ 0	.000	5/ 6	.833	6/13	3	2	1	0	3	11	.333
CORCHIANI, CHRIS	39	7/ 8	.875	3/ 3	1.000	8/ 8	1.000	0/ 3	11	4	2	2	0	25	.641
MONROE, RODNEY	39	8/22	.364	1/ 9	.111	8/ 8	1.000	2/ 5	3	0	1	0	1	25	.641
BAKALLI, MIGJEN	18	6/ 7	.857	6/ 6	1.000	0/ 0	.000	0/ 2	0	1	3	0	0	18	1.000
LEE, DAVID	5	0/ 1	.000	0/ 0	.000	0/ 0	.000	0/ 1	0	1	0	0	0	0	.000
ROBINSON, ANTHONY	3	1/ 1	1.000	0/ 0	.000	0/ 0	.000	0/ 1	0	0	0	0	0	2	.667
RITTER, CHRIS	1	0/ 1	.000	0/ 0	.000	0/ 0	.000	0/ 0	0	0	0	0	0	0	.000
CAMPION, PAUL	1	0/ 0	.000	0/ 0	.000	0/ 0	.000	0/ 0	0	0	0	0	0	0	.000
LEWIS, MARC	1	0/ 0	.000	0/ 0	.000	0/ 0	.000	0/ 0	0	0	0	0	0	0	.000
FLETCHER, ADAM	1	1/ 1	1.000	0/ 0	.000	0/ 0	.000	0/ 1	0	0	0	0	0	2	2.000
Totals	200	38/70	.543	12/25	.480	26/28	.929	13/39	21	9	10	4	6	114	.570

Southern Miss. (85)   Coach: M.K. Turk

	Min.	Total FG/FGA	Pct.	3-Pt. FG/FGA	Pct.	FT/FTA	Pct.	Reb. O/T	A	TO	PF	S	Blk	TP	PPM
CHANCELLOR, DARRIN	37	11/19	.579	2/ 6	.333	0/ 2	.000	1/ 2	3	0	2	0	0	24	.649
WEATHERSPOON, CLAREN	35	10/16	.625	0/ 1	.000	1/ 3	.333	7/12	3	2	2	0	2	21	.600
JENKINS, DARON	27	4/ 7	.571	0/ 0	.000	4/ 4	1.000	0/ 3	1	1	2	0	1	12	.444
HASLETT, BERNARD	29	6/11	.545	4/ 8	.500	0/ 0	.000	2/ 3	5	2	1	1	0	16	.552
JOHNSON, RUSSELL	26	1/ 5	.200	0/ 3	.000	2/ 3	.667	0/ 0	4	0	4	2	0	4	.154
COURTNEY, JOE	17	1/ 7	.143	0/ 0	.000	0/ 0	.000	3/ 3	1	3	1	0	1	2	.118
DALE, DALLAS	6	1/ 4	.250	1/ 3	.333	0/ 0	.000	0/ 0	1	0	2	0	0	3	.500
REMBERT, RON	5	0/ 2	.000	0/ 0	.000	0/ 0	.000	1/ 2	0	0	0	0	0	0	.000
LACEY, JOHN	15	0/ 4	.000	0/ 0	.000	0/ 0	.000	2/ 4	0	1	3	0	0	0	.000
MEALER, NEWTON	1	1/ 2	.500	1/ 1	1.000	0/ 0	.000	0/ 0	0	0	0	0	0	3	3.000
DUNN, JASON	1	0/ 0	.000	0/ 0	.000	0/ 0	.000	0/ 0	0	0	0	0	0	0	.000
JONES, RICKEY	1	0/ 0	.000	0/ 0	.000	0/ 0	.000	0/ 1	0	0	0	0	0	0	.000
Totals	200	35/77	.455	8/22	.364	7/12	.583	16/30	18	9	17	3	4	85	.425

Team Rebounds: N.C. State 5; Southern Miss. 3. Deadball Rebounds: N.C. State 1; Southern Miss. 3. Disqualified: None. Technical Fouls: Southern Miss.—Coach Turk.

	1st Half	2nd Half	Final
N.C. State	50	64	114
Southern Miss.	44	41	85

Oklahoma State (67)   Coach: Eddie Sutton   Season Record: 22-7

	Min.	Total FG/FGA	Pct.	3-Pt. FG/FGA	Pct.	FT/FTA	Pct.	Reb. O/T	A	TO	PF	S	Blk	TP	PPM
POTTER, JOHN	25	4/ 9	.444	1/ 2	.500	0/ 0	.000	1/ 5	2	3	0	1	0	9	.360
HOUSTON, BYRON	34	7/19	.368	0/ 0	.000	7/ 9	.778	8/17	1	5	4	0	2	21	.618
PITTMAN, JOHNNY	35	3/12	.250	0/ 0	.000	1/ 4	.250	6/13	0	3	4	0	1	7	.200
ALEXANDER, DARWYN	36	1/ 7	.143	0/ 1	.000	6/ 6	1.000	0/ 1	2	4	1	0	0	8	.222
SUTTON, SEAN	30	2/ 6	.333	1/ 1	1.000	3/ 3	1.000	0/ 2	1	0	2	0	0	8	.267
WILLIAMS, COREY	13	2/ 3	.667	1/ 2	.500	0/ 1	.000	0/ 2	1	0	0	0	0	5	.385
HATCHER, CORNELL	16	1/ 2	.500	0/ 0	.000	5/ 6	.833	1/ 3	1	1	1	3	0	7	.438
SAHLSTROM, MATTIAS	11	1/ 4	.250	0/ 0	.000	0/ 0	.000	0/ 1	1	0	3	1	1	2	.182
Totals	200	21/62	.339	3/ 6	.500	22/29	.759	16/44	9	17	15	5	4	67	.335

New Mexico (54)   Coach: Dave Bliss   Season Record: 20-9

	Min.	Total FG/FGA	Pct.	3-Pt. FG/FGA	Pct.	FT/FTA	Pct.	Reb. O/T	A	TO	PF	S	Blk	TP	PPM
MCCRARY, VLADIMIR	25	1/ 6	.167	0/ 0	.000	0/ 0	.000	1/ 6	1	3	4	0	1	2	.080
LONGLEY, LUC	36	6/13	.462	0/ 1	.000	4/ 6	.667	2/ 9	1	3	3	2	3	16	.444
WILLIAMS, IKE	20	5/ 7	.714	1/ 1	1.000	1/ 2	.500	0/ 3	1	7	2	0	0	12	.600
BANKS, WILLIE	40	5/11	.455	0/ 2	.000	0/ 0	.000	1/ 4	4	1	0	4	0	10	.250
ROBBINS, ROB	31	2/ 7	.286	1/ 5	.200	0/ 0	.000	1/ 5	2	1	1	0	0	5	.161
JAXON, KHARI	7	0/ 0	.000	0/ 0	.000	0/ 0	.000	0/ 0	0	1	5	0	0	0	.000
TAYLOR, JIMMY	20	1/ 2	.500	0/ 0	.000	0/ 0	.000	0/ 3	0	2	2	1	0	2	.100
NEWTON, ROB	5	0/ 3	.000	0/ 0	.000	0/ 0	.000	0/ 0	0	0	1	0	1	0	.000
MCBURROWS, MARVIN	9	1/ 1	1.000	1/ 1	1.000	0/ 0	.000	0/ 1	0	0	2	0	0	3	.333
MILLER, KURT	6	1/ 6	.167	0/ 2	.000	2/ 2	1.000	0/ 0	0	0	3	0	0	4	.667
MILFORD, LANCE	1	0/ 0	.000	0/ 0	.000	0/ 0	.000	0/ 0	0	0	0	0	0	0	.000
Totals	200	22/56	.393	3/12	.250	7/10	.700	5/31	9	18	23	7	5	54	.270

Team Rebounds: Oklahoma State 3; New Mexico 3. Deadball Rebounds: Oklahoma State 3; New Mexico 1. Team Turnovers: Oklahoma State 1. Disqualified: New Mexico—Jaxon. Technical Fouls: None.

	1st Half	2nd Half	Final
Oklahoma State	26	41	67
New Mexico	26	28	54

Purdue (63)

Coach: Gene Keady

Season Record: 17-11

	Min.	Total FG / FGA	Pct.	3–Pt. FG / FGA	Pct.	FT / FTA	Pct.	Reb. O / T	A	TO	PF	S	Blk	TP	PPM
WHITE, CHUCKIE	39	3/ 7	.429	0/ 0	.000	1/ 3	.333	5/13	1	2	1	0	1	7	.179
OLIVER, JIMMY	40	8/19	.421	5/10	.500	0/ 0	.000	1/ 2	2	2	1	0	0	21	.525
RILEY, CRAIG	19	4/ 6	.667	0/ 0	.000	0/ 0	.000	1/ 2	0	3	1	0	0	8	.421
PAINTER, MATT	28	2/ 5	.400	0/ 2	.000	0/ 0	.000	0/ 1	2	2	4	0	0	4	.143
BARRETT, DAVE	15	1/ 2	.500	0/ 0	.000	4/ 4	1.000	0/ 0	2	0	1	2	0	6	.400
STANBACK, IAN	22	1/ 3	.333	0/ 0	.000	2/ 3	.667	2/ 4	1	2	3	0	0	4	.182
DARNER, LINC	23	3/ 5	.600	2/ 3	.667	0/ 0	.000	0/ 0	4	1	0	1	0	8	.348
TRICE, TRAVIS	14	2/ 3	.667	1/ 2	.500	0/ 0	.000	1/ 1	3	1	5	0	0	5	.357
Totals	200	24/50	.480	8/17	.471	7/10	.700	10/23	15	13	16	3	1	63	.315

Temple (80)

Coach: John Chaney

Season Record: 21-9

	Min.	Total FG / FGA	Pct.	3–Pt. FG / FGA	Pct.	FT / FTA	Pct.	Reb. O / T	A	TO	PF	S	Blk	TP	PPM
KILGORE, MIK	40	8/11	.727	3/ 4	.750	6/ 6	1.000	1/ 4	5	0	1	0	0	25	.625
STRICKLAND, MARK	40	5/ 9	.556	0/ 0	.000	0/ 1	.000	1/ 5	0	0	0	0	2	10	.250
HODGE, DONALD	29	3/ 3	1.000	0/ 0	.000	0/ 2	.000	2/ 4	1	1	3	0	0	6	.207
CARSTARPHEN, VIC	38	7/ 9	.778	2/ 4	.500	2/ 3	.667	0/ 3	3	3	1	0	0	18	.474
MACON, MARK	34	6/12	.500	1/ 2	.500	6/ 6	1.000	1/ 2	4	2	3	3	0	19	.559
HARDEN, MICHAEL	8	0/ 0	.000	0/ 0	.000	0/ 0	.000	0/ 0	1	0	1	0	0	0	.000
SPEARS, JAMES	8	1/ 1	1.000	0/ 0	.000	0/ 0	.000	0/ 3	0	1	1	0	0	2	.250
LOVELACE, CHRIS	3	0/ 1	.000	0/ 0	.000	0/ 0	.000	0/ 0	0	0	1	1	0	0	.000
Totals	200	30/46	.652	6/10	.600	14/18	.778	5/21	14	7	11	4	2	80	.400

Team Rebounds: Temple 2; Purdue 1. Deadball Rebounds: Temple 1; Purdue 1. Disqualified: Purdue—Trice.

	1st Half	2nd Half	Final
Purdue	27	36	63
Temple	37	43	80

Syracuse (69)   Coach: Jim Boeheim   Season Record: 26-5

	Min.	Total FG / FGA	Pct.	3–Pt. FG / FGA	Pct.	FT / FTA	Pct.	Reb. O / T	A	TO	PF	S	Blk	TP	PPM
JOHNSON, DAVE	30	4/ 8	.500	0/ 4	.000	5/ 6	.833	3/ 4	2	1	5	0	0	13	.433
OWENS, BILLY	40	9/19	.474	1/ 3	.333	3/ 4	.750	4/ 7	1	3	3	0	1	22	.550
ELLIS, LERON	37	4/ 5	.800	0/ 0	.000	4/ 6	.667	3/ 5	0	1	2	0	3	12	.324
AUTRY, ADRIAN	36	3/ 7	.429	0/ 3	.000	1/ 2	.500	2/ 7	9	4	5	2	0	7	.194
EDWARDS, MICHAEL	32	4/13	.308	4/10	.400	0/ 0	.000	0/ 2	0	3	1	1	0	12	.375
MCRAE, CONRAD	13	1/ 1	1.000	0/ 0	.000	1/ 1	1.000	1/ 4	0	0	0	0	0	3	.231
HOPKINS, MIKE	7	0/ 1	.000	0/ 1	.000	0/ 0	.000	1/ 1	0	0	2	0	0	0	.000
MCCORKLE, SCOTT	5	0/ 1	.000	0/ 0	.000	0/ 0	.000	0/ 0	0	1	1	0	0	0	.000
Totals	200	25/55	.455	5/21	.238	14/19	.737	14/30	12	13	19	3	4	69	.345

Richmond (73)   Coach: Dick Tarrant   Season Record: 21-9

	Min.	Total FG / FGA	Pct.	3–Pt. FG / FGA	Pct.	FT / FTA	Pct.	Reb. O / T	A	TO	PF	S	Blk	TP	PPM
SHIELDS, JIM	24	3/ 4	.750	0/ 0	.000	0/ 0	.000	3/ 3	3	2	4	1	0	6	.250
WOODS, KENNY	31	6/11	.545	0/ 1	.000	0/ 1	.000	2/ 7	0	2	3	0	0	12	.387
WEATHERS, TIM	15	0/ 5	.000	0/ 3	.000	0/ 0	.000	1/ 3	0	1	1	0	0	0	.000
JARMON, GERALD	26	2/ 3	.667	1/ 2	.500	1/ 2	.500	0/ 0	3	1	0	0	0	5	.192
BLAIR, CURTIS	39	5/ 9	.556	1/ 3	.333	7/ 8	.875	0/ 3	6	1	3	3	0	18	.462
SPRINGER, JIM	16	3/ 5	.600	0/ 0	.000	2/ 2	1.000	1/ 2	0	0	2	2	0	8	.500
CONNOLLY, TERRY	30	4/ 9	.444	1/ 5	.200	5/ 6	.833	2/ 7	5	1	4	0	1	14	.467
BURROUGHS, EUGENE	6	0/ 0	.000	0/ 0	.000	2/ 2	1.000	0/ 0	1	1	0	0	0	2	.333
FLEMING, CHRIS	13	2/ 5	.400	2/ 3	.667	2/ 2	1.000	0/ 0	0	0	1	0	0	8	.615
Totals	200	25/51	.490	5/17	.294	18/22	.818	9/25	18	9	18	6	1	73	.365

Team Rebounds: Richmond 3; Syracuse 4. Deadball Rebounds: Richmond 1; Syracuse 2. Disqualified: Syracuse—Johnson, Autry.

	1st Half	2nd Half	Final
Syracuse	36	33	69
Richmond	44	29	73

FIRST ROUND SOUTHEAST

Arkansas (117)   Coach: Nolan Richardson

Season Record: 31-3

	Min.	Total FG / FGA	Pct.	3–Pt. FG / FGA	Pct.	FT / FTA	Pct.	Reb. O / T	A	TO	PF	S	Blk	TP	PPM
DAY, TODD	22	3/ 9	.333	2/ 4	.500	4/ 4	1.000	1/ 4	2	4	4	4	1	12	.545
MORRIS, ISAIAH	11	2/ 6	.333	0/ 0	.000	0/ 0	.000	3/ 4	0	2	4	0	0	4	.364
MILLER, OLIVER	16	7/ 9	.778	0/ 1	.000	6/ 9	.667	1/ 5	1	2	3	2	1	20	1.250
MAYBERRY, LEE	28	8/12	.667	2/ 4	.500	0/ 0	.000	1/ 3	5	3	0	0	0	18	.643
BOWERS, ARLYN	27	4/10	.400	0/ 3	.000	6/ 7	.857	1/ 2	6	1	2	3	0	14	.519
WALLACE, ROOSEVELT	14	2/ 9	.222	2/ 3	.667	6/ 6	1.000	4/14	2	3	2	1	0	12	.857
HUERY, RON	18	8/12	.667	0/ 2	.000	5/ 6	.833	4/ 6	4	4	3	0	4	21	1.167
MURRY, ERNIE	26	1/ 2	.500	0/ 1	.000	0/ 2	.000	2/ 3	11	1	0	2	0	2	.077
FLETCHER, CLYDE	15	3/ 7	.429	0/ 0	.000	0/ 0	.000	2/ 3	1	0	2	3	0	6	.400
DAVIS, SHAWN	13	1/ 4	.250	0/ 0	.000	2/ 4	.500	2/ 3	0	1	1	0	2	4	.308
BILEY, KEN	10	1/ 2	.500	0/ 1	.000	2/ 4	.500	2/ 6	0	1	3	1	0	4	.400
Totals	200	40/82	.488	6/19	.316	31/42	.738	23/53	32	22	24	16	8	117	.585

Georgia State (76)   Coach: Bob Reinhart

Season Record: 16-14

	Min.	Total FG / FGA	Pct.	3–Pt. FG / FGA	Pct.	FT / FTA	Pct.	Reb. O / T	A	TO	PF	S	Blk	TP	PPM
COLLIER, CHRIS	34	9/16	.563	0/ 0	.000	4/ 7	.571	4/13	0	5	3	2	1	22	.647
LUCKYDO, PHILLIP	33	6/16	.375	0/ 4	.000	4/ 6	.667	3/ 4	3	8	3	2	0	16	.485
SMITH, ZAVIAN	24	5/10	.500	0/ 0	.000	4/ 9	.444	6/ 9	2	3	5	3	6	14	.583
WILDER, SAM	22	2/11	.182	2/ 5	.400	1/ 2	.500	0/ 1	2	3	4	0	0	7	.318
COLEY, GARRETT	26	2/ 5	.400	0/ 1	.000	0/ 0	.000	4/ 9	1	4	5	0	0	4	.154
GAUFF, COREY	22	2/ 7	.286	0/ 0	.000	2/ 4	.500	0/ 2	5	3	3	3	0	6	.273
NALLS, MIKE	17	1/ 3	.333	0/ 0	.000	1/ 2	.500	3/ 4	0	4	2	0	0	3	.176
COLE, ARTE	5	1/ 1	1.000	0/ 0	.000	0/ 0	.000	1/ 1	0	0	2	0	0	2	.400
O'BRIEN, MATT	10	0/ 4	.000	0/ 0	.000	0/ 0	.000	1/ 1	3	0	0	0	0	0	.000
BROOKS, COURTNEY	5	0/ 1	.000	0/ 1	.000	0/ 0	.000	0/ 0	0	1	1	0	0	0	.000
MONROE, ESELL	2	1/ 1	1.000	0/ 0	.000	0/ 0	.000	0/ 0	0	0	0	0	0	2	1.000
Totals	200	29/75	.387	2/11	.182	16/30	.533	22/44	16	32	28	10	7	76	.380

Team Rebounds: Arkansas 1; Georgia State 4. Deadball Rebounds: Arkansas 5; Georgia State 6. Team Turnovers: Georgia State 1. Disqualified: Georgia State—Smith, Coley.

	1st Half	2nd Half	Final
Arkansas	52	65	117
Georgia State	35	41	76

Arizona State (79)   Coach: Bill Frieder   Season Record: 19-9

	Min.	Total FG/FGA	Pct.	3-Pt. FG/FGA	Pct.	FT/FTA	Pct.	Reb. O/T	A	TO	PF	S	Blk	TP	PPM
FONTANA, DWAYNE	30	2/ 4	.500	0/ 0	.000	1/ 2	.500	3/ 6	4	1	4	0	1	5	.167
FAULKNER, JAMAL	39	4/11	.364	0/ 2	.000	1/ 2	.500	0/ 6	2	3	2	3	3	9	.231
AUSTIN, ISAAC	38	11/15	.733	0/ 0	.000	3/ 6	.500	3/ 8	1	5	3	0	0	25	.658
COLLINS, LYNN	19	1/ 2	.500	0/ 0	.000	0/ 0	.000	1/ 1	4	2	1	0	0	2	.105
WHEELER, TARENCE	32	8/13	.615	5/ 8	.625	4/ 5	.800	0/ 4	4	2	2	2	0	25	.781
SMITH, STEVIN	30	2/ 7	.286	2/ 7	.286	4/ 6	.667	1/ 4	2	3	2	5	0	10	.333
ANDERSON, MATT	10	1/ 2	.500	1/ 2	.500	0/ 0	.000	0/ 0	0	1	1	1	0	3	.300
LEWIS, EMORY	1	0/ 0	.000	0/ 0	.000	0/ 0	.000	0/ 0	0	1	0	0	0	0	.000
CONLISK, ROBERT	1	0/ 0	.000	0/ 0	.000	0/ 0	.000	0/ 0	0	0	0	0	0	0	.000
Totals	200	29/54	.537	8/19	.421	13/21	.619	8/29	17	18	15	11	4	79	.395

Rutgers (76)   Coach: Bob Wenzel   Season Record: 19-9

	Min.	Total FG/FGA	Pct.	3-Pt. FG/FGA	Pct.	FT/FTA	Pct.	Reb. O/T	A	TO	PF	S	Blk	TP	PPM
HUGHES, KEITH	37	8/21	.381	1/ 3	.333	4/ 4	1.000	6/11	0	1	2	1	1	21	.568
SMITH, DARYL	27	3/10	.300	0/ 0	.000	3/ 3	1.000	6/ 8	1	2	3	2	0	9	.333
DABBS, BRENT	26	5/12	.417	2/ 4	.500	0/ 0	.000	2/ 6	0	2	3	2	0	12	.462
DUNCAN, EARL	36	6/11	.545	3/ 4	.750	5/ 5	1.000	1/ 2	2	5	2	0	0	20	.556
JONES, MIKE	25	1/ 3	.333	0/ 0	.000	0/ 0	.000	0/ 0	0	1	4	0	0	2	.080
CARTER, CRAIG	20	1/ 7	.143	0/ 0	.000	2/ 2	1.000	1/ 3	4	3	3	0	0	4	.200
LAMOUREAUX, ANDRE	11	1/ 1	1.000	0/ 0	.000	0/ 0	.000	0/ 1	1	0	2	0	0	2	.182
LUMPKIN, DONNELL	12	1/ 4	.250	1/ 2	.500	0/ 0	.000	1/ 4	3	2	1	0	0	3	.250
WEILER, CHARLES	5	1/ 2	.500	0/ 0	.000	1/ 2	.500	1/ 2	0	0	1	0	0	3	.600
REDDEN, MARC	1	0/ 0	.000	0/ 0	.000	0/ 0	.000	0/ 0	0	0	0	0	0	0	.000
Totals	200	27/71	.380	7/13	.538	15/16	.938	18/37	11	16	21	5	1	76	.380

Team Rebounds: Arizona St. 3; Rutgers 5. Deadball Rebounds: Arizona St. 3; Rutgers 1. Disqualified: None.
Technical Fouls: Rutgers—bench.

	1st Half	2nd Half	Final
Arizona St.	30	49	79
Rutgers	36	40	76

Wake Forest (71)   Coach: Dave Odom   Season Record: 18-10

	Min.	Total FG/FGA	Pct.	3–Pt. FG/FGA	Pct.	FT/FTA	Pct.	Reb. O/T	A	TO	PF	S	Blk	TP	PPM
TUCKER, ANTHONY	37	5/ 9	.556	1/ 2	.500	6/ 9	.667	3/ 7	2	2	4	0	0	17	.459
KING, CHRIS	32	3/11	.273	0/ 1	.000	3/ 8	.375	1/ 9	1	1	3	2	1	9	.281
ROGERS, RODNEY	34	6/14	.429	0/ 0	.000	4/ 7	.667	4/ 7	1	3	5	3	0	14	.412
MCQUEEN, DERRICK	36	2/ 4	.500	1/ 1	1.000	0/ 0	.000	0/ 3	7	1	2	1	0	5	.139
SILER, ROBERT	19	2/ 7	.286	1/ 2	.500	1/ 2	.500	0/ 0	3	0	1	3	0	6	.316
CHILDRESS, RANDOLPH	25	6/11	.545	0/ 4	.000	6/10	.600	2/ 6	2	2	3	1	0	18	.720
OWENS, TRELONNIE	8	1/ 3	.333	0/ 0	.000	0/ 0	.000	1/ 2	0	1	2	0	0	2	.250
WISE, TOM	6	0/ 0	.000	0/ 0	.000	0/ 0	.000	1/ 2	0	0	2	0	0	0	.000
MEDLIN, PHIL	1	0/ 0	.000	0/ 0	.000	0/ 0	.000	0/ 0	0	0	0	0	0	0	.000
RAY, STEVE	1	0/ 0	.000	0/ 0	.000	0/ 0	.000	0/ 0	0	0	0	0	0	0	.000
SANDERS, TODD	1	0/ 0	.000	0/ 0	.000	0/ 0	.000	0/ 0	0	0	0	0	0	0	.000
Totals	200	25/59	.424	3/10	.300	18/32	.563	12/36	16	10	22	10	1	71	.355

Louisiana Tech (65)   Coach: Jerry Lloyd   Season Record: 21-9

	Min.	Total FG/FGA	Pct.	3–Pt. FG/FGA	Pct.	FT/FTA	Pct.	Reb. O/T	A	TO	PF	S	Blk	TP	PPM
DADE, ANTHONY	37	11/18	.611	0/ 0	.000	3/ 7	.429	7/14	3	5	2	1	2	25	.676
ELLIS, RONALD	21	2/ 4	.500	0/ 0	.000	2/ 6	.333	1/ 3	1	1	5	0	0	6	.286
BROWN, P.J.	40	5/12	.417	0/ 2	.000	2/ 4	.500	1/ 9	2	2	3	1	4	12	.300
MASON, RENI	32	2/ 4	.500	0/ 0	.000	0/ 0	.000	0/ 4	4	2	5	1	0	4	.125
POWELL, ROOSEVELT	35	1/ 7	.143	0/ 3	.000	4/ 4	1.000	0/ 2	3	1	4	1	1	6	.171
HEAPS, BRYAN	5	0/ 1	.000	0/ 1	.000	0/ 0	.000	0/ 0	0	1	3	0	0	0	.000
SPRALDING, MARK	2	0/ 0	.000	0/ 0	.000	0/ 0	.000	0/ 1	0	2	0	0	0	0	.000
BROWN, ERIC	22	3/ 6	.500	2/ 5	.400	2/ 4	.500	1/ 1	1	2	1	0	0	10	.455
MORRIS, ANTUAN	6	0/ 3	.000	0/ 3	.000	2/ 4	.500	1/ 2	0	0	0	0	0	2	.333
Totals	200	24/55	.436	2/14	.143	15/29	.517	11/36	14	16	23	4	7	65	.325

Team Rebounds: Wake Forest 4; Louisiana Tech 4. Deadball Rebounds: Wake Forest 7; Louisiana Tech 6. Disqualified: Wake Forest—Rogers; Louisiana Tech—Ellis, Mason. Technical Foul: Wake Forest—bench.

	1st Half	2nd Half	Final
Wake Forest	37	34	71
Louisiana Tech	36	29	65

Alabama (89)   Coach: Wimp Sanderson   Season Record: 21-9

	Min.	Total FG / FGA	Pct.	3-Pt. FG / FGA	Pct.	FT / FTA	Pct.	Reb. O/T	A	TO	PF	S	Blk	TP	PPM
HORRY, ROBERT	27	8/12	.667	3/ 5	.600	2/ 3	.667	1/ 5	3	0	4	2	2	21	.778
SPREWELL, LATRELL	34	5/ 7	.714	1/ 2	.500	1/ 2	.500	2/ 9	2	2	0	3	1	12	.353
CHEATUM, MELVIN	34	11/15	.733	0/ 0	.000	1/ 2	.500	3/ 9	2	4	1	3	0	23	.676
WAITES, GARY	30	3/ 8	.375	0/ 5	.000	0/ 0	.000	0/ 5	9	2	2	0	0	6	.200
LANCASTER, BRYANT	21	0/ 3	.000	0/ 0	.000	0/ 0	.000	1/ 2	4	1	1	0	0	0	.000
ROBINSON, JAMES	16	6/11	.545	3/ 4	.750	0/ 0	.000	0/ 1	1	2	5	1	0	15	.938
WEBB, MARCUS	14	2/ 3	.667	0/ 0	.000	1/ 2	.500	1/ 3	1	2	2	0	0	5	.357
JONES, MARCUS	13	3/ 5	.600	0/ 0	.000	0/ 0	.000	0/ 0	1	1	2	0	0	6	.462
CAMPBELL, MARCUS	7	0/ 1	.000	0/ 0	.000	0/ 0	.000	0/ 1	0	0	1	0	0	0	.000
RICH, DARBY	2	0/ 0	.000	0/ 0	.000	0/ 0	.000	0/ 0	0	0	2	0	0	0	.000
RICE, KENNETH	2	0/ 1	.000	0/ 0	.000	1/ 2	.500	0/ 0	0	2	0	0	0	1	.500
Totals	200	38/66	.576	7/16	.438	6/11	.545	8/35	23	16	20	9	3	89	.445

Murray State (79)   Coach: Steve Newton   Season Record: 24-8

	Min.	Total FG / FGA	Pct.	3-Pt. FG / FGA	Pct.	FT / FTA	Pct.	Reb. O/T	A	TO	PF	S	Blk	TP	PPM
COBLE, GREG	38	9/16	.563	4/ 8	.500	0/ 0	.000	3/ 5	4	5	2	1	0	22	.579
JACKSON, JOHN	33	6/10	.600	0/ 0	.000	0/ 0	.000	4/ 7	1	3	1	1	0	12	.364
JONES, POPEYE	36	5/16	.313	0/ 1	.000	1/ 4	.250	0/ 8	6	2	3	1	2	11	.306
KING, PAUL	38	6/13	.462	3/ 9	.333	10/12	.833	1/ 3	0	2	1	3	1	25	.658
ALLEN, FRANK	30	2/14	.143	0/ 5	.000	0/ 0	.000	0/ 0	3	2	1	3	0	4	.133
ADAMS, SCOTT	7	0/ 0	.000	0/ 0	.000	0/ 0	.000	0/ 1	0	1	3	0	0	0	.000
GUMM, CEDRIC	10	0/ 1	.000	0/ 0	.000	3/ 4	.750	3/ 4	1	0	0	0	0	3	.300
OVERSTREET, DONALD	3	0/ 0	.000	0/ 0	.000	0/ 0	.000	0/ 1	0	0	1	0	0	0	.000
SIVILLS, SCOTT	3	0/ 1	.000	0/ 0	.000	2/ 2	1.000	0/ 1	1	0	0	1	0	2	.667
GOLD, DOUG	1	0/ 0	.000	0/ 0	.000	0/ 0	.000	0/ 0	0	0	0	0	0	0	.000
BIRDSONG, TERRY	1	0/ 1	.000	0/ 0	.000	0/ 0	.000	2/ 2	0	0	0	0	0	0	.000
Totals	200	28/72	.389	7/23	.304	16/22	.727	13/32	16	15	12	10	3	79	.395

Team Rebounds: Alabama 3; Murray State 10. Deadball Rebounds: Alabama 1; Murray State 0. Disqualified: Alabama—Robinson.

	1st Half	2nd Half	Final
Alabama	46	43	89
Murray State	30	49	79

Pittsburgh (76)   Coach: Paul Evans

Season Record: 20-11

	Min.	Total FG / FGA	Pct.	3–Pt. FG / FGA	Pct.	FT / FTA	Pct.	Reb. O / T	A	TO	PF	S	Blk	TP	PPM
SHORTER, BRIAN	39	8/12	.667	0/ 0	.000	7/10	.700	3/13	0	1	2	0	0	23	.590
JONES, ANTOINE	27	1/ 3	.333	0/ 0	.000	0/ 0	.000	1/ 2	1	0	1	1	0	2	.074
MARTIN, BOBBY	21	2/ 5	.400	0/ 0	.000	1/ 2	.500	0/ 4	0	1	5	0	0	5	.238
MILLER, SEAN	29	2/ 6	.333	2/ 6	.333	4/ 4	1.000	1/ 2	6	3	0	0	0	10	.345
MATTHEWS, JASON	23	3/ 9	.333	2/ 6	.333	2/ 3	.667	0/ 1	1	2	3	0	0	10	.435
PORTER, DARELLE	22	1/ 7	.143	0/ 1	.000	6/ 6	1.000	1/ 5	6	0	0	1	0	8	.364
MORNINGSTAR, DARREN	14	1/ 3	.333	0/ 0	.000	1/ 2	.500	4/ 5	0	1	4	0	1	3	.214
MORGAN, JERMAINE	4	0/ 0	.000	0/ 0	.000	0/ 0	.000	1/ 1	0	1	0	0	0	0	.000
SHAREEF, AHMAD	3	0/ 1	.000	0/ 0	.000	0/ 0	.000	0/ 0	0	0	0	0	0	0	.000
MCNEAL, CHRIS	25	0/ 4	.000	0/ 0	.000	3/ 4	.750	2/ 6	1	0	2	1	0	3	.120
GLOVER, TIM	18	4/ 6	.667	4/ 6	.667	0/ 0	.000	0/ 2	1	0	1	0	1	12	.667
Totals	225	22/56	.393	8/19	.421	24/31	.774	13/41	16	9	18	3	2	76	.338

Georgia (68)   Coach: Hugh Durham

Season Record: 17-12

	Min.	Total FG / FGA	Pct.	3–Pt. FG / FGA	Pct.	FT / FTA	Pct.	Reb. O / T	A	TO	PF	S	Blk	TP	PPM
HARVEY, ANTONIO	38	5/13	.385	0/ 0	.000	1/ 3	.333	2/ 4	3	1	4	1	1	11	.289
WILSON, MARSHALL	34	9/21	.429	4/13	.308	0/ 0	.000	3/ 6	0	1	0	0	1	22	.647
AUSTIN, NEVILLE	23	1/ 2	.500	0/ 0	.000	0/ 0	.000	0/ 8	2	0	5	0	0	2	.087
PATTON, JODY	37	5/14	.357	3/12	.250	1/ 1	1.000	2/ 4	4	1	1	0	0	14	.378
COLE, ROD	35	1/ 4	.250	0/ 2	.000	4/ 4	1.000	0/ 2	4	4	5	0	0	6	.171
TINCH, REGGIE	21	2/ 4	.500	0/ 0	.000	1/ 3	.333	1/ 3	1	2	2	2	0	5	.238
BENNETT, ARLANDO	25	1/ 3	.333	0/ 0	.000	2/ 4	.500	3/ 6	0	0	3	0	1	4	.160
GOLDEN, SHAUN	11	2/ 2	1.000	0/ 0	.000	0/ 1	.000	0/ 0	0	1	3	0	0	4	.364
HOWARD, LEM	1	0/ 0	.000	0/ 0	.000	0/ 0	.000	0/ 0	0	0	0	0	0	0	.000
Totals	225	26/63	.413	7/27	.259	9/16	.563	11/33	14	10	23	3	3	68	.302

Team Rebounds: Pittsburgh 0; Georgia 5. Deadball Rebounds: Pittsburgh 3; Georgia 3. Disqualified: Pittsburgh—Martin; Georgia— Austin, Cole. Technical Fouls: None.

	1st Half	2nd Half	1 OT	Final
Pittsburgh	30	36	10	76
Georgia	29	37	2	68

Kansas (55)   Coach: Roy Williams   Season Record: 22-7

	Min.	Total FG / FGA	Pct.	3–Pt. FG / FGA	Pct.	FT / FTA	Pct.	Reb. O / T	A	TO	PF	S	Blk	TP	PPM
JAMISON, ALONZO	24	2/ 5	.400	0/ 0	.000	1/ 2	.500	0/ 3	5	3	4	2	0	5	.208
MADDOX, MIKE	22	6/12	.500	0/ 0	.000	0/ 0	.000	4/ 6	3	1	4	0	0	12	.545
RANDALL, MARK	36	5/13	.385	0/ 0	.000	0/ 2	.000	3/ 8	1	1	3	1	0	10	.278
BROWN, TERRY	19	1/ 5	.200	0/ 2	.000	0/ 0	.000	1/ 1	0	1	3	0	0	2	.105
JORDAN, ADONIS	37	3/ 9	.333	1/ 3	.333	2/ 2	1.000	1/ 2	2	1	1	4	0	9	.243
WOODBERRY, STEVE	21	2/ 5	.400	0/ 1	.000	0/ 0	.000	1/ 4	0	3	4	3	0	4	.190
TUNSTALL, SEAN	21	3/ 4	.750	1/ 2	.500	0/ 0	.000	2/ 4	0	3	1	0	0	7	.333
SCOTT, RICHARD	12	2/ 3	.667	0/ 0	.000	2/ 4	.500	2/ 3	0	2	2	0	0	6	.500
WAGNER, KIRK	5	0/ 1	.000	0/ 0	.000	0/ 0	.000	0/ 0	0	0	0	0	0	0	.000
JOHANNING, DAVID	3	0/ 1	.000	0/ 0	.000	0/ 0	.000	1/ 1	0	0	0	0	0	0	.000
Totals	200	24/58	.414	2/ 8	.250	5/10	.500	15/32	11	15	22	10	0	55	.275

New Orleans (49)   Coach: Tim Floyd   Season Record: 23-7

	Min.	Total FG / FGA	Pct.	3–Pt. FG / FGA	Pct.	FT / FTA	Pct.	Reb. O / T	A	TO	PF	S	Blk	TP	PPM
COLLINS, TANK	31	3/11	.273	0/ 0	.000	7/10	.700	2/ 3	2	4	4	2	0	13	.419
RICE, SYDNEY	15	1/ 1	1.000	0/ 0	.000	2/ 3	.667	0/ 0	0	1	1	0	2	4	.267
JOHNSON, ERVIN	33	5/ 7	.714	0/ 0	.000	3/ 4	.750	6/14	0	0	3	0	1	13	.394
CLARKE, CASS	27	0/ 1	.000	0/ 0	.000	0/ 0	.000	0/ 3	3	7	1	2	0	0	.000
BENNETT, LEONARD	26	2/ 8	.250	0/ 3	.000	0/ 0	.000	1/ 4	0	4	1	0	0	4	.154
SIMON, MELVIN	31	3/ 7	.429	0/ 0	.000	3/ 5	.600	2/ 9	1	3	4	0	0	9	.290
DYER, LOUWEEGI	15	0/ 1	.000	0/ 0	.000	2/ 2	1.000	0/ 1	1	2	0	0	0	2	.133
MYVETT, DWIGHT	21	2/ 5	.400	0/ 1	.000	0/ 0	.000	0/ 1	1	0	1	1	0	4	.190
HILL, FRED	1	0/ 0	.000	0/ 0	.000	0/ 0	.000	0/ 0	0	0	1	0	0	0	.000
Totals	200	16/41	.390	0/ 4	.000	17/24	.708	11/35	8	21	16	5	3	49	.245

Team Rebounds: None. Deadball Rebounds: Kansas 1; New Orleans 3. Disqualified: None.
Technical Fouls: None.

	1st Half	2nd Half	Final
Kansas	26	29	55
New Orleans	26	23	49

Florida State (75)   Coach: Pat Kennedy   Season Record: 20-10

	Min.	Total FG / FGA	Pct.	3-Pt. FG / FGA	Pct.	FT / FTA	Pct.	Reb. O / T	A	TO	PF	S	Blk	TP	PPM
EDWARDS, DOUGLAS	35	9/13	.692	0/ 0	.000	6/10	.600	2/ 9	2	2	4	3	0	24	.686
POLITE, MICHAEL	35	4/10	.400	0/ 0	.000	3/ 5	.600	1/ 6	0	2	0	1	0	11	.314
DOBARD, RODNEY	31	2/ 3	.667	0/ 0	.000	2/ 4	.500	1/ 8	2	2	4	1	2	6	.194
WARD, CHARLIE	37	3/ 5	.600	2/ 3	.667	3/ 4	.750	1/ 4	5	2	2	3	0	11	.297
BOYD, AUBRY	30	2/10	.200	0/ 5	.000	8/12	.667	2/ 3	2	4	3	0	0	12	.400
GRAHAM, CHUCK	18	4/ 8	.500	1/ 2	.500	0/ 0	.000	2/ 4	2	3	2	0	0	9	.500
MYERS, DERRICK	2	0/ 0	.000	0/ 0	.000	0/ 0	.000	0/ 0	0	0	0	0	0	0	.000
SALTERS, JESSE	3	0/ 1	.000	0/ 0	.000	0/ 0	.000	0/ 0	0	1	1	0	0	0	.000
REID, ANDRE	1	0/ 0	.000	0/ 0	.000	0/ 0	.000	0/ 0	0	0	1	0	0	0	.000
WHITE, DAVID	8	1/ 1	1.000	0/ 0	.000	0/ 0	.000	0/ 1	0	0	0	0	0	2	.250
Totals	200	25/51	.490	3/10	.300	22/35	.629	9/35	13	16	17	8	2	75	.375

USC (72)   Coach: George Raveling   Season Record: 19-9

	Min.	Total FG / FGA	Pct.	3-Pt. FG / FGA	Pct.	FT / FTA	Pct.	Reb. O / T	A	TO	PF	S	Blk	TP	PPM
BANKS, CALVIN	11	1/ 3	.333	0/ 0	.000	0/ 0	.000	1/ 3	0	1	1	0	0	2	.182
COLEMAN, RONNIE	31	6/14	.429	0/ 0	.000	3/ 7	.429	4/ 8	0	2	5	1	0	15	.484
COOPER, DUANE	34	2/ 4	.500	2/ 4	.500	0/ 0	.000	2/ 5	4	2	2	1	0	6	.176
MINER, HAROLD	39	7/27	.259	2/12	.167	0/ 0	.000	2/ 6	1	3	3	1	0	16	.410
PACK, ROBERT	29	6/ 9	.667	0/ 0	.000	8/ 8	1.000	0/ 1	4	4	5	0	0	20	.690
BOYD, MARK	18	0/ 0	.000	0/ 0	.000	2/ 2	1.000	2/ 3	0	2	4	0	0	2	.111
CHATMAN, RODNEY	15	0/ 1	.000	0/ 1	.000	0/ 0	.000	0/ 1	4	1	3	1	0	0	.000
SANDERS, YAMEN	20	4/ 5	.800	0/ 0	.000	3/ 4	.750	2/ 7	0	1	4	1	0	11	.550
GLENN, PHIL	3	0/ 0	.000	0/ 0	.000	0/ 0	.000	0/ 0	0	0	0	1	0	0	.000
Totals	200	26/63	.413	4/17	.235	16/21	.762	13/34	13	16	27	6	0	72	.360

Team Rebounds: Florida State 1; USC 2. Deadball Rebounds: Florida State 7; USC 2. Disqualified: USC—Coleman, Pack.

	1st Half	2nd Half	Final
Florida State	38	37	75
USC	38	34	72

Indiana (79)   Coach: Bob Knight   Season Record: 27-4

	Min.	Total FG / FGA	Pct.	3–Pt. FG / FGA	Pct.	FT / FTA	Pct.	Reb. O / T	A	TO	PF	S	Blk	TP	PPM
ANDERSON, ERIC	33	8/12	.667	0/ 0	.000	6/ 6	1.000	4/ 7	2	0	2	1	0	22	.667
CHEANEY, CALBERT	32	7/15	.467	1/ 2	.500	2/ 2	1.000	3/14	2	2	2	1	0	17	.531
NOVER, MATT	31	4/ 6	.667	0/ 0	.000	7/ 8	.875	2/ 3	2	1	1	0	2	15	.484
GRAHAM, GREG	13	1/ 2	.500	0/ 1	.000	1/ 2	.500	2/ 2	3	1	1	2	0	3	.231
MEEKS, JAMAL	29	0/ 3	.000	0/ 0	.000	2/ 2	1.000	1/ 6	6	4	2	2	0	2	.069
BAILEY, DAMON	33	3/ 9	.333	1/ 2	.500	2/ 3	.667	1/ 2	1	1	1	0	1	9	.273
GRAHAM, PAT	15	2/ 5	.400	0/ 1	.000	5/ 6	.833	0/ 1	2	2	1	1	0	9	.600
REYNOLDS, CHRIS	12	1/ 2	.500	0/ 0	.000	0/ 2	.000	0/ 1	0	1	2	3	0	2	.167
JONES, LYNDON	2	0/ 1	.000	0/ 0	.000	0/ 0	.000	0/ 0	0	0	0	0	0	0	.000
Totals	200	26/55	.473	2/ 6	.333	25/31	.806	13/36	18	12	12	10	3	79	.395

Coastal Caro. (69)   Coach: Russ Bergman   Season Record: 24-7

	Min.	Total FG / FGA	Pct.	3–Pt. FG / FGA	Pct.	FT / FTA	Pct.	Reb. O / T	A	TO	PF	S	Blk	TP	PPM
DUNKIN, TONY	38	4/14	.286	1/ 2	.500	2/ 2	1.000	1/ 5	0	3	4	1	0	11	.289
LESAINE, EDDIE	31	1/ 4	.250	1/ 2	.500	2/ 2	1.000	2/ 7	3	2	4	0	2	5	.161
CHEATAM, DUWAYNE	17	1/ 3	.333	0/ 0	.000	0/ 0	.000	2/ 5	2	2	5	0	0	2	.118
DOWDELL, ROBERT	40	5/13	.385	2/ 7	.286	2/ 2	1.000	3/ 5	6	3	4	2	0	14	.350
PENNY, BRIAN	38	13/15	.867	5/ 6	.833	3/ 4	.750	1/ 5	1	5	4	0	0	34	.895
FOSTER, J.J.	22	1/ 5	.200	1/ 2	.500	0/ 0	.000	0/ 1	3	0	3	0	0	3	.136
WILLIAMS, ERNIE	10	0/ 3	.000	0/ 1	.000	0/ 1	.000	0/ 0	0	0	1	1	0	0	.000
POLL, RON	4	0/ 0	.000	0/ 0	.000	0/ 0	.000	0/ 0	0	1	0	0	0	0	.000
Totals	200	25/57	.439	10/20	.500	9/11	.818	9/28	15	16	25	4	2	69	.345

Team Rebounds: Indiana 0; Coastal Caro. 1. Deadball Rebounds: Indiana 3; Coastal Caro. 1. Disqualified: Coastal Caro.—Cheatam.

	1st Half	2nd Half	Final
Indiana	46	33	79
Coastal Caro.	30	39	69

FIRST ROUND WEST

UNLV (99) Coach: Jerry Tarkanian   Season Record: 30-0

	Min.	Total FG / FGA	Pct.	3–Pt. FG / FGA	Pct.	FT / FTA	Pct.	Reb. O / T	A	TO	PF	S	Blk	TP	PPM
JOHNSON, LARRY	30	9/16	.563	0/ 1	.000	5/ 5	1.000	4/ 9	6	2	1	3	1	23	.767
AUGMON, STACEY	29	8/ 9	.889	2/ 2	1.000	2/ 3	.667	3/ 6	3	2	0	1	1	20	.690
ACKLES, GEORGE	14	2/ 2	1.000	0/ 0	.000	0/ 0	.000	1/ 3	0	2	1	1	1	4	.286
HUNT, ANDERSON	27	4/10	.400	0/ 4	.000	0/ 1	.000	1/ 2	0	2	1	2	0	8	.296
ANTHONY, GREG	31	7/15	.467	2/ 4	.500	4/ 4	1.000	0/ 2	9	1	1	1	0	20	.645
SPENCER, ELMORE	21	1/ 4	.250	0/ 0	.000	3/ 5	.600	1/ 4	2	1	2	0	6	5	.238
GRAY, EVRIC	16	5/11	.455	0/ 0	.000	3/ 4	.750	5/ 8	1	1	4	2	0	13	.813
BICE, TRAVIS	11	1/ 2	.500	1/ 1	1.000	0/ 0	.000	1/ 2	0	0	0	0	0	3	.273
WALDMAN, H	9	0/ 1	.000	0/ 1	.000	0/ 0	.000	0/ 0	2	1	1	1	0	0	.000
RICE, DAVE	5	0/ 2	.000	0/ 1	.000	0/ 0	.000	0/ 0	0	0	0	0	0	0	.000
LOVE, MELVIN	5	0/ 1	.000	0/ 0	.000	1/ 2	.500	0/ 3	0	0	1	0	0	1	.200
JETER, CHRIS	2	1/ 2	.500	0/ 0	.000	0/ 0	.000	1/ 1	0	0	0	0	0	2	1.000
Totals	200	38/75	.507	5/14	.357	18/24	.750	17/40	23	12	12	11	9	99	.495

Montana (65) Coach: Stew Morrill   Season Record: 23-7

	Min.	Total FG / FGA	Pct.	3–Pt. FG / FGA	Pct.	FT / FTA	Pct.	Reb. O / T	A	TO	PF	S	Blk	TP	PPM
ANDERSON, DELVON	32	6/18	.333	2/ 4	.500	0/ 2	.000	4/ 7	0	3	3	2	0	14	.438
KEARNEY, KEVIN	33	5/13	.385	1/ 1	1.000	2/ 2	1.000	2/ 3	2	4	2	0	0	13	.394
ENGELLANT, DAREN	27	6/ 7	.857	0/ 0	.000	1/ 1	1.000	4/ 6	5	1	1	1	1	13	.481
JORDAN, ERIC	24	0/ 4	.000	0/ 0	.000	0/ 0	.000	1/ 1	4	5	5	0	0	0	.000
FASTING, ROGER	33	3/ 4	.750	0/ 1	.000	0/ 0	.000	1/ 5	3	5	3	0	0	6	.182
KANE, GARY	30	5/13	.385	3/ 7	.429	2/ 2	1.000	1/ 5	2	4	3	1	0	15	.500
ATCHISON, NATE	14	2/ 4	.500	0/ 0	.000	0/ 0	.000	0/ 2	0	1	1	0	0	4	.286
LACHEUR, JOSH	5	0/ 0	.000	0/ 0	.000	0/ 0	.000	1/ 1	0	0	1	0	3	0	.000
BROWN, AL	2	0/ 0	.000	0/ 0	.000	0/ 0	.000	0/ 0	0	1	0	0	0	0	.000
Totals	200	27/63	.429	6/13	.462	5/ 7	.714	14/30	16	24	19	4	4	65	.325

Team Rebounds: UNLV 3; Montana 1. Deadball Rebounds: UNLV 4; Montana 3. Disqualified: Montana—Jordan.
Technical Fouls: Montana—Atchison.

	1st Half	2nd Half	Final
UNLV	48	51	99
Montana	32	33	65

Georgetown (70)   Coach: John Thompson   Season Record: 18-12

	Min.	Total FG / FGA	Pct.	3–Pt. FG / FGA	Pct.	FT / FTA	Pct.	Reb. O / T	A	TO	PF	S	Blk	TP	PPM
CHURCHWELL, ROBERT	28	2/ 8	.250	0/ 0	.000	0/ 0	.000	1/ 3	5	1	2	1	0	4	.143
MOURNING, ALONZO	26	7/ 9	.778	0/ 0	.000	9/10	.900	3/ 8	3	2	4	1	3	23	.885
MUTOMBO, DIKEMBE	38	4/ 8	.500	0/ 0	.000	6/ 7	.857	4/12	1	5	2	1	3	14	.368
BROWN, JOEY	39	6/10	.600	1/ 2	.500	1/ 1	1.000	1/ 7	4	4	1	1	0	14	.359
HARRISON, CHARLES	22	4/ 9	.444	0/ 2	.000	1/ 2	.500	1/ 3	0	2	0	0	0	9	.409
MORGAN, LAMONT	16	0/ 0	.000	0/ 0	.000	1/ 2	.500	3/ 3	1	2	2	0	0	1	.063
THOMPSON, RONNY	15	0/ 3	.000	0/ 0	.000	0/ 0	.000	0/ 1	1	0	0	1	1	0	.000
KELLY, BRIAN	16	2/ 2	1.000	0/ 0	.000	1/ 2	.500	0/ 0	0	1	1	0	0	5	.313
Totals	200	25/49	.510	1/ 4	.250	19/24	.792	13/37	15	17	12	5	7	70	.350

Vanderbilt (60)   Coach: Eddie Fogler   Season Record: 17-12

	Min.	Total FG / FGA	Pct.	3–Pt. FG / FGA	Pct.	FT / FTA	Pct.	Reb. O / T	A	TO	PF	S	Blk	TP	PPM
ELDER, BRUCE	33	2/ 6	.333	0/ 0	.000	2/ 2	1.000	3/ 4	4	3	3	2	0	6	.182
MAYES, CHARLES	32	2/ 8	.250	1/ 4	.250	3/ 4	.750	1/ 5	1	1	5	0	0	8	.250
GRANT, STEVE	21	3/ 7	.429	0/ 0	.000	1/ 1	1.000	2/ 2	0	2	5	2	1	7	.333
ANGLIN, KEVIN	28	1/ 4	.250	0/ 2	.000	0/ 0	.000	1/ 2	2	2	4	0	0	2	.071
DRAUD, SCOTT	32	6/16	.375	5/12	.417	5/ 6	.833	0/ 1	0	0	2	1	0	22	.688
MILHOLLAND, TODD	21	4/ 8	.500	0/ 1	.000	0/ 0	.000	1/ 2	0	2	3	0	0	8	.381
MALONEY, MATT	23	2/ 5	.400	1/ 3	.333	0/ 0	.000	0/ 2	4	1	1	2	0	5	.217
DAUNIC, WILLY	4	0/ 0	.000	0/ 0	.000	0/ 0	.000	0/ 0	0	0	1	0	0	0	.000
BETH, AARON	3	0/ 0	.000	0/ 0	.000	0/ 0	.000	0/ 1	0	0	1	0	0	0	.000
BENHAMIN, FRED	3	1/ 2	.500	0/ 0	.000	0/ 0	.000	1/ 2	0	0	0	0	0	2	.667
Totals	200	21/56	.375	7/22	.318	11/13	.846	9/21	11	11	25	7	1	60	.300

Team Rebounds: Georgetown 2; Vanderbilt 1. Deadball Rebounds: Georgetown 3; Vanderbilt 2. Disqualified: Vanderbilt—Mayes, Grant. Technical Fouls: Georgetown—Coach Thompson.

	1st Half	2nd Half	Final
Georgetown	35	35	70
Vanderbilt	25	35	60

Michigan State (60)   Coach: Jud Heathcote

Season Record: 18-10

	Min.	Total FG/FGA	Pct.	3-Pt. FG/FGA	Pct.	FT/FTA	Pct.	Reb. O/T	A	TO	PF	S	Blk	TP	PPM
STEPHENS, DWAYNE	35	3/6	.500	0/0	.000	0/0	.000	0/1	3	2	3	0	1	6	.171
STEIGENGA, MATT	32	5/9	.556	0/0	.000	2/2	1.000	1/2	0	0	0	0	1	12	.375
PEPLOWSKI, MIKE	33	5/8	.625	0/0	.000	2/2	1.000	5/12	1	0	1	0	1	12	.364
MONTGOMERY, MARK	30	0/3	.000	0/2	.000	0/0	.000	0/1	4	1	5	0	1	0	.000
SMITH, STEVE	33	7/15	.467	3/7	.429	2/3	.667	0/5	1	3	1	0	0	19	.576
ZULAUF, JON	11	2/2	1.000	0/0	.000	0/0	.000	2/2	0	0	0	0	0	4	.364
HICKMAN, PARISH	12	2/4	.500	0/0	.000	0/0	.000	1/1	0	0	0	0	0	4	.333
PENICK, ANDY	13	1/2	.500	1/1	1.000	0/0	.000	0/0	4	0	0	0	0	3	.231
WESHINSKEY, KRIS	1	0/0	.000	0/0	.000	0/0	.000	0/0	0	0	0	0	0	0	.000
Totals	200	25/49	.510	4/10	.400	6/7	.857	9/24	13	6	10	0	4	60	.300

Wis.-Green Bay (58)   Coach: Dick Bennett

Season Record: 24-6

	Min.	Total FG/FGA	Pct.	3-Pt. FG/FGA	Pct.	FT/FTA	Pct.	Reb. O/T	A	TO	PF	S	Blk	TP	PPM
VANDER PLAS, DEAN	34	6/11	.545	1/2	.500	4/4	1.000	0/1	0	0	0	0	0	17	.500
JOHNSON, BEN	30	1/4	.250	1/2	.500	0/0	.000	2/4	1	0	3	0	0	3	.100
LUDVIGSON, JEREMY	26	1/2	.500	0/0	.000	1/1	1.000	1/2	0	0	1	0	0	3	.115
MARTINEZ, JOHN	30	3/8	.375	2/4	.500	2/2	1.000	1/2	3	1	1	1	0	10	.333
BENNETT, TONY	32	3/12	.250	3/7	.429	0/0	.000	0/2	10	4	4	1	0	9	.281
VANDER VELDEN, LOGAN	11	0/0	.000	0/0	.000	0/0	.000	1/1	0	0	0	0	0	0	.000
LEMOINE, SCOTT	7	0/0	.000	0/0	.000	0/0	.000	0/1	0	1	1	0	0	0	.000
RONDORF, DEAN	30	6/8	.750	4/5	.800	0/0	.000	1/3	1	0	0	0	0	16	.533
Totals	200	20/45	.444	11/20	.550	7/7	1.000	6/16	15	6	10	2	0	58	.290

Team Rebounds: Michigan St. 2; Wis.-Green Bay 6. Deadball Rebounds: Michigan St. 1; Wis.-Green Bay 1. Disqualified: Michigan St.—Montgomery.

	1st Half	2nd Half	Final
Michigan St.	30	30	60
Wis.-Green Bay	35	23	58

Utah (82)

Coach: Rick Majerus　　　　　　　　　　　　　　　　Season Record: 28-3

	Min.	Total FG/FGA	Pct.	3-Pt. FG/FGA	Pct.	FT/FTA	Pct.	Reb. O/T	A	TO	PF	S	Blk	TP	PPM
GRANT, JOSH	26	7/12	.583	1/ 4	.250	7/ 7	1.000	3/11	4	5	3	1	0	22	.846
MCGRATH, M'KAY	23	2/ 4	.500	0/ 0	.000	2/ 4	.500	1/ 6	2	1	1	0	0	6	.261
WATTS, WALTER	22	5/ 9	.556	0/ 0	.000	4/ 6	.667	3/11	1	1	1	1	1	14	.636
TATE, TYRONE	30	2/ 4	.500	0/ 0	.000	5/ 9	.556	0/ 1	4	2	1	1	0	9	.300
WILSON, BYRON	27	5/ 8	.625	1/ 1	1.000	2/ 3	.667	0/ 2	1	4	1	0	0	13	.481
SOTO, JIMMY	22	2/ 4	.500	0/ 1	.000	0/ 0	.000	1/ 3	4	5	2	2	0	4	.182
RYDALCH, CRAIG	22	2/ 7	.286	2/ 5	.400	0/ 0	.000	0/ 3	1	3	3	1	0	6	.273
DIXON, PHIL	12	1/ 5	.200	1/ 2	.500	0/ 0	.000	1/ 3	0	0	2	0	0	3	.250
AFEAKI, PAUL	15	1/ 5	.200	0/ 0	.000	3/ 3	1.000	2/ 2	0	2	2	0	1	5	.333
HOWARD, BARRY	1	0/ 0	.000	0/ 0	.000	0/ 0	.000	0/ 0	0	0	0	0	0	0	.000
Totals	200	27/58	.466	5/13	.385	23/32	.719	11/42	17	23	16	6	2	82	.410

South Alabama (72)

Coach: Ronnie Arrow　　　　　　　　　　　　　　　　Season Record: 22-8

	Min.	Total FG/FGA	Pct.	3-Pt. FG/FGA	Pct.	FT/FTA	Pct.	Reb. O/T	A	TO	PF	S	Blk	TP	PPM
EACKLES, MARVIN	23	5/ 8	.625	0/ 0	.000	4/ 5	.800	1/ 4	3	0	0	0	0	14	.609
CURTIS, BOBBY	22	3/ 8	.375	0/ 0	.000	1/ 2	.500	0/ 5	0	1	3	1	1	7	.318
ADAMS, THOMAS	25	3/ 5	.600	1/ 1	1.000	3/ 3	1.000	2/ 4	0	4	2	2	0	10	.400
MCDANIELS, KEVIN	29	3/ 9	.333	0/ 1	.000	0/ 1	.000	1/ 2	2	2	3	3	0	6	.207
YELDING, CEDRIC	30	0/ 6	.000	0/ 2	.000	0/ 0	.000	0/ 4	6	3	1	2	0	0	.000
PORTILLO, CESAR	10	1/ 6	.167	0/ 0	.000	1/ 4	.250	0/ 0	0	1	3	0	1	3	.300
JAMES, BOOBIE	23	7/10	.700	0/ 2	.000	1/ 2	.500	0/ 1	4	2	4	1	0	15	.652
HINES, SAMUEL	16	4/ 7	.571	0/ 0	.000	0/ 0	.000	4/ 6	0	1	5	1	0	8	.500
TURNER, DEREK	11	4/10	.400	1/ 6	.167	0/ 0	.000	0/ 0	0	0	3	0	0	9	.818
MITCHELL, ALONZO	6	0/ 4	.000	0/ 0	.000	0/ 0	.000	2/ 2	1	1	2	0	1	0	.000
WASHINGTON, DERELL	5	0/ 0	.000	0/ 0	.000	0/ 0	.000	0/ 1	1	0	0	0	0	0	.000
Totals	200	30/73	.411	2/12	.167	10/17	.588	10/29	17	16	26	10	3	72	.360

Team Rebounds: Utah 6; South Alabama 4. Deadball Rebounds: Utah 3; South Alabama 1. Team Turnovers: South Alabama 1. Disqualified: South Alabama—Hines.

	1st Half	2nd Half	Final
Utah	34	48	82
South Alabama	41	31	72

New Mexico State (56)   Coach: Neil McCarthy

Season Record: 23-5

	Min.	Total FG/FGA	Pct.	3–Pt. FG/FGA	Pct.	FT/FTA	Pct.	Reb. O/T	A	TO	PF	S	Blk	TP	PPM
JORDAN, REGGIE	25	2/ 7	.286	0/ 0	.000	1/ 2	.500	0/ 3	2	0	3	1	0	5	.200
WARE, TRACY	33	3/ 8	.375	0/ 0	.000	0/ 0	.000	3/13	0	0	2	1	2	6	.182
NEW, MICHAEL	37	4/10	.400	1/ 2	.500	0/ 1	.000	4/ 9	1	6	1	0	1	9	.243
BROWN, RANDY	30	3/ 7	.429	1/ 2	.500	5/ 6	.833	0/ 3	4	2	5	1	1	12	.400
BENJAMIN, WILLIAM	32	2/ 9	.222	1/ 3	.333	0/ 0	.000	1/ 1	5	2	2	2	0	5	.156
BENNETT, TERRY	13	3/13	.231	3/11	.273	0/ 0	.000	0/ 0	0	0	1	0	0	9	.692
PUTZI, RON	16	2/ 7	.286	2/ 6	.333	0/ 0	.000	0/ 0	0	2	1	0	1	6	.375
HICKMAN, CHRIS	14	1/ 4	.250	0/ 0	.000	2/ 2	1.000	4/ 6	0	2	4	0	1	4	.286
Totals	200	20/65	.308	8/24	.333	8/11	.727	12/35	12	14	19	5	6	56	.280

Creighton (64)   Coach: Tony Barone

Season Record: 23-7

	Min.	Total FG/FGA	Pct.	3–Pt. FG/FGA	Pct.	FT/FTA	Pct.	Reb. O/T	A	TO	PF	S	Blk	TP	PPM
HARSTAD, BOB	37	5/11	.455	0/ 0	.000	3/ 6	.500	3/16	1	4	3	1	0	13	.351
PLAUTZ, DARIN	12	0/ 1	.000	0/ 1	.000	0/ 0	.000	1/ 3	3	0	1	0	2	0	.000
GALLAGHER, CHAD	37	9/17	.529	0/ 0	.000	0/ 0	.000	5/14	0	1	2	1	4	18	.486
PETTY, MATT	16	1/ 2	.500	1/ 2	.500	0/ 0	.000	0/ 1	1	1	0	0	0	3	.188
COLE, DUAN	37	6/12	.500	3/ 4	.750	2/ 2	1.000	0/ 1	4	3	1	2	0	17	.459
EISNER, TODD	32	1/ 9	.111	1/ 8	.125	2/ 2	1.000	0/ 1	4	3	4	2	0	5	.156
WRIGHTSELL, LATRELL	27	1/ 3	.333	0/ 0	.000	6/ 8	.750	1/ 6	7	1	0	2	0	8	.296
RODGERS, CHRIS	2	0/ 1	.000	0/ 0	.000	0/ 0	.000	0/ 0	0	0	1	0	0	0	.000
Totals	200	23/56	.411	5/15	.333	13/18	.722	10/42	20	13	12	8	6	64	.320

Team Rebounds: Creighton 3; New Mexico St. 2. Deadball Rebounds: Creighton 3; New Mexico St. 1. Disqualified: New Mexico St.—Brown.

	1st Half	2nd Half	Final
New Mexico St.	19	37	56
Creighton	24	40	64

Seton Hall (71)   Coach: P. J. Carlesimo   Season Record: 22-8

	Min.	Total FG/FGA	Pct.	3–Pt. FG/FGA	Pct.	FT/FTA	Pct.	Reb. O/T	A	TO	PF	S	Blk	TP	PPM
WINCHESTER, GORDON	36	1/2	.500	0/0	.000	2/4	.500	1/4	4	3	2	2	3	4	.111
KARNISHOVAS, ARTURAS	30	3/6	.500	2/4	.500	0/0	.000	2/4	2	1	3	5	0	8	.267
AVENT, ANTHONY	19	6/9	.667	0/0	.000	1/1	1.000	1/4	0	1	4	1	1	13	.684
TAYLOR, OLIVER	23	3/7	.429	1/2	.500	0/0	.000	0/1	3	1	0	2	0	7	.304
DEHERE, TERRY	35	9/17	.529	4/8	.500	4/5	.800	1/4	2	3	1	3	0	26	.743
CAVER, BRYAN	19	2/4	.500	1/1	1.000	0/0	.000	0/0	3	2	1	3	0	5	.263
CRIST, DARYL	2	0/0	.000	0/0	.000	0/0	.000	0/0	0	0	0	0	0	0	.000
WALKER, JERRY	23	2/2	1.000	0/0	.000	4/6	.667	0/3	0	1	3	1	0	8	.348
BARNEA, ASSAF	11	0/1	.000	0/0	.000	0/0	.000	0/0	0	1	1	0	0	0	.000
DAVIS, CHRIS	2	0/0	.000	0/0	.000	0/0	.000	0/0	0	0	1	0	0	0	.000
Totals	200	26/48	.542	8/15	.533	11/16	.688	5/20	14	13	16	17	4	71	.355

Pepperdine (51)   Coach: Tom Asbury   Season Record: 22-8

	Min.	Total FG/FGA	Pct.	3–Pt. FG/FGA	Pct.	FT/FTA	Pct.	Reb. O/T	A	TO	PF	S	Blk	TP	PPM
JONES, DANA	35	5/8	.625	0/0	.000	0/0	.000	2/9	5	5	2	0	1	10	.286
LEAR, GEOFF	35	5/10	.500	0/0	.000	4/9	.444	2/7	0	5	4	0	0	14	.400
NOETHER, DEREK	10	0/1	.000	0/0	.000	0/0	.000	0/1	0	2	0	0	0	0	.000
LOPEZ, DAMIN	32	2/6	.333	2/6	.333	0/0	.000	0/0	2	3	1	1	0	6	.188
WELCH, RICK	35	3/10	.300	2/6	.333	2/2	1.000	0/1	3	3	3	3	0	10	.286
GUILD, STEVE	30	2/8	.250	1/4	.250	0/0	.000	3/4	3	4	1	2	0	5	.167
CLOVER, STEVE	2	0/0	.000	0/0	.000	0/0	.000	0/0	0	0	1	0	0	0	.000
SANDERS, RODNEY	3	1/1	1.000	1/1	1.000	0/0	.000	0/0	0	0	0	0	0	3	1.000
MANU, REX	18	0/4	.000	0/0	.000	3/4	.750	3/4	1	1	2	1	0	3	.167
Totals	200	18/48	.375	6/17	.353	9/15	.600	10/26	14	23	14	7	1	51	.255

Team Rebounds: Seton Hall 4; Pepperdine 4. Deadball Rebounds: Seton Hall 5; Pepperdine 4. Disqualified: None.
Technical Fouls: Seton Hall—Coach Carlesimo.

	1st Half	2nd Half	Final
Seton Hall	32	39	71
Pepperdine	25	26	51

Virginia (48)   Coach: Jeff Jones   Season Record: 21-11

	Min.	Total FG/FGA	Pct.	3–Pt. FG/FGA	Pct.	FT/FTA	Pct.	Reb. O/T	A	TO	PF	S	Blk	TP	PPM
TURNER, KENNY	32	3/17	.176	1/6	.167	1/2	.500	7/8	0	1	5	3	0	8	.250
STITH, BRYANT	38	4/13	.308	0/3	.000	5/5	1.000	4/8	0	4	2	2	1	13	.342
JEFFRIES, TED	34	3/9	.333	0/0	.000	0/0	.000	3/6	0	2	2	1	0	6	.176
OLIVER, ANTHONY	20	0/5	.000	0/1	.000	0/0	.000	0/0	2	1	5	1	0	0	.000
CROTTY, JOHN	40	8/18	.444	0/3	.000	4/5	.800	1/3	4	0	3	3	0	20	.500
FLORIANI, BERNIE	1	0/0	.000	0/0	.000	0/0	.000	0/0	0	0	0	0	0	0	.000
SMITH, DOUG	9	0/1	.000	0/1	.000	0/0	.000	0/0	1	0	1	0	0	0	.000
KATSTRA, DIRK	4	0/2	.000	0/1	.000	0/0	.000	0/0	0	0	0	0	0	0	.000
BLUNDIN, MATT	12	0/0	.000	0/0	.000	0/0	.000	0/2	0	0	1	0	0	0	.000
PARKER, CORNEL	10	0/0	.000	0/0	.000	1/2	.500	0/1	0	0	4	1	0	1	.100
Totals	200	18/65	.277	1/15	.067	11/14	.786	15/28	7	8	23	11	1	48	.240

Brigham Young (61)   Coach: Roger Reid   Season Record: 20-12

	Min.	Total FG/FGA	Pct.	3–Pt. FG/FGA	Pct.	FT/FTA	Pct.	Reb. O/T	A	TO	PF	S	Blk	TP	PPM
ROBERTS, KENNETH	24	1/1	1.000	0/0	.000	0/0	.000	0/3	1	4	0	0	1	2	.083
SCHREINER, STEVE	21	5/6	.833	0/0	.000	2/4	.500	1/4	0	4	1	0	0	12	.571
BRADLEY, SHAWN	37	3/10	.300	0/0	.000	2/2	1.000	0/5	1	2	3	0	10	8	.216
CALL, NATHAN	33	2/3	.667	1/2	.500	2/2	1.000	2/4	5	3	3	1	0	7	.212
MOON, SCOTT	22	2/6	.333	1/1	1.000	5/6	.833	0/0	1	1	3	0	1	10	.455
HESLOP, MARK	22	1/3	.333	0/2	.000	5/5	1.000	0/3	1	1	2	0	0	7	.318
SANTIAGO, MARK	7	0/0	.000	0/0	.000	0/0	.000	0/1	1	1	0	0	0	0	.000
TROST, GARY	27	4/6	.667	0/0	.000	5/6	.833	3/11	2	3	2	0	1	13	.481
MILLER, JARED	7	1/2	.500	0/0	.000	0/0	.000	0/2	0	0	1	0	0	2	.286
Totals	200	19/37	.514	2/5	.400	21/25	.840	6/33	12	19	15	1	13	61	.305

Team Rebounds: Brigham Young 3; Virginia 4. Deadball Rebounds: Brigham Young 2; Virginia 2. Disqualified: Virginia—Turner, Oliver.

	1st Half	2nd Half	Final
Virginia	22	26	48
Brigham Young	19	42	61

Arizona (93)   Coach: Lute Olson   Season Record: 26-6

	Min.	Total FG/FGA	Pct.	3–Pt. FG/FGA	Pct.	FT/FTA	Pct.	Reb. O/T	A	TO	PF	S	Blk	TP	PPM
MILLS, CHRIS	37	7/12	.583	1/3	.333	6/7	.857	3/8	2	2	4	0	1	21	.568
ROOKS, SEAN	29	4/11	.364	0/0	.000	1/3	.333	2/6	0	3	2	0	4	9	.310
WILLIAMS, BRIAN	23	2/5	.400	0/0	.000	0/0	.000	1/6	1	1	3	0	1	4	.174
OTHICK, MATT	33	8/10	.800	5/7	.714	4/6	.667	0/0	7	1	1	4	0	25	.758
MUEHLEBACH, MATT	31	6/8	.750	2/3	.667	2/2	1.000	0/1	7	1	1	2	0	16	.516
REEVES, KHALID	19	4/6	.667	0/1	.000	3/4	.750	0/2	2	3	0	1	1	11	.579
SCHMIDT, CASEY	1	0/0	.000	0/0	.000	0/0	.000	0/0	0	0	0	0	0	0	.000
JOHNSON, DERON	1	0/0	.000	0/0	.000	0/0	.000	0/0	0	0	0	0	0	0	.000
WOMACK, WAYNE	9	0/0	.000	0/0	.000	1/2	.500	1/1	0	2	3	0	0	1	.111
STOKES, ED	16	2/4	.500	0/0	.000	2/2	1.000	0/4	1	0	3	0	1	6	.375
FLANAGAN, KEVIN	1	0/0	.000	0/0	.000	0/0	.000	0/0	0	0	0	0	0	0	.000
Totals	200	33/56	.589	8/14	.571	19/26	.731	7/28	20	13	17	7	8	93	.465

St. Francis-Pa. (80)   Coach: Jim Baron   Season Record: 24-7

	Min.	Total FG/FGA	Pct.	3–Pt. FG/FGA	Pct.	FT/FTA	Pct.	Reb. O/T	A	TO	PF	S	Blk	TP	PPM
BENNETCH, TOM	29	2/6	.333	0/1	.000	0/0	.000	0/3	1	1	4	0	0	4	.138
ANDERSON, JOE	37	11/20	.550	5/7	.714	2/2	1.000	4/12	1	7	2	3	0	29	.784
FINK, MIKE	25	2/7	.286	0/0	.000	2/4	.500	2/2	1	1	4	0	0	6	.240
HILVERT, JOHN	33	6/12	.500	5/8	.625	0/0	.000	5/7	3	1	1	0	0	17	.515
IUZZOLINO, MIKE	35	7/13	.538	3/8	.375	3/4	.750	0/1	6	5	4	0	0	20	.571
STRACHAN, STEVE	11	0/0	.000	0/0	.000	0/0	.000	0/1	1	0	1	1	0	0	.000
CLORAN, STEVE	1	0/0	.000	0/0	.000	0/0	.000	0/0	0	0	0	0	0	0	.000
PACSI, ROBERT	1	0/1	.000	0/0	.000	0/0	.000	0/0	0	0	0	0	0	0	.000
SMITH, WILLIE	1	0/1	.000	0/1	.000	0/0	.000	0/0	0	0	0	0	0	0	.000
HORN, JIM	1	0/0	.000	0/0	.000	0/0	.000	1/1	0	0	0	0	0	0	.000
PATTERSON, ANTOINE	16	1/4	.250	0/0	.000	0/0	.000	0/1	1	1	4	0	0	2	.125
SEAWARD, BILL	1	0/0	.000	0/0	.000	0/0	.000	0/1	0	0	0	0	0	0	.000
GEORGE, DEON	9	0/2	.000	0/0	.000	2/2	1.000	2/4	0	1	3	0	0	2	.222
Totals	200	29/66	.439	13/25	.520	9/12	.750	14/33	14	17	23	4	0	80	.400

Team Rebounds: Arizona 2; St. Francis-Pa. 2. Deadball Rebounds: Arizona 3; St. Francis-Pa. 2. Disqualified: None. Technical Fouls: Arizona—Williams.

	1st Half	2nd Half	Final
Arizona	43	50	93
St. Francis-Pa.	29	51	80

FIRST ROUND MIDWEST

Ohio State (97)   Coach: Randy Ayers

Season Record: 25-3

	Min.	Total FG/FGA	Pct.	3-Pt. FG/FGA	Pct.	FT/FTA	Pct.	Reb. O/T	A	TO	PF	S	Blk	TP	PPM
JACKSON, JIM	32	10/17	.588	1/ 3	.333	3/ 5	.600	3/ 8	5	1	4	0	2	24	.750
JENT, CHRIS	30	5/11	.455	3/ 5	.600	4/ 4	1.000	0/ 3	3	1	2	1	0	17	.567
CARTER, PERRY	31	7/12	.583	0/ 0	.000	1/ 8	.125	6/11	0	1	3	1	1	15	.484
BAKER, MARK	36	4/ 6	.667	0/ 0	.000	4/ 8	.500	0/ 5	9	6	3	4	2	12	.333
BROWN, JAMAAL	26	3/ 8	.375	1/ 1	1.000	8/11	.727	1/ 4	2	3	4	0	0	15	.577
ROBINSON, BILL	8	1/ 1	1.000	0/ 0	.000	0/ 0	.000	1/ 4	0	1	4	0	0	2	.250
DAVIS, ALEX	8	1/ 2	.500	0/ 1	.000	0/ 0	.000	0/ 1	1	1	0	1	0	2	.250
LEE, TREG	14	4/ 6	.667	0/ 0	.000	2/ 2	1.000	0/ 4	0	0	5	0	0	10	.714
BRANDEWIE, TOM	9	0/ 0	.000	0/ 0	.000	0/ 1	.000	1/ 4	0	0	0	0	1	0	.000
SKELTON, JAMIE	6	0/ 0	.000	0/ 0	.000	0/ 0	.000	0/ 0	0	1	0	0	0	0	.000
Totals	200	35/63	.556	5/10	.500	22/39	.564	12/44	20	15	25	7	6	97	.485

Towson State (86)   Coach: Terry Truax

Season Record: 19-10

	Min.	Total FG/FGA	Pct.	3-Pt. FG/FGA	Pct.	FT/FTA	Pct.	Reb. O/T	A	TO	PF	S	Blk	TP	PPM
LIGHTENING, CHUCK	35	8/24	.333	1/ 2	.500	9/13	.692	4/ 6	0	1	2	1	0	26	.743
BROWN, LARRY	24	2/ 4	.500	0/ 0	.000	0/ 0	.000	3/ 4	1	1	3	0	0	4	.167
JAMES, JOHN	33	2/ 2	1.000	0/ 0	.000	2/ 4	.500	2/11	2	2	3	1	0	6	.182
BOYD, DEVIN	21	5/11	.455	1/ 5	.200	1/ 2	1.000	1/ 2	0	5	5	0	0	17	.810
JACOBS, TERRANCE	34	8/17	.471	2/ 2	1.000	4/ 7	.571	3/ 5	3	2	5	2	0	22	.647
WALLER, LEWIS	27	1/ 5	.200	0/ 2	.000	4/ 4	1.000	1/ 2	6	5	1	0	0	6	.222
CAMPBELL, MATT	15	0/ 1	.000	0/ 0	.000	0/ 0	.000	0/ 3	0	0	3	0	0	0	.000
GRIFFIN, WILLIAM	5	1/ 3	.333	0/ 0	.000	0/ 0	.000	1/ 1	0	0	3	0	1	2	.400
RAY, MYRON	2	0/ 2	.000	0/ 2	.000	0/ 0	.000	0/ 0	0	0	3	0	0	0	.000
MANNING, PATRICK	1	1/ 1	1.000	0/ 0	.000	0/ 0	.000	1/ 1	0	0	0	0	0	2	2.000
VALENTINE, CRAIG	1	0/ 0	.000	0/ 0	.000	1/ 2	.500	0/ 1	0	0	0	0	0	1	1.000
CALDWELL, TOM	1	0/ 1	.000	0/ 0	.000	0/ 0	.000	1/ 1	0	0	0	0	0	0	.000
MASON, ANDREW	1	0/ 1	.000	0/ 0	.000	0/ 0	.000	0/ 0	0	0	0	0	0	0	.000
Totals	200	28/72	.389	4/13	.308	26/36	.722	17/37	12	16	28	4	1	86	.430

Team Rebounds: Ohio State 0; Towson State 6. Deadball Rebounds: Ohio State 10; Towson State 2. Team Turnovers: Towson State 1. Disqualified: Ohio State—Lee; Towson State—Boyd, Jacobs. Technical Fouls: Towson State—bench.

	1st Half	2nd Half	Final
Ohio State	45	52	97
Towson State	37	49	86

Georgia Tech (87)   Coach: Bobby Cremins   Season Record: 16-12

	Min.	Total FG / FGA	Pct.	3–Pt. FG / FGA	Pct.	FT / FTA	Pct.	Reb. O / T	A	TO	PF	S	Blk	TP	PPM
HILL, BRYAN	34	2/ 2	1.000	1/ 1	1.000	5/ 8	.625	2/ 7	6	0	2	0	0	10	.294
MACKEY, MALCOLM	29	6/12	.500	0/ 0	.000	0/ 2	.000	5/ 8	0	3	4	0	1	12	.414
GEIGER, MATT	28	4/ 5	.800	0/ 0	.000	0/ 0	.000	1/ 3	1	1	4	0	1	8	.286
ANDERSON, KENNY	37	12/23	.522	3/ 8	.375	4/ 4	1.000	1/ 4	5	3	2	2	0	31	.838
BARRY, JON	36	9/13	.692	2/ 4	.500	2/ 3	.667	0/ 3	3	2	2	0	0	22	.611
DOMALIK, BRIAN	13	0/ 1	.000	0/ 1	.000	1/ 2	.500	0/ 1	1	1	0	0	0	1	.077
NEWBILL, IVANO	23	1/ 2	.500	0/ 0	.000	1/ 2	.500	3/ 6	0	1	2	0	0	3	.130
Totals	200	34/58	.586	6/14	.429	13/21	.619	12/32	16	11	16	2	2	87	.435

DePaul (70)   Coach: Joey Meyer   Season Record: 20-8

	Min.	Total FG / FGA	Pct.	3–Pt. FG / FGA	Pct.	FT / FTA	Pct.	Reb. O / T	A	TO	PF	S	Blk	TP	PPM
DAVIS, TERRY	29	5/12	.417	0/ 2	.000	0/ 0	.000	1/ 1	1	3	1	0	0	10	.345
BOOTH, DAVID	29	2/ 8	.250	0/ 2	.000	1/ 2	.500	0/ 5	0	3	1	0	0	5	.172
STERN, JEFF	19	3/ 6	.500	0/ 0	.000	1/ 4	.250	3/ 4	1	1	2	0	0	7	.368
DAUGHIRTY, JOE	24	2/ 5	.400	1/ 3	.333	1/ 2	.500	0/ 0	4	2	3	0	0	6	.250
FOSTER, MELVON	16	0/ 4	.000	0/ 1	.000	0/ 1	.000	1/ 3	0	0	2	0	0	0	.000
HOWARD, STEPHEN	31	5/13	.385	1/ 2	.500	3/ 6	.500	5/ 7	0	2	3	1	0	14	.452
HOLLAND, KEVIN	21	4/ 6	.667	0/ 0	.000	3/ 4	.750	5/10	0	0	2	0	0	11	.524
NIEMANN, BRAD	10	1/ 3	.333	1/ 3	.333	0/ 0	.000	0/ 0	1	0	1	0	0	3	.300
PRICE, CURTIS	8	0/ 0	.000	0/ 0	.000	0/ 0	.000	0/ 0	0	1	0	0	0	0	.000
MURPHY, CHUCK	12	5/ 5	1.000	4/ 4	1.000	0/ 0	.000	0/ 0	4	1	2	0	0	14	1.167
RAVIZEE, MICHAEL	1	0/ 0	.000	0/ 0	.000	0/ 0	.000	0/ 0	0	0	0	0	0	0	.000
Totals	200	27/62	.435	7/17	.412	9/19	.474	15/30	10	14	16	1	0	70	.350

Team Rebounds: Georgia Tech 1; DePaul 3. Deadball Rebounds: Georgia Tech 4; DePaul 7. Disqualified: None.

	1st Half	2nd Half	Final
Georgia Tech	35	52	87
DePaul	26	44	70

Texas (73) Coach: Tom Penders

Season Record: 22-8

	Min.	Total FG/FGA	Pct.	3–Pt. FG/FGA	Pct.	FT/FTA	Pct.	Reb. O/T	A	TO	PF	S	Blk	TP	PPM
WILLIAMS, BENFORD	36	7/12	.583	0/ 0	.000	1/ 2	.500	2/ 8	5	4	3	0	0	15	.417
COLLIE, LOCKSLEY	15	3/ 6	.500	0/ 1	.000	0/ 0	.000	1/ 2	0	2	2	0	0	6	.400
MYERS, GUILLERMO	27	4/ 5	.800	0/ 0	.000	1/ 4	.250	5/17	1	2	2	0	4	9	.333
JEANS, COURTNEY	23	3/ 5	.600	0/ 0	.000	1/ 2	.500	2/ 3	1	2	3	0	0	7	.304
WRIGHT, JOEY	40	4/10	.400	0/ 1	.000	0/ 0	.000	0/ 2	2	3	2	0	0	8	.200
CAMBRIDGE, DEXTER	25	6/10	.600	0/ 2	.000	6/ 6	1.000	1/ 5	4	2	2	1	0	18	.720
BURDITT, ALBERT	12	1/ 1	1.000	0/ 0	.000	0/ 0	.000	1/ 3	1	0	2	0	0	2	.167
MCCOY, TEYON	18	3/ 4	.750	2/ 2	1.000	0/ 1	.000	0/ 0	1	1	0	0	0	8	.444
SHEPARD, WINN	3	0/ 0	.000	0/ 0	.000	0/ 3	.000	1/ 1	0	0	1	0	0	0	.000
DUDEK, HANK	1	0/ 0	.000	0/ 0	.000	0/ 0	.000	0/ 0	0	0	0	0	0	0	.000
Totals	200	31/53	.585	2/ 6	.333	9/18	.500	13/41	15	16	17	1	4	73	.365

St. Peter's (65) Coach: Ted Fiore

Season Record: 24-6

	Min.	Total FG/FGA	Pct.	3–Pt. FG/FGA	Pct.	FT/FTA	Pct.	Reb. O/T	A	TO	PF	S	Blk	TP	PPM
WALKER, TONY	35	10/17	.588	0/ 1	.000	1/ 3	.333	1/ 6	0	2	3	0	0	21	.600
ANDREWS, MARVIN	40	3/ 9	.333	0/ 1	.000	6/ 9	.667	4/ 7	6	1	4	0	1	12	.300
CONNELL, JOHN	13	2/ 4	.500	0/ 0	.000	0/ 0	.000	2/ 2	0	0	4	0	0	4	.308
WALKER, JASPER	33	1/ 7	.143	1/ 4	.250	0/ 0	.000	0/ 0	6	3	4	2	0	3	.091
ALLEN, ANTOINE	39	4/ 8	.500	1/ 4	.250	0/ 0	.000	0/ 3	1	0	1	2	0	9	.231
MERRIMAN, OYANGO	27	6/10	.600	0/ 0	.000	1/ 5	.200	3/ 6	0	2	3	1	0	13	.481
GIBSON, WALTER	9	1/ 3	.333	1/ 3	.333	0/ 0	.000	0/ 0	1	0	0	0	0	3	.333
MACK, KEN	4	0/ 1	.000	0/ 0	.000	0/ 0	.000	0/ 1	0	1	1	0	0	0	.000
Totals	200	27/59	.458	3/13	.231	8/17	.471	10/25	14	9	20	5	1	65	.325

Team Rebounds: Texas 0; St. Peter's 1; Deadball Rebounds: Texas 1; St. Peter's 2. Disqualified: None.

	1st Half	2nd Half	Final
Texas	32	41	73
St. Peter's	30	35	65

St. John's (75)   Coach: Lou Carnesecca

Season Record: 20-8

	Min.	Total FG/FGA	Pct.	3-Pt. FG/FGA	Pct.	FT/FTA	Pct.	Reb. O/T	A	TO	PF	S	Blk	TP	PPM
SEALY, MALIK	40	8/16	.500	0/ 0	.000	3/ 6	.500	2/ 8	4	2	2	4	1	19	.475
SINGLETON, BILLY	35	3/ 5	.600	0/ 0	.000	7/ 8	.875	0/ 2	1	1	2	0	0	13	.371
WERDANN, ROBERT	14	4/ 6	.667	0/ 0	.000	4/ 4	1.000	1/ 3	0	0	3	0	2	12	.857
BUCHANAN, JASON	39	5/11	.455	3/ 6	.500	7/ 8	.875	2/ 4	5	1	2	3	0	20	.513
SPROLING, CHUCKY	22	1/ 3	.333	1/ 2	.500	2/ 4	.500	1/ 1	5	0	4	0	0	5	.227
MUTO, SEAN	11	0/ 1	.000	0/ 0	.000	0/ 0	.000	0/ 1	0	1	2	0	0	0	.000
CAIN, DAVID	19	1/ 3	.333	0/ 0	.000	0/ 4	.000	0/ 1	2	0	3	1	0	2	.105
SCOTT, SHAWNELLE	20	2/ 5	.400	0/ 0	.000	0/ 0	.000	2/ 5	0	0	2	0	0	4	.200
Totals	200	24/50	.480	4/ 8	.500	23/34	.676	8/25	17	5	20	8	3	75	.375

Northern Ill. (68)   Coach: Jim Molinari

Season Record: 25-5

	Min.	Total FG/FGA	Pct.	3-Pt. FG/FGA	Pct.	FT/FTA	Pct.	Reb. O/T	A	TO	PF	S	Blk	TP	PPM
HARMON, ANTWON	21	0/ 3	.000	0/ 0	.000	1/ 2	.500	3/ 4	0	1	4	0	0	1	.048
THOMAS, DONNELL	36	9/14	.643	1/ 1	1.000	4/ 6	.667	3/12	0	2	3	0	0	23	.639
WELLS, ANDREW	22	2/ 4	.500	0/ 0	.000	1/ 2	.500	0/ 5	0	2	1	0	3	5	.227
WHITESIDE, DONALD	39	8/15	.533	3/ 8	.375	1/ 2	.500	1/ 1	5	3	4	0	1	20	.513
LIPNISKY, MIKE	17	0/ 2	.000	0/ 0	.000	5/ 6	.833	0/ 1	1	2	3	0	0	5	.294
MOLIS, BRIAN	15	0/ 2	.000	0/ 2	.000	0/ 0	.000	0/ 2	0	1	2	0	0	0	.000
HIDDEN, MIKE	24	3/ 6	.500	1/ 2	.500	3/ 5	.600	1/ 3	3	1	5	0	0	10	.417
FENS, RANDY	19	1/ 3	.333	0/ 0	.000	0/ 0	.000	1/ 5	2	0	1	0	1	2	.105
ARRINGTON, STACY	7	1/ 2	.500	0/ 0	.000	0/ 0	.000	0/ 0	2	1	2	0	0	2	.286
Totals	200	24/51	.471	5/13	.385	15/23	.652	9/33	13	13	25	0	5	68	.340

Team Rebounds: St. John's 2; Northern Ill. 5. Deadball Rebounds: St. John's 3; Northern Ill. 4. Disqualified: Northern Ill.—Hidden.

	1st Half	2nd Half	Final
St. John's	41	34	75
Northern Ill.	25	43	68

Louisiana State (62) Coach: Dale Brown

Season Record: 20-9

	Min.	Total FG / FGA	Pct.	3–Pt. FG / FGA	Pct.	FT / FTA	Pct.	Reb. O / T	A	TO	PF	S	Blk	TP	PPM
SINGLETON, VERNEL	32	2/ 9	.222	0/ 0	.000	3/ 6	.500	3/ 4	0	2	1	0	0	7	.219
BOUDREAUX, HAROLD	20	1/ 8	.125	1/ 5	.200	0/ 0	.000	3/ 4	1	3	3	0	0	3	.150
O'NEAL, SHAQUILLE	35	11/22	.500	0/ 0	.000	5/ 6	.833	6/16	0	2	4	1	5	27	.771
HANSEN, MIKE	21	2/ 9	.222	1/ 5	.200	0/ 0	.000	1/ 2	1	0	0	1	0	5	.238
PUGH, T.J.	24	0/ 6	.000	0/ 4	.000	0/ 0	.000	0/ 2	4	4	1	2	0	0	.000
SIMS, WAYNE	16	1/ 4	.250	0/ 2	.000	0/ 0	.000	1/ 2	1	0	0	0	1	2	.125
BURNS, LENEAR	9	1/ 2	.500	0/ 1	.000	0/ 0	.000	0/ 1	1	0	1	0	0	2	.222
GRIGGS, SHAWN	22	3/ 9	.333	1/ 1	1.000	0/ 0	.000	5/ 7	3	0	5	3	0	7	.318
PICOU, JOHN	15	1/ 1	1.000	1/ 1	1.000	0/ 1	.000	1/ 1	2	2	4	0	0	3	.200
HAMMINK, GEERT	5	1/ 4	.250	0/ 0	.000	2/ 2	1.000	2/ 5	0	1	0	0	0	4	.800
KRAJEWSKI, RICHARD	1	1/ 1	1.000	0/ 0	.000	0/ 0	.000	1/ 1	0	0	0	0	0	2	2.000
Totals	200	24/75	.320	4/19	.211	10/15	.667	23/45	13	14	19	7	6	62	.310

U. Conn. (79) Coach: Jim Calhoun

Season Record: 18-10

	Min.	Total FG / FGA	Pct.	3–Pt. FG / FGA	Pct.	FT / FTA	Pct.	Reb. O / T	A	TO	PF	S	Blk	TP	PPM
BURRELL, SCOTT	39	4/10	.400	1/ 4	.250	0/ 0	.000	1/ 8	2	1	0	1	4	9	.231
WALKER, TORAINO	16	4/ 5	.800	0/ 0	.000	0/ 1	.000	3/ 5	3	2	3	0	0	8	.500
SELLERS, ROD	32	6/10	.600	0/ 0	.000	1/ 4	.250	3/10	3	2	3	2	0	13	.406
PIKIELL, STEVE	19	1/ 1	1.000	0/ 0	.000	1/ 2	.500	0/ 0	0	1	0	0	3	.158	
SMITH, CHRIS	40	10/16	.625	3/ 4	.750	2/ 5	.400	1/ 4	5	5	1	2	0	25	.625
DEPRIEST, LYMAN	19	1/ 4	.250	0/ 0	.000	0/ 1	.000	1/ 3	3	2	2	3	0	2	.105
GWYNN, JOHN	24	4/11	.364	0/ 0	.000	9/11	.818	1/ 2	3	1	2	1	0	17	.708
CYRULIK, DAN	11	1/ 2	.500	0/ 0	.000	0/ 0	.000	1/ 3	2	1	4	0	1	2	.182
Totals	200	31/59	.525	4/ 8	.500	13/24	.542	11/35	21	14	16	9	5	79	.395

Team Rebounds: U. Conn. 9; Louisiana St. 1. Disqualified: Louisiana St.—Griggs.

	1st Half	2nd Half	Final
Louisiana St.	25	37	62
U. Conn.	36	43	79

Nebraska (84)   Coach: Danny Nee   Season Record: 26-7

	Min.	Total FG / FGA	Pct.	3-Pt. FG / FGA	Pct.	FT / FTA	Pct.	Reb. O / T	A	TO	PF	S	Blk	TP	PPM
FARMER, TONY	27	5/ 9	.556	0/ 1	.000	5/ 8	.625	2/ 3	1	0	5	2	0	15	.556
REID, BEAU	27	2/12	.167	0/ 3	.000	2/ 4	.500	3/ 7	2	5	3	1	0	6	.222
KING, RICH	33	11/17	.647	1/ 1	1.000	2/ 7	.286	8/12	4	0	4	2	2	25	.758
MOODY, KEITH	19	1/ 3	.333	0/ 0	.000	0/ 0	.000	0/ 2	3	4	3	1	0	2	.105
SCALES, CLIFFORD	32	4/ 5	.800	1/ 2	.500	3/ 4	.750	2/ 4	3	3	4	1	0	12	.375
HAYES, CARL	29	7/12	.583	0/ 0	.000	1/ 3	.333	4/ 6	2	3	3	0	0	15	.517
OWENS, DAPREIS	10	0/ 1	.000	0/ 0	.000	0/ 0	.000	0/ 1	0	1	1	0	1	0	.000
PIATKOWSKI, ERIC	23	3/10	.300	2/ 6	.333	1/ 1	1.000	1/ 3	2	1	2	1	2	9	.391
Totals	200	33/69	.478	4/13	.308	14/27	.519	20/38	17	18	25	8	5	84	.420

Xavier (Ohio) (89)   Coach: Pete Gillen   Season Record: 21-9

	Min.	Total FG / FGA	Pct.	3-Pt. FG / FGA	Pct.	FT / FTA	Pct.	Reb. O / T	A	TO	PF	S	Blk	TP	PPM
DAVENPORT, MICHAEL	35	5/13	.385	3/ 8	.375	4/ 4	1.000	0/ 2	1	2	2	2	0	17	.486
WILLIAMS, AARON	20	0/ 1	.000	0/ 0	.000	4/ 4	1.000	0/ 2	0	2	5	1	1	4	.200
GRANT, BRIAN	32	3/ 6	.500	0/ 0	.000	9/12	.750	1/10	0	3	4	0	0	15	.469
WALKER, JAMAL	33	5/ 9	.556	1/ 2	.500	7/11	.636	1/ 3	8	2	3	2	0	18	.545
GLADDEN, JAMIE	38	9/15	.600	2/ 3	.667	0/ 0	.000	1/ 3	3	3	0	1	0	20	.526
BRANTLEY, MAURICE	12	2/ 3	.667	0/ 1	.000	2/ 4	.500	1/ 1	2	2	4	2	0	6	.500
WILSON, DWAYNE	21	2/ 2	1.000	0/ 0	.000	1/ 2	.500	2/ 2	0	0	2	1	0	5	.238
EDWARDS, ERIK	7	1/ 1	1.000	0/ 0	.000	0/ 0	.000	1/ 1	0	0	2	0	1	2	.286
PARKER, COLIN	2	0/ 0	.000	0/ 0	.000	2/ 3	.667	0/ 1	0	0	0	0	0	2	1.000
Totals	200	27/50	.540	6/14	.429	29/40	.725	7/25	14	15	22	9	2	89	.445

Team Rebounds: Xavier (Ohio) 5; Nebraska 3. Deadball Rebounds: Xavier (Ohio) 6; Nebraska 6. Team Turnovers: Xavier (Ohio) 1; Nebraska 1. Disqualified: Xavier (Ohio)—Williams; Nebraska—Farmer.

	1st Half	2nd Half	Final
Nebraska	42	42	84
Xavier (Ohio)	45	44	89

Iowa (76)   Coach: Tom Davis

Season Record: 20-10

	Min.	Total FG/FGA	Pct.	3-Pt. FG/FGA	Pct.	FT/FTA	Pct.	Reb. O/T	A	TO	PF	S	Blk	TP	PPM
DAVIS, RODELL	20	3/ 4	.750	1/ 1	1.000	4/ 4	1.000	2/ 4	0	2	1	2	0	11	.550
STREET, CHRIS	23	0/ 3	.000	0/ 0	.000	2/ 4	.500	1/ 7	3	2	2	5	0	2	.087
WINTERS, JAMES	20	3/ 4	.750	0/ 0	.000	0/ 0	.000	3/ 6	1	6	2	0	1	6	.300
SKINNER, TROY	29	4/ 4	1.000	4/ 4	1.000	2/ 2	1.000	1/ 3	3	3	4	0	0	14	.483
MOSES, JAMES	34	5/ 9	.556	2/ 3	.667	2/ 2	1.000	1/ 5	0	4	1	2	0	14	.412
EARL, ACIE	32	4/ 9	.444	0/ 0	.000	10/14	.714	3/ 6	1	3	4	0	2	18	.563
SMITH, KEVIN	15	2/ 5	.400	0/ 1	.000	1/ 2	.500	0/ 2	1	2	1	0	0	5	.333
BARNES, VAL	22	3/10	.300	0/ 1	.000	0/ 0	.000	2/ 3	1	0	0	2	0	6	.273
WEBB, JAY	5	0/ 0	.000	0/ 0	.000	0/ 0	.000	0/ 1	0	0	0	0	0	0	.000
Totals	200	24/48	.500	7/10	.700	21/28	.750	13/37	10	22	15	11	3	76	.380

East Tenn. State (73)   Coach: Alan Leforce

Season Record: 28-4

	Min.	Total FG/FGA	Pct.	3-Pt. FG/FGA	Pct.	FT/FTA	Pct.	Reb. O/T	A	TO	PF	S	Blk	TP	PPM
ENGLISH, RODNEY	36	11/17	.647	0/ 0	.000	3/ 3	1.000	3/10	0	3	3	3	0	25	.694
STORY, MARTY	22	2/ 5	.400	0/ 1	.000	3/ 4	.750	2/ 4	0	1	5	3	0	7	.318
JONES, DARELL	22	1/ 2	.500	0/ 0	.000	1/ 4	.250	3/ 3	1	1	4	2	1	3	.136
JENNINGS, KEITH	37	4/13	.308	3/ 8	.375	0/ 0	.000	0/ 4	13	0	3	2	0	11	.297
GEER, MAJOR	22	3/ 7	.429	1/ 4	.250	0/ 1	.000	1/ 1	0	1	1	1	0	7	.318
PELPHREY, JERRY	27	3/10	.300	2/ 6	.333	0/ 0	.000	0/ 1	1	4	5	1	0	8	.296
SILVERS, TRAZEL	10	2/ 4	.500	0/ 0	.000	0/ 0	.000	0/ 0	1	2	0	1	0	4	.400
WEST, ALVIN	20	3/ 7	.429	2/ 6	.333	0/ 0	.000	1/ 1	1	1	1	1	0	8	.400
PALMER, ERIC	3	0/ 0	.000	0/ 0	.000	0/ 0	.000	0/ 0	1	0	0	0	0	0	.000
HAYES, MAURICE	1	0/ 0	.000	0/ 0	.000	0/ 0	.000	0/ 0	0	0	0	0	0	0	.000
Totals	200	29/65	.446	8/25	.320	7/12	.583	10/24	18	13	22	14	1	73	.365

Team Rebounds: Iowa 2; East Tenn. St. 2. Deadball Rebounds: Iowa 4; East Tenn. St. 3. Disqualified: East Tenn. St.—Story, Pelphrey.

	1st Half	2nd Half	Final
Iowa	33	43	76
East Tenn. St.	37	36	73

Duke (102)   Coach: Mike Krzyzewski

Season Record: 26-7

	Min.	Total FG / FGA	Pct.	3–Pt. FG / FGA	Pct.	FT / FTA	Pct.	Reb. O / T	A	TO	PF	S	Blk	TP	PPM
HILL, GRANT	26	4/ 7	.571	0/ 0	.000	1/ 3	.333	1/ 5	4	3	0	3	1	9	.346
KOUBEK, GREG	11	0/ 4	.000	0/ 1	.000	0/ 0	.000	0/ 1	1	0	3	0	0	0	.000
LAETTNER, CHRISTIAN	29	8/12	.667	0/ 0	.000	6/ 6	1.000	1/ 4	3	1	3	1	1	22	.759
HILL, THOMAS	31	8/14	.571	1/ 1	1.000	1/ 1	1.000	1/ 3	3	0	2	4	0	18	.581
HURLEY, BOBBY	30	2/ 5	.400	1/ 4	.250	0/ 0	.000	0/ 2	8	2	5	1	0	5	.167
DAVIS, BRIAN	27	6/ 9	.667	0/ 0	.000	3/ 4	.750	6/ 9	2	3	3	0	0	15	.556
MCCAFFREY, BILL	24	7/11	.636	1/ 1	1.000	2/ 2	1.000	1/ 1	0	1	1	0	0	17	.708
LANG, ANTONIO	13	4/ 5	.800	0/ 0	.000	0/ 0	.000	2/ 4	1	0	2	0	1	8	.615
BUCKLEY, CLAY	3	1/ 1	1.000	0/ 0	.000	0/ 0	.000	1/ 2	0	1	0	0	0	2	.667
AST, CHRISTIAN	1	1/ 1	1.000	0/ 0	.000	0/ 0	.000	0/ 0	0	0	0	0	0	2	2.000
CLARK, MARTY	3	0/ 1	.000	0/ 1	.000	0/ 0	.000	0/ 1	1	0	0	0	0	0	.000
PALMER, CRAWFORD	2	2/ 2	1.000	0/ 0	.000	0/ 0	.000	0/ 0	0	0	1	0	0	4	2.000
Totals	200	43/72	.597	3/ 8	.375	13/16	.813	13/32	23	11	20	9	3	102	.510

Northeast La. (73)   Coach: Mike Vining

Season Record: 25-7

	Min.	Total FG FGA	Pct.	3–Pt. FG / FGA	Pct.	FT / FTA	Pct.	Reb. O / T	A	TO	PF	S	Blk	TP	PPM
FUNCHESS, CARLOS	37	8/16	.500	0/ 1	.000	3/ 4	.750	4/ 6	3	1	3	2	0	19	.514
JACOBS, CHAD	18	0/ 4	.000	0/ 0	.000	0/ 0	.000	1/ 2	0	1	2	1	0	0	.000
CRAIG, PHILLIP	25	1/ 2	.500	0/ 0	.000	0/ 0	.000	1/ 2	1	0	3	1	0	2	.080
JONES, ANTHONY	36	10/17	.588	1/ 3	.333	3/ 3	1.000	3/ 5	2	5	1	3	0	24	.667
JONES, CASEY	35	4/ 5	.800	2/ 2	1.000	4/ 5	.800	1/ 4	1	5	3	1	0	14	.400
CREASE, CHRIS	24	3/ 8	.375	0/ 0	.000	4/ 6	.667	2/ 5	1	1	4	1	0	10	.417
REDMOND, RODNEY	14	1/ 3	.333	0/ 2	.000	0/ 0	.000	0/ 0	0	4	2	0	0	2	.143
SMITH, ANTHONY	5	0/ 0	.000	0/ 0	.000	0/ 0	.000	0/ 0	0	0	0	1	0	0	.000
ENLOE, TODD	2	0/ 1	.000	0/ 0	.000	0/ 0	.000	0/ 0	0	0	0	0	0	0	.000
MARSHALL, ANTOINE	1	0/ 1	.000	0/ 1	.000	0/ 0	.000	0/ 0	0	0	0	0	0	0	.000
BYRD, SCOTT	1	0/ 1	.000	0/ 0	.000	1/ 2	.500	2/ 2	0	0	0	0	0	1	1.000
WILLIAMS, CHARLES	2	0/ 1	.000	0/ 0	.000	1/ 2	.500	0/ 0	0	0	0	0	0	1	.500
Totals	200	27/59	.458	3/ 9	.333	16/22	.727	14/26	8	19	18	9	1	73	.365

Team Rebounds: Duke 4; Northeast La. 4. Deadball Rebounds: Duke 1; Northeast La. 3. Team Turnovers: Northeast La. 2. Disqualified: Duke—Hurley. Technical Foul: Northeast La.—Coach Vining.

	1st Half	2nd Half	Final
Duke	46	56	102
Northeast La.	40	33	73

SECOND ROUND EAST

N. Carolina (84)   Coach: Dean Smith

	Min.	Total FG/FGA	Pct.	3-Pt. FG/FGA	Pct.	FT/FTA	Pct.	Reb. O/T	A	TO	PF	S	Blk	TP	PPM
FOX, RICK	32	6/12	.500	2/7	.286	0/0	.000	1/2	8	2	3	2	1	14	.438
CHILCUTT, PETE	26	4/10	.400	0/1	.000	3/5	.600	0/5	1	2	3	3	1	11	.423
MONTROSS, ERIC	13	2/3	.667	0/0	.000	0/0	.000	2/5	1	0	1	0	0	4	.308
DAVIS, HUBERT	31	6/11	.545	3/4	.750	3/4	.750	2/3	4	1	0	1	0	18	.581
RICE, KING	28	3/8	.375	1/1	1.000	1/2	.500	1/1	9	2	1	2	0	8	.286
LYNCH, GEORGE	32	8/11	.727	0/0	.000	3/4	.750	4/10	0	2	1	2	1	19	.594
RODL, HENRIK	6	1/1	1.000	0/0	.000	0/0	.000	0/0	2	1	0	1	0	2	.333
PHELPS, DERRICK	11	2/4	.500	0/0	.000	3/4	.750	0/3	2	2	0	2	0	7	.636
ROZIER, CLIFFORD	6	0/1	.000	0/0	.000	1/2	.500	0/0	0	2	1	0	0	1	.167
REESE, BRIAN	10	0/0	.000	0/0	.000	0/0	.000	0/1	0	1	2	0	0	0	.000
SULLIVAN, PAT	1	0/0	.000	0/0	.000	0/0	.000	0/0	0	0	0	0	0	0	.000
HARRIS, KENNY	1	0/0	.000	0/0	.000	0/0	.000	0/0	0	0	0	0	0	0	.000
CHERRY, SCOTT	1	0/0	.000	0/0	.000	0/0	.000	0/0	0	1	0	0	0	0	.000
SALVADORI, KEVIN	1	0/0	.000	0/0	.000	0/0	.000	0/0	0	0	0	0	0	0	.000
WENSTROM, MATT	1	0/0	.000	0/0	.000	0/0	.000	0/1	0	0	0	0	0	0	.000
Totals	200	32/61	.525	6/13	.462	14/21	.667	10/31	27	16	12	13	3	84	.420

Villanova (69)   Coach: Rollie Massimino

	Min.	Total FG/FGA	Pct.	3-Pt. FG/FGA	Pct.	FT/FTA	Pct.	Reb. O/T	A	TO	PF	S	Blk	TP	PPM
BAIN, ARRON	24	2/7	.286	0/2	.000	2/2	1.000	0/3	1	2	4	0	1	6	.250
MILLER, LANCE	35	6/12	.500	1/2	.500	4/4	1.000	3/7	3	6	1	5	1	17	.486
DOWDELL, MARC	26	3/8	.375	0/0	.000	2/2	1.000	4/6	3	0	5	0	1	8	.308
WOODARD, GREG	32	5/11	.455	3/7	.429	2/2	1.000	0/3	1	4	3	1	0	15	.469
WALKER, CHRIS	21	4/9	.444	3/6	.500	0/0	.000	0/1	1	4	3	0	0	11	.524
BYRD, CALVIN	28	1/4	.250	0/0	.000	0/0	.000	1/2	0	2	1	0	0	2	.071
BRYSON, JAMES	7	0/0	.000	0/0	.000	0/0	.000	0/0	0	1	0	0	0	0	.000
MUMFORD, LLOYD	12	3/4	.750	2/2	1.000	2/2	1.000	0/0	2	2	2	1	0	10	.833
MILLER, DAVID	1	0/1	.000	0/1	.000	0/0	.000	0/0	0	0	0	1	0	0	.000
PELLE, ANTHONY	11	0/0	.000	0/0	.000	0/0	.000	0/4	0	1	1	0	2	0	.000
MASOTTI, CHRIS	1	0/1	.000	0/0	.000	0/0	.000	0/1	0	0	0	0	0	0	.000
VRIND, PAUL	1	0/0	.000	0/0	.000	0/0	.000	0/0	0	0	1	0	0	0	.000
MULLER, TIM	1	0/1	.000	0/1	.000	0/0	.000	0/0	0	0	0	0	0	0	.000
Totals	200	24/58	.414	9/21	.429	12/12	1.000	8/27	11	22	21	8	5	69	.345

Team Rebounds: N. Carolina 4; Villanova 7. Deadball Rebounds: N. Carolina 1; Villanova 0. Disqualified: Villanova—Dowdell. Technical Fouls: None.

	1st Half	2nd Half	Final
N. Carolina	44	40	84
Villanova	32	37	69

Eastern Mich. (71)   Coach: Ben Braun

	Min.	Total FG/FGA	Pct.	3-Pt. FG/FGA	Pct.	FT/FTA	Pct.	Reb. O/T	A	TO	PF	S	Blk	TP	PPM
HALLAS, KORY	35	4/10	.400	0/ 0	.000	4/ 4	1.000	4/ 8	3	1	5	1	1	12	.343
THOMAS, CARL	42	2/ 8	.250	1/ 6	.167	2/ 4	.500	0/ 7	4	3	3	0	0	7	.167
KENNEDY, MARCUS	30	8/13	.615	0/ 0	.000	5/ 7	.714	2/ 5	0	1	5	0	0	21	.700
THOMAS, CHARLES	43	3/ 7	.429	2/ 6	.333	3/ 3	1.000	1/ 6	3	2	2	2	0	11	.256
NEELY, LORENZO	42	5/10	.500	1/ 1	1.000	7/ 8	.875	0/ 3	4	1	3	2	1	18	.429
BOYKIN, MIKE	13	0/ 1	.000	0/ 0	.000	0/ 0	.000	0/ 3	0	0	3	0	1	0	.000
LEWIS, ROGER	9	1/ 1	1.000	0/ 0	.000	0/ 0	.000	0/ 0	2	0	0	0	0	2	.222
FELDER, KAHLIL	3	0/ 0	.000	0/ 0	.000	0/ 0	.000	0/ 0	0	0	0	0	0	0	.000
PEARSON, FENORRIS	8	0/ 0	.000	0/ 0	.000	0/ 0	.000	0/ 0	0	0	0	0	0	0	.000
Totals	225	23/50	.460	4/13	.308	21/26	.808	7/32	16	8	21	5	3	71	.316

Penn State (68)   Coach: Bruce Parkhill

	Min.	Total FG/FGA	Pct.	3-Pt. FG/FGA	Pct.	FT/FTA	Pct.	Reb. O/T	A	TO	PF	S	Blk	TP	PPM
BARNES, JAMES	38	3/ 6	.500	0/ 0	.000	6/ 7	.857	3/ 8	2	2	3	1	0	12	.316
HAYES, DERON	43	6/13	.462	0/ 0	.000	0/ 0	.000	0/ 0	3	0	3	0	0	12	.279
DEGITZ, DAVE	36	3/ 9	.333	0/ 0	.000	2/ 5	.400	3/ 6	0	1	2	1	0	8	.222
BARNES, FREDDIE	42	3/11	.273	3/ 8	.375	3/ 4	.750	1/ 6	4	2	1	0	0	12	.286
BROWN, MONROE	37	5/ 6	.833	2/ 2	1.000	0/ 1	.000	1/ 2	4	1	4	2	1	12	.324
JENNINGS, MICHAEL	9	1/ 2	.500	1/ 2	.500	1/ 2	.500	0/ 0	0	0	0	1	0	4	.444
JOHNSON, C.J.	15	2/ 4	.500	0/ 0	.000	2/ 2	1.000	1/ 3	0	0	2	1	0	6	.400
CARTER, ELTON	3	1/ 2	.500	0/ 0	.000	0/ 0	.000	0/ 0	0	0	2	0	0	2	.667
DIETZ, JON	2	0/ 3	.000	0/ 0	.000	0/ 0	.000	0/ 1	0	0	1	0	0	0	.000
Totals	225	24/56	.429	6/12	.500	14/21	.667	9/26	13	6	18	6	1	68	.302

Team Rebounds: Eastern Mich. 3; Penn State 6. Deadball Rebounds: Eastern Mich. 3; Penn State 1. Disqualified: Eastern Mich.—Hallas, Kennedy.

	1st Half	2nd Half	1 OT	Final
Eastern Mich.	29	29	13	71
Penn State	33	25	10	68

N.C. State (64)   Coach: Les Robinson

	Min.	Total FG / FGA	Pct.	3-Pt. FG / FGA	Pct.	FT / FTA	Pct.	Reb. O / T	A	TO	PF	S	Blk	TP	PPM
GUGLIOTTA, TOM	40	3/ 8	.375	1/ 4	.250	3/ 4	.750	1/ 5	1	1	2	1	1	10	.250
FEGGINS, BRYANT	38	3/ 8	.375	0/ 0	.000	2/ 2	1.000	2/ 5	1	1	3	0	0	8	.211
THOMPSON, KEVIN	37	6/ 7	.857	0/ 0	.000	0/ 1	.000	3/ 8	1	3	3	1	3	12	.324
CORCHIANI, CHRIS	37	4/ 9	.444	2/ 3	.667	5/ 6	.833	0/ 3	6	7	5	2	0	15	.405
MONROE, RODNEY	37	4/16	.250	2/ 5	.400	9/ 9	1.000	2/ 3	0	3	3	1	0	19	.514
BAKALLI, MIGJEN	9	0/ 2	.000	0/ 0	.000	0/ 0	.000	1/ 1	0	1	5	0	0	0	.000
LEE, DAVID	1	0/ 0	.000	0/ 0	.000	0/ 0	.000	0/ 0	0	0	0	0	0	0	.000
ROBINSON, ANTHONY	1	0/ 0	.000	0/ 0	.000	0/ 0	.000	0/ 0	0	0	0	0	0	0	.000
Totals	200	20/50	.400	5/12	.417	19/22	.864	9/25	9	16	21	5	4	64	.320

Oklahoma State (73)   Coach: Eddie Sutton

	Min.	Total FG / FGA	Pct.	3-Pt. FG / FGA	Pct.	FT / FTA	Pct.	Reb. O / T	A	TO	PF	S	Blk	TP	PPM
POTTER, JOHN	23	2/ 5	.400	0/ 2	.000	9/10	.900	0/ 1	1	2	2	0	0	13	.565
HOUSTON, BYRON	39	7/11	.636	0/ 0	.000	10/11	.909	2/12	4	3	2	0	2	24	.615
PITTMAN, JOHNNY	24	2/ 4	.500	0/ 0	.000	0/ 0	.000	2/ 5	0	1	1	0	0	4	.167
ALEXANDER, DARWYN	28	2/ 8	.250	0/ 2	.000	2/ 2	1.000	1/ 1	4	2	4	0	0	6	.214
SUTTON, SEAN	30	5/10	.500	2/ 3	.667	2/ 2	1.000	0/ 1	2	1	3	1	0	14	.467
WILLIAMS, COREY	20	1/ 5	.200	0/ 2	.000	2/ 2	1.000	0/ 0	1	1	2	0	0	4	.200
HATCHER, CORNELL	20	2/ 3	.667	0/ 1	.000	2/ 2	1.000	2/ 4	4	3	4	3	0	6	.300
SAHLSTROM, MATTIAS	12	1/ 2	.500	0/ 0	.000	0/ 0	.000	1/ 2	1	0	1	0	0	2	.167
JONES, EARL	1	0/ 1	.000	0/ 1	.000	0/ 0	.000	0/ 0	0	0	0	0	0	0	.000
PHILPOTT, MIKE	1	0/ 0	.000	0/ 0	.000	0/ 0	.000	0/ 0	0	0	0	0	0	0	.000
BROWN, MILTON	1	0/ 0	.000	0/ 0	.000	0/ 0	.000	0/ 0	0	0	0	0	0	0	.000
BURBANK, DENNIS	1	0/ 0	.000	0/ 0	.000	0/ 0	.000	0/ 0	0	0	0	0	0	0	.000
Totals	200	22/49	.449	2/11	.182	27/29	.931	8/26	17	13	19	4	2	73	.365

Team Rebounds: Oklahoma State 4; N.C. State 4. Deadball Rebounds: Oklahoma State 2; N.C. State 1. Disqualified: N.C. State—Corchiani, Bakalli. Technical Fouls: None.

	1st Half	2nd Half	Final
N.C. State	34	30	64
Oklahoma State	37	36	73

Temple (77)   Coach: John Chaney

	Min.	Total FG / FGA	Pct.	3-Pt. FG / FGA	Pct.	FT / FTA	Pct.	Reb. O / T	A	TO	PF	S	Blk	TP	PPM
KILGORE, MIK	34	5/11	.455	1/ 2	.500	7/ 7	1.000	2/ 7	3	2	3	1	1	18	.529
STRICKLAND, MARK	36	3/ 9	.333	0/ 0	.000	3/ 4	.750	6/10	0	0	5	1	2	9	.250
HODGE, DONALD	37	5/ 7	.714	0/ 0	.000	5/ 5	1.000	2/ 7	2	2	3	1	2	15	.405
CARSTARPHEN, VIC	34	3/ 7	.429	2/ 6	.333	1/ 2	.500	0/ 0	0	0	0	0	0	9	.265
MACON, MARK	40	7/18	.389	2/ 4	.500	4/ 7	.571	0/ 4	2	2	2	0	0	20	.500
HARDEN, MICHAEL	14	0/ 0	.000	0/ 0	.000	6/ 6	1.000	0/ 0	0	0	1	0	0	6	.429
SPEARS, JAMES	5	0/ 2	.000	0/ 0	.000	0/ 0	.000	3/ 3	0	1	1	1	0	0	.000
Totals	200	23/54	.426	5/12	.417	26/31	.839	13/31	7	7	15	4	5	77	.385

Richmond (64)   Coach: Dick Tarrant

	Min.	Total FG / FGA	Pct.	3-Pt. FG / FGA	Pct.	FT / FTA	Pct.	Reb. O / T	A	TO	PF	S	Blk	TP	PPM
WEATHERS, TIM	13	2/ 6	.333	1/ 5	.200	1/ 2	.500	0/ 3	3	2	3	0	0	6	.462
WOOD, KENNY	34	5/ 8	.625	0/ 0	.000	0/ 0	.000	4/ 7	2	2	1	0	1	10	.294
SHIELDS, JIM	28	0/ 4	.000	0/ 0	.000	1/ 2	.500	3/ 3	1	2	4	0	1	1	.036
JARMON, GERALD	25	1/ 4	.250	1/ 3	.333	0/ 0	.000	0/ 2	4	3	1	0	0	3	.120
BLAIR, CURTIS	34	3/ 9	.333	1/ 3	.333	0/ 0	.000	0/ 2	2	2	4	0	0	7	.206
BURROUGHS, EUGENE	12	0/ 4	.000	0/ 4	.000	0/ 0	.000	0/ 1	2	0	0	0	0	0	.000
CONNOLLY, TERRY	21	4/ 7	.571	2/ 3	.667	2/ 2	1.000	3/ 4	2	0	5	0	0	12	.571
SPRINGER, JIM	5	0/ 0	.000	0/ 0	.000	0/ 0	.000	0/ 1	0	1	1	0	0	0	.000
FLEMING, CHRIS	28	8/11	.727	7/10	.700	2/ 3	.667	1/ 4	0	2	4	0	0	25	.893
Totals	200	23/53	.434	12/28	.429	6/ 9	.667	11/27	16	14	23	0	2	64	.320

Team Rebounds: Temple 4; Richmond 3. Deadball Rebounds: Temple 3; Richmond 1. Disqualified: Temple—Strickland; Richmond—Connolly. Technical Fouls: None.

	1st Half	2nd Half	Final
Temple	32	45	77
Richmond	31	33	64

SECOND ROUND SOUTHEAST

Arkansas (97) Coach: Nolan Richardson

	Min.	Total FG/FGA	Pct.	3-Pt. FG/FGA	Pct.	FT/FTA	Pct.	Reb. O/T	A	TO	PF	S	Blk	TP	PPM
DAY, TODD	30	6/14	.429	2/6	.333	3/5	.600	4/8	1	3	4	3	0	17	.567
MORRIS, ISAIAH	16	1/2	.500	0/0	.000	0/0	.000	1/2	3	1	1	0	0	2	.125
MILLER, OLIVER	32	8/12	.667	0/0	.000	3/6	.500	2/10	4	2	3	0	4	19	.594
MAYBERRY, LEE	38	5/10	.500	2/4	.500	2/7	.286	1/9	4	2	3	0	0	14	.368
BOWERS, ARLYN	31	5/8	.625	2/3	.667	2/2	1.000	1/1	5	2	3	2	0	14	.452
WALLACE, ROOSEVELT	14	2/9	.222	0/1	.000	2/2	1.000	4/7	3	0	2	1	0	6	.429
HUERY, RON	18	5/7	.714	1/1	1.000	2/3	.667	1/3	4	0	5	0	1	13	.722
MURRY, ERNIE	20	4/9	.444	3/5	.600	1/1	1.000	1/1	0	2	1	1	0	12	.600
FLETCHER, CLYDE	1	0/0	.000	0/0	.000	0/0	.000	0/0	0	1	1	0	0	0	.000
Totals	200	36/71	.507	10/20	.500	15/26	.577	15/41	24	13	23	7	5	97	.485

Arizona State (90) Coach: Bill Frieder

	Min.	Total FG/FGA	Pct.	3-Pt. FG/FGA	Pct.	FT/FTA	Pct.	Reb. O/T	A	TO	PF	S	Blk	TP	PPM
FONTANA, DWAYNE	31	6/12	.500	0/0	.000	6/7	.857	3/6	1	2	1	0	0	18	.581
FAULKNER, JAMAL	36	11/23	.478	0/2	.000	7/9	.778	3/8	3	1	4	0	1	29	.806
AUSTIN, ISAAC	29	5/9	.556	0/0	.000	3/5	.600	1/10	1	5	3	2	0	13	.448
COLLINS, LYNN	28	1/5	.200	0/0	.000	0/1	.000	3/6	5	1	1	1	0	2	.071
WHEELER, TARENCE	32	3/12	.250	2/7	.286	4/4	1.000	0/2	5	1	4	1	0	12	.375
SMITH, STEVIN	27	4/8	.500	3/4	.750	0/1	.000	0/2	7	2	5	2	0	11	.407
ANDERSON, MATT	5	1/2	.500	1/1	1.000	0/0	.000	1/1	0	1	2	0	0	3	.600
LEWIS, EMORY	11	0/1	.000	0/0	.000	2/2	1.000	1/1	1	1	1	0	0	2	.182
CAMPER, BRIAN	1	0/0	.000	0/0	.000	0/0	.000	0/0	0	0	0	0	0	0	.000
Totals	200	31/72	.431	6/14	.429	22/29	.759	12/36	23	14	21	6	1	90	.450

Team Rebounds: Arkansas 1; Arizona St. 6. Deadball Rebounds: Arkansas 6; Arizona St. 4. Disqualified: Arkansas—Huery; Arizona St.—Smith. Technical Fouls: None.

	1st Half	2nd Half	Final
Arkansas	58	39	97
Arizona St.	54	36	90

Wake Forest (88)   Coach: Dave Odom

	Min.	Total FG / FGA	Pct.	3–Pt. FG / FGA	Pct.	FT / FTA	Pct.	Reb. O / T	A	TO	PF	S	Blk	TP	PPM
TUCKER, ANTHONY	28	2/ 3	.667	0/ 0	.000	1/ 3	.333	1/ 5	3	1	1	0	0	5	.179
KING, CHRIS	37	13/22	.591	0/ 1	.000	3/ 6	.500	1/ 4	5	2	3	1	1	29	.784
ROGERS, RODNEY	39	8/12	.667	0/ 1	.000	0/ 0	.000	3/12	4	5	3	0	0	16	.410
MCQUEEN, DERRICK	38	4/ 8	.500	1/ 2	.500	0/ 0	.000	1/ 4	7	0	2	0	0	9	.237
SILER, ROBERT	29	4/ 7	.571	1/ 3	.333	2/ 2	1.000	0/ 1	1	0	4	1	0	11	.379
OWENS, TRELONNIE	5	2/ 2	1.000	0/ 0	.000	0/ 0	.000	1/ 2	1	3	2	0	0	4	.800
CHILDRESS, RANDOLPH	23	5/10	.500	1/ 5	.200	3/ 3	1.000	0/ 0	6	2	3	1	0	14	.609
WISE, TOM	1	0/ 0	.000	0/ 0	.000	0/ 0	.000	0/ 0	0	0	1	0	0	0	.000
Totals	200	38/64	.594	3/12	.250	9/14	.643	7/28	27	13	19	3	1	88	.440

Alabama (96)   Coach: Wimp Sanderson

	Min.	Total FG / FGA	Pct.	3–Pt. FG / FGA	Pct.	FT / FTA	Pct.	Reb. O / T	A	TO	PF	S	Blk	TP	PPM
HORRY, ROBERT	28	6/ 9	.667	2/ 4	.500	2/ 2	1.000	2/ 7	2	1	3	1	0	16	.571
SPREWELL, LATRELL	40	7/17	.412	0/ 1	.000	7/ 7	1.000	3/ 6	6	1	2	0	0	21	.525
CHEATUM, MELVIN	39	8/17	.471	0/ 0	.000	5/ 7	.714	5/ 9	1	2	3	0	0	21	.538
WAITES, GARY	39	8/11	.727	5/ 6	.833	0/ 0	.000	0/ 2	10	2	0	2	0	21	.538
LANCASTER, BRYANT	5	0/ 2	.000	0/ 1	.000	0/ 0	.000	1/ 1	1	0	0	1	0	0	.000
ROBINSON, JAMES	35	5/14	.357	2/ 6	.333	3/ 4	.750	1/ 6	2	2	3	1	0	15	.429
WEBB, MARCUS	12	1/ 1	1.000	0/ 0	.000	0/ 0	.000	1/ 2	1	0	3	0	0	2	.167
JONES, MARCUS	1	0/ 1	.000	0/ 0	.000	0/ 0	.000	0/ 0	1	0	0	0	0	0	.000
CAMPBELL, MARCUS	1	0/ 0	.000	0/ 0	.000	0/ 0	.000	0/ 0	0	0	0	0	0	0	.000
Totals	200	35/72	.486	9/18	.500	17/20	.850	13/33	24	8	14	5	0	96	.480

Team Rebounds: Alabama 4; Wake Forest 3. Deadball Rebounds: Alabama 1; Wake Forest 2. Disqualified: None.
Technical Fouls: None.

	1st Half	2nd Half	Final
Wake Forest	45	43	88
Alabama	48	48	96

Pittsburgh (66)   Coach: Paul Evans

	Min.	Total FG / FGA	Pct.	3–Pt. FG / FGA	Pct.	FT / FTA	Pct.	Reb. O / T	A	TO	PF	S	Blk	TP	PPM
SHORTER, BRIAN	21	2/ 7	.286	0/ 0	.000	2/ 2	1.000	1/ 3	1	2	4	1	0	6	.286
JONES, ANTOINE	10	1/ 1	1.000	0/ 0	.000	0/ 0	.000	0/ 0	0	0	1	0	0	2	.200
MARTIN, BOBBY	25	3/ 5	.600	0/ 0	.000	3/ 4	.750	3/ 7	0	3	3	1	0	9	.360
MILLER, SEAN	36	4/ 9	.444	3/ 5	.600	0/ 0	.000	2/ 4	6	1	1	0	0	11	.306
MATTHEWS, JASON	30	5/15	.333	3/ 9	.333	4/ 4	1.000	1/ 2	0	1	3	2	0	17	.567
PORTER, DARELLE	30	2/ 9	.222	2/ 3	.667	1/ 2	.500	1/ 4	5	2	1	3	0	7	.233
MORNINGSTAR, DARREN	26	2/ 2	1.000	0/ 0	.000	2/ 3	.667	0/ 5	3	0	4	0	0	6	.231
SHAREEF, AHMAD	1	0/ 0	.000	0/ 0	.000	0/ 0	.000	0/ 0	0	0	1	0	0	0	.000
MCNEAL, CHRIS	11	0/ 1	.000	0/ 0	.000	2/ 2	1.000	1/ 1	0	2	3	1	0	2	.182
GLOVER, TIM	10	2/ 6	.333	2/ 6	.333	0/ 0	.000	0/ 0	0	0	0	0	0	6	.600
Totals	200	21/55	.382	10/23	.435	14/17	.824	9/26	15	11	21	8	0	66	.330

Kansas (77)   Coach: Roy Williams

	Min.	Total FG / FGA	Pct.	3–Pt. FG / FGA	Pct.	FT / FTA	Pct.	Reb. O / T	A	TO	PF	S	Blk	TP	PPM
JAMISON, ALONZO	27	6/ 7	.857	0/ 0	.000	1/ 4	.250	5/ 8	3	2	4	2	0	13	.481
MADDOX, MIKE	25	4/ 5	.800	0/ 0	.000	0/ 0	.000	1/ 2	3	1	4	0	0	8	.320
RANDALL, MARK	35	2/ 6	.333	0/ 0	.000	2/ 2	1.000	1/ 7	5	1	3	0	0	6	.171
BROWN, TERRY	30	6/17	.353	4/12	.333	6/ 8	.750	0/ 4	1	1	1	0	1	22	.733
JORDAN, ADONIS	34	6/ 8	.750	4/ 5	.800	0/ 0	.000	1/ 5	5	5	1	1	0	16	.471
WOODBERRY, STEVE	17	0/ 1	.000	0/ 0	.000	1/ 2	.500	0/ 4	2	1	0	0	0	1	.059
TUNSTALL, SEAN	10	1/ 2	.500	1/ 2	.500	0/ 0	.000	1/ 2	0	0	0	0	0	3	.300
SCOTT, RICHARD	10	1/ 3	.333	0/ 0	.000	0/ 0	.000	0/ 1	0	1	4	0	1	2	.200
WAGNER, KIRK	3	0/ 1	.000	0/ 0	.000	4/ 4	1.000	1/ 1	0	2	0	0	0	4	1.333
JOHANNING, DAVID	2	0/ 0	.000	0/ 0	.000	0/ 0	.000	0/ 0	0	0	0	0	0	0	.000
RICHEY, PATRICK	7	1/ 1	1.000	0/ 0	.000	0/ 0	.000	0/ 0	0	1	0	0	0	2	.286
Totals	200	27/51	.529	9/19	.474	14/20	.700	10/34	19	15	17	3	2	77	.385

Team Rebounds: Kansas 3; Pittsburgh 1. Deadball Rebounds: Kansas 1; Pittsburgh 2. Disqualified: None.
Technical Fouls: None.

	1st Half	2nd Half	Final
Pittsburgh	32	34	66
Kansas	34	43	77

Florida State (60)   Coach: Pat Kennedy

	Min.	Total FG/FGA	Pct.	3–Pt. FG/FGA	Pct.	FT/FTA	Pct.	Reb. O/T	A	TO	PF	S	Blk	TP	PPM
EDWARDS, DOUGLAS	39	8/16	.500	1/ 1	1.000	1/ 3	.333	6/14	0	3	3	0	2	18	.462
POLITE, MICHAEL	36	5/13	.385	0/ 0	.000	2/ 5	.400	5/ 9	1	1	2	0	0	12	.333
DOBARD, RODNEY	21	2/ 3	.667	0/ 0	.000	1/ 2	.500	2/ 3	0	2	5	1	1	5	.238
WARD, CHARLIE	28	3/ 9	.333	0/ 1	.000	2/ 2	1.000	2/ 4	4	3	5	5	0	8	.286
BOYD, AUBRY	28	2/ 8	.250	0/ 3	.000	2/ 2	1.000	0/ 0	2	0	3	0	0	6	.214
GRAHAM, CHUCK	21	3/ 8	.375	1/ 4	.250	1/ 1	1.000	0/ 2	0	1	4	0	0	8	.381
REID, ANDRE	6	0/ 2	.000	0/ 0	.000	0/ 0	.000	0/ 0	0	0	1	0	1	0	.000
MYERS, DERRICK	13	1/ 2	.500	1/ 2	.500	0/ 0	.000	1/ 1	1	0	0	0	0	3	.231
WHITE, DAVID	5	0/ 2	.000	0/ 1	.000	0/ 0	.000	1/ 1	0	1	0	0	0	0	.000
SALTERS, JESSE	3	0/ 2	.000	0/ 0	.000	0/ 0	.000	0/ 0	0	0	0	0	0	0	.000
Totals	200	24/65	.369	3/12	.250	9/15	.600	17/34	8	11	23	6	4	60	.300

Indiana (82)   Coach: Bob Knight

	Min.	Total FG/FGA	Pct.	3–Pt. FG/FGA	Pct.	FT/FTA	Pct.	Reb. O/T	A	TO	PF	S	Blk	TP	PPM
ANDERSON, ERIC	32	4/11	.364	0/ 0	.000	5/ 8	.625	2/ 7	2	4	2	1	0	13	.406
CHEANEY, CALBERT	37	11/14	.786	2/ 3	.667	0/ 0	.000	2/10	3	1	4	1	0	24	.649
NOVER, MATT	12	1/ 1	1.000	0/ 0	.000	0/ 0	.000	0/ 0	0	0	2	0	0	2	.167
GRAHAM, GREG	32	5/ 8	.625	1/ 3	.333	3/ 5	.600	0/ 2	3	0	2	2	0	14	.438
MEEKS, JAMAL	21	2/ 3	.667	0/ 1	.000	0/ 0	.000	0/ 1	4	1	1	1	0	4	.190
BAILEY, DAMON	31	3/ 6	.500	1/ 2	.500	5/ 9	.556	1/ 5	3	0	3	0	0	12	.387
REYNOLDS, CHRIS	2	0/ 0	.000	0/ 0	.000	0/ 0	.000	0/ 0	0	1	0	0	0	0	.000
GRAHAM, PAT	21	4/ 6	.667	3/ 3	1.000	2/ 2	1.000	1/ 4	6	0	1	0	0	13	.619
LAWSON, CHRIS	5	0/ 2	.000	0/ 0	.000	0/ 0	.000	1/ 1	0	1	0	0	1	0	.000
JONES, LYNDON	7	0/ 1	.000	0/ 1	.000	0/ 0	.000	0/ 0	3	0	0	0	0	0	.000
Totals	200	30/52	.577	7/13	.538	15/25	.600	7/30	24	8	15	5	1	82	.410

Team Rebounds: Indiana 4; Florida State 3. Deadball Rebounds: Indiana 4; Florida State 4. Disqualified: Florida State—Dobard, Ward. Technical Fouls: None.

	1st Half	2nd Half	Final
Florida State	38	22	60
Indiana	32	50	82

SECOND ROUND WEST

UNLV (62)   Coach: Jerry Tarkanian

	Min.	Total FG / FGA	Pct.	3–Pt. FG / FGA	Pct.	FT / FTA	Pct.	Reb. O / T	A	TO	PF	S	Blk	TP	PPM
JOHNSON, LARRY	40	7/14	.500	1/ 6	.167	5/ 6	.833	5/10	2	4	1	1	1	20	.500
AUGMON, STACEY	39	4/12	.333	0/ 3	.000	1/ 2	.500	6/10	0	1	1	0	0	9	.231
ACKLES, GEORGE	13	1/ 3	.333	0/ 0	.000	0/ 0	.000	0/ 1	0	0	3	0	1	2	.154
HUNT, ANDERSON	40	5/11	.455	2/ 5	.400	2/ 2	1.000	0/ 2	1	3	1	2	0	14	.350
ANTHONY, GREG	38	4/10	.400	0/ 2	.000	7/ 8	.875	1/ 3	4	2	2	1	0	15	.395
SPENCER, ELMORE	27	1/ 8	.125	0/ 0	.000	0/ 0	.000	2/ 5	1	1	3	0	6	2	.074
GRAY, EVRIC	1	0/ 0	.000	0/ 0	.000	0/ 0	.000	0/ 0	0	0	0	0	0	0	.000
WALDMAN, H	2	0/ 0	.000	0/ 0	.000	0/ 0	.000	0/ 0	0	0	0	0	0	0	.000
Totals	200	22/58	.379	3/16	.188	15/18	.833	14/31	8	11	11	4	8	62	.310

Georgetown (54)   Coach: John Thompson

	Min.	Total FG / FGA	Pct.	3–Pt. FG / FGA	Pct.	FT / FTA	Pct.	Reb. O / T	A	TO	PF	S	Blk	TP	PPM
CHURCHWELL, ROBERT	32	1/10	.100	0/ 0	.000	0/ 0	.000	2/ 4	2	1	1	0	1	2	.063
MOURNING, ALONZO	24	2/ 5	.400	0/ 1	.000	3/ 4	.750	1/11	0	4	5	0	1	7	.292
MUTOMBO, DIKEMBE	39	8/13	.615	0/ 0	.000	0/ 0	.000	5/ 9	0	3	3	0	3	16	.410
BROWN, JOEY	38	2/10	.200	0/ 5	.000	3/ 3	1.000	1/ 2	2	3	5	0	0	7	.184
HARRISON, CHARLES	24	3/ 7	.429	1/ 4	.250	2/ 2	1.000	2/ 5	4	1	0	1	0	9	.375
MORGAN, LAMONT	9	3/ 6	.500	0/ 1	.000	0/ 0	.000	4/ 4	2	0	1	1	0	6	.667
THOMPSON, RONNY	16	3/ 5	.600	0/ 1	.000	0/ 0	.000	0/ 1	0	2	1	0	0	6	.375
KELLY, BRIAN	17	0/ 1	.000	0/ 0	.000	1/ 2	.500	0/ 1	1	2	2	0	0	1	.059
FLEURY, PASCAL	1	0/ 0	.000	0/ 0	.000	0/ 0	.000	0/ 0	0	0	0	0	1	0	.000
Totals	200	22/57	.386	1/12	.083	9/11	.818	15/37	11	16	18	2	6	54	.270

Team Rebounds: UNLV 2; Georgetown 3. Deadball Rebounds: UNLV 1; Georgetown 2. Disqualified: Georgetown—Brown, Mourning. Technical Fouls: UNLV—Johnson.

	1st Half	2nd Half	Final
UNLV	29	33	62
Georgetown	19	35	54

Michigan State (84) Coach: Jud Heathcote

	Min.	Total FG/FGA	Pct.	3–Pt. FG/FGA	Pct.	FT/FTA	Pct.	Reb. O/T	A	TO	PF	S	Blk	TP	PPM
STEPHENS, DWAYNE	41	2/ 3	.667	0/ 0	.000	2/ 2	1.000	1/ 5	2	4	3	4	0	6	.146
STEIGENGA, MATT	31	7/14	.500	1/ 2	.500	2/ 2	1.000	4/ 6	2	3	5	0	0	17	.548
PEPLOWSKI, MIKE	32	7/11	.636	0/ 0	.000	0/ 2	.000	6/11	2	2	4	0	0	14	.438
MONTGOMERY, MARK	40	4/ 9	.444	1/ 2	.500	0/ 0	.000	1/ 7	7	2	5	2	1	9	.225
SMITH, STEVE	47	10/21	.476	3/ 8	.375	5/ 6	.833	0/ 5	4	2	4	1	0	28	.596
ZULAUF, JON	6	1/ 4	.250	0/ 0	.000	0/ 0	.000	3/ 3	2	0	2	1	0	2	.333
HICKMAN, PARISH	25	1/ 3	.333	0/ 0	.000	0/ 0	.000	0/ 2	0	1	1	0	1	2	.080
PENICK, ANDY	26	1/ 7	.143	0/ 2	.000	4/ 5	.800	0/ 2	0	1	4	0	0	6	.231
WESHINSKEY, KRIS	2	0/ 0	.000	0/ 0	.000	0/ 0	.000	0/ 0	0	0	0	0	0	0	.000
Totals	250	33/72	.458	5/14	.357	13/17	.765	15/41	19	15	28	8	2	84	.336

Utah (85) Coach: Rick Majerus

	Min.	Total FG/FGA	Pct.	3–Pt. FG/FGA	Pct.	FT/FTA	Pct.	Reb. O/T	A	TO	PF	S	Blk	TP	PPM
GRANT, JOSH	43	10/17	.588	3/ 6	.500	6/ 8	.750	3/10	4	3	2	5	0	29	.674
MCGRATH, M'KAY	21	1/ 1	1.000	0/ 0	.000	1/ 2	.500	1/ 2	1	1	4	0	0	3	.143
WATTS, WALTER	36	3/ 9	.333	0/ 0	.000	8/16	.500	4/10	0	0	0	0	0	14	.389
TATE, TYRONE	29	3/ 5	.600	0/ 0	.000	0/ 0	.000	0/ 0	5	0	2	1	0	6	.207
WILSON, BYRON	27	3/ 7	.429	1/ 4	.250	1/ 2	.500	0/ 1	2	2	5	1	1	8	.296
SOTO, JIMMY	35	3/ 8	.375	2/ 4	.500	8/12	.667	0/ 2	2	1	4	1	0	16	.457
RYDALCH, CRAIG	28	1/ 4	.250	1/ 4	.250	1/ 2	.500	0/ 2	0	3	1	2	0	4	.143
DIXON, PHIL	13	0/ 4	.000	0/ 3	.000	0/ 0	.000	0/ 0	1	1	0	0	0	0	.000
AFEAKI, PAUL	14	1/ 4	.250	0/ 0	.000	3/ 4	.750	4/ 6	0	1	2	0	0	5	.357
HOWARD, BARRY	4	0/ 0	.000	0/ 0	.000	0/ 0	.000	0/ 1	0	0	0	0	0	0	.000
Totals	250	25/59	.424	7/21	.333	28/46	.609	12/34	15	12	20	10	1	85	.340

Team Rebounds: Utah 2; Michigan St. 2. Deadball Rebounds: Utah 10; Michigan St. 6. Disqualified: Utah—Wilson; Michigan St.—Steigenga, Montgomery. Technical Fouls: Michigan St.—Coach Heathcote, Montgomery.

	1st Half	2nd Half	1 OT	2 OT	Final
Michigan St.	33	31	11	9	84
Utah	29	35	11	10	85

Creighton (69)   Coach: Tony Barone

	Min.	Total FG / FGA	Pct.	3–Pt. FG / FGA	Pct.	FT / FTA	Pct.	Reb. O / T	A	TO	PF	S	Blk	TP	PPM
HARSTAD, BOB	34	6/16	.375	0/ 0	.000	1/ 3	.333	3/ 8	0	1	3	0	0	13	.382
PLAUTZ, DARIN	31	2/ 8	.250	1/ 5	.200	2/ 2	1.000	2/ 7	4	3	2	1	1	7	.226
GALLAGHER, CHAD	38	8/16	.500	1/ 2	.500	0/ 0	.000	4/12	4	3	1	0	2	17	.447
PETTY, MATT	17	3/ 9	.333	3/ 7	.429	0/ 0	.000	2/ 3	3	3	4	0	0	9	.529
COLE, DUAN	27	2/ 3	.667	1/ 2	.500	2/ 2	1.000	0/ 0	0	3	2	0	0	7	.259
WILLIAMS, JOHNNIE	2	0/ 0	.000	0/ 0	.000	0/ 0	.000	0/ 0	0	0	0	0	0	0	.000
EISNER, TODD	11	2/ 3	.667	2/ 3	.667	0/ 0	.000	0/ 0	0	2	2	0	0	6	.545
WRIGHTSELL, LATRELL	34	3/ 8	.375	1/ 2	.500	3/ 4	.750	1/ 1	9	2	3	1	0	10	.294
O'DOWD, BILL	2	0/ 0	.000	0/ 0	.000	0/ 0	.000	0/ 0	0	0	2	0	0	0	.000
RODGERS, CHRIS	4	0/ 1	.000	0/ 0	.000	0/ 0	.000	0/ 2	0	0	0	0	0	0	.000
Totals	200	26/64	.406	9/21	.429	8/11	.727	12/33	20	17	19	2	3	69	.345

Seton Hall (81)   Coach: P. J. Carlesimo

	Min.	Total FG / FGA	Pct.	3–Pt. FG / FGA	Pct.	FT / FTA	Pct.	Reb. O / T	A	TO	PF	S	Blk	TP	PPM
WINCHESTER, GORDON	31	6/ 9	.667	0/ 0	.000	0/ 0	.000	2/ 5	4	4	2	0	0	12	.387
KARNISHOVAS, ARTURAS	23	1/ 3	.333	0/ 2	.000	4/ 4	1.000	1/ 5	4	0	3	1	0	6	.261
AVENT, ANTHONY	30	7/15	.467	0/ 0	.000	3/ 6	.500	3/11	3	2	0	2	3	17	.567
TAYLOR, OLIVER	25	4/ 7	.571	1/ 3	.333	0/ 0	.000	0/ 1	3	1	2	2	0	9	.360
DEHERE, TERRY	32	12/18	.667	4/ 7	.571	0/ 1	.000	2/ 3	0	2	2	2	0	28	.875
CAVER, BRYAN	19	2/ 3	.667	0/ 1	.000	3/ 6	.500	0/ 2	3	1	0	0	2	7	.368
CRIST, DARYL	4	0/ 0	.000	0/ 0	.000	0/ 1	.000	0/ 0	0	1	0	0	0	0	.000
WALKER, JERRY	22	0/ 3	.000	0/ 0	.000	2/ 2	1.000	2/ 7	2	1	4	1	3	2	.091
BARNEA, ASSAF	11	0/ 0	.000	0/ 0	.000	0/ 0	.000	0/ 1	0	2	1	0	1	0	.000
DAVIS, CHRIS	3	0/ 1	.000	0/ 0	.000	0/ 0	.000	0/ 0	0	1	1	0	1	0	.000
Totals	200	32/59	.542	5/13	.385	12/20	.600	10/35	19	15	15	8	10	81	.405

Team Rebounds: Seton Hall 2; Creighton 2. Deadball Rebounds: Seton Hall 3; Creighton 1. Disqualified: None.
Technical Fouls: None.

	1st Half	2nd Half	Final
Creighton	32	37	69
Seton Hall	31	50	81

Brigham Young (61)   Coach: Roger Reid

	Min.	Total FG/FGA	Pct.	3-Pt. FG/FGA	Pct.	FT/FTA	Pct.	Reb. O/T	A	TO	PF	S	Blk	TP	PPM
ROBERTS, KENNETH	19	1/ 2	.500	0/ 0	.000	0/ 0	.000	0/ 1	1	2	0	0	2	2	.105
SCHREINER, STEVE	28	4/ 7	.571	0/ 0	.000	0/ 0	.000	1/ 3	0	1	4	0	2	8	.286
BRADLEY, SHAWN	27	4/11	.364	0/ 0	.000	2/ 3	.667	1/ 9	0	2	5	2	2	10	.370
CALL, NATHAN	36	4/ 9	.444	1/ 3	.333	3/ 3	1.000	2/ 3	7	3	2	1	0	12	.333
MOON, SCOTT	24	1/ 7	.143	0/ 0	.000	0/ 0	.000	2/ 2	4	1	3	0	0	2	.083
HESLOP, MARK	20	2/ 7	.286	1/ 4	.250	0/ 0	.000	0/ 1	2	2	4	2	0	5	.250
SANTIAGO, MARK	4	1/ 3	.333	1/ 2	.500	0/ 0	.000	0/ 0	0	0	1	0	0	3	.750
TROST, GARY	26	4/ 7	.571	0/ 2	.000	2/ 2	1.000	3/11	3	1	3	0	1	10	.385
MILLER, JARED	12	3/ 6	.500	0/ 0	.000	1/ 5	.200	2/ 5	0	1	4	0	2	7	.583
KANE, KEEGAN	1	0/ 1	.000	0/ 1	.000	0/ 0	.000	0/ 0	0	0	0	0	0	0	.000
JONES, ROBERT	1	1/ 1	1.000	0/ 0	.000	0/ 0	.000	1/ 1	0	0	0	0	0	2	2.000
CAMPBELL, JEFF	1	0/ 0	.000	0/ 0	.000	0/ 0	.000	0/ 0	0	0	0	0	0	0	.000
ASTLE, DAVID	1	0/ 1	.000	0/ 1	.000	0/ 0	.000	1/ 1	1	0	0	0	0	0	.000
Totals	200	25/62	.403	3/13	.231	8/13	.615	13/37	18	13	26	5	9	61	.305

Arizona (76)   Coach: Lute Olson

	Min.	Total FG/FGA	Pct.	3-Pt. FG/FGA	Pct.	FT/FTA	Pct.	Reb. O/T	A	TO	PF	S	Blk	TP	PPM
MILLS, CHRIS	29	3/ 8	.375	1/ 3	.333	2/ 2	1.000	3/ 8	1	2	3	2	0	9	.310
ROOKS, SEAN	25	3/ 7	.429	0/ 0	.000	2/ 2	1.000	1/ 2	0	2	4	0	0	8	.320
WILLIAMS, BRIAN	34	9/18	.500	0/ 0	.000	6/ 8	.750	3/11	0	1	2	2	3	24	.706
OTHICK, MATT	29	0/ 3	.000	0/ 2	.000	8/ 8	1.000	0/ 2	6	0	0	1	0	8	.276
MUEHLEBACH, MATT	31	1/ 2	.500	0/ 1	.000	4/ 5	.800	0/ 2	3	1	2	0	0	6	.194
REEVES, KHALID	24	3/ 7	.429	1/ 2	.500	4/ 5	.800	0/ 0	5	1	0	1	0	11	.458
SCHMIDT, CASEY	1	0/ 0	.000	0/ 0	.000	0/ 0	.000	0/ 0	0	0	0	0	0	0	.000
JOHNSON, DERON	1	0/ 1	.000	0/ 0	.000	0/ 0	.000	0/ 0	0	0	0	0	0	0	.000
WOMACK, WAYNE	10	0/ 0	.000	0/ 0	.000	0/ 0	.000	0/ 1	0	0	1	0	0	0	.000
STOKES, ED	15	2/ 4	.500	0/ 0	.000	4/ 8	.500	3/ 5	0	1	3	0	1	8	.533
FLANAGAN, KEVIN	1	1/ 1	1.000	0/ 0	.000	0/ 0	.000	0/ 0	0	0	0	0	0	2	2.000
Totals	200	22/51	.431	2/ 8	.250	30/38	.789	10/31	15	8	15	6	4	76	.380

Team Rebounds: Arizona 3; Brigham Young 5. Deadball Rebounds: Arizona 1; Brigham Young 2. Disqualified: Brigham Young—Bradley. Technical Fouls: None.

	1st Half	2nd Half	Final
Brigham Young	27	34	61
Arizona	30	46	76

SECOND ROUND MIDWEST

Ohio State (65)   Coach: Randy Ayers

	Min.	Total FG/FGA	Pct.	3-Pt. FG/FGA	Pct.	FT/FTA	Pct.	Reb. O/T	A	TO	PF	S	Blk	TP	PPM
JACKSON, JIM	34	5/17	.294	1/3	.333	5/8	.625	5/8	6	4	1	1	0	16	.471
LEE, TREG	33	3/12	.250	0/0	.000	3/4	.750	5/13	4	2	3	0	1	9	.273
CARTER, PERRY	30	8/14	.571	0/0	.000	3/8	.375	5/18	0	2	3	0	0	19	.633
BAKER, MARK	31	2/4	.500	0/0	.000	2/4	.500	0/1	1	1	5	0	0	6	.194
BROWN, JAMAAL	27	1/9	.111	0/3	.000	2/3	.667	3/4	1	1	2	0	0	4	.148
ROBINSON, BILL	14	2/3	.667	0/0	.000	0/0	.000	1/4	0	0	4	0	0	4	.286
JENT, CHRIS	20	2/4	.500	1/2	.500	0/0	.000	1/2	1	1	0	0	0	5	.250
SKELTON, JAMIE	10	1/2	.500	0/0	.000	0/0	.000	0/0	0	0	2	1	0	2	.200
BRANDEWIE, TOM	1	0/0	.000	0/0	.000	0/0	.000	0/0	0	0	0	0	0	0	.000
Totals	200	24/65	.369	2/8	.250	15/27	.556	20/50	13	11	20	2	1	65	.325

Georgia Tech (61)   Coach: Bobby Cremins

	Min.	Total FG/FGA	Pct.	3-Pt. FG/FGA	Pct.	FT/FTA	Pct.	Reb. O/T	A	TO	PF	S	Blk	TP	PPM
HILL, BRYAN	26	3/6	.500	1/1	1.000	2/4	.500	3/6	1	3	4	1	0	9	.346
MACKEY, MALCOLM	40	5/10	.500	0/0	.000	0/0	.000	5/19	1	2	4	1	2	10	.250
GEIGER, MATT	16	3/5	.600	0/0	.000	0/0	.000	0/2	0	3	5	0	2	6	.375
ANDERSON, KENNY	37	8/28	.286	0/1	.000	9/10	.900	3/6	2	0	4	0	0	25	.676
BARRY, JON	38	4/13	.308	1/8	.125	0/0	.000	1/4	5	1	2	0	0	9	.237
DOMALIK, BRIAN	17	0/1	.000	0/1	.000	0/0	.000	0/0	3	0	0	0	0	0	.000
NEWBILL, IVANO	26	1/2	.500	0/0	.000	0/2	.000	1/6	1	0	3	0	0	2	.077
Totals	200	24/65	.369	2/11	.182	11/16	.688	13/43	13	9	22	2	4	61	.305

Team Rebounds: Ohio State 0; Georgia Tech 1. Deadball Rebounds: Ohio State 4; Georgia Tech 1. Disqualified: Ohio State—Baker; Georgia Tech—Geiger. Technical Fouls: Georgia Tech—bench 2.

	1st Half	2nd Half	Final
Ohio State	36	29	65
Georgia Tech	28	33	61

Texas (76)　Coach: Tom Penders

	Min.	Total FG/FGA	Pct.	3–Pt. FG/FGA	Pct.	FT/FTA	Pct.	Reb. O/T	A	TO	PF	S	Blk	TP	PPM
WILLIAMS, BENFORD	34	2/ 7	.286	0/ 0	.000	0/ 0	.000	3/ 6	3	1	2	1	0	4	.118
COLLIE, LOCKSLEY	20	2/ 4	.500	0/ 1	.000	2/ 2	1.000	1/ 2	0	3	1	0	0	6	.300
MYERS, GUILLERMO	27	3/ 4	.750	0/ 0	.000	1/ 2	.500	4/ 9	0	1	4	3	0	7	.259
JEANS, COURTNEY	21	1/ 4	.250	0/ 2	.000	0/ 0	.000	2/ 2	2	1	2	0	0	2	.095
WRIGHT, JOEY	38	10/23	.435	2/ 5	.400	10/10	1.000	0/ 6	2	2	4	1	1	32	.842
CAMBRIDGE, DEXTER	27	6/16	.375	2/ 5	.400	3/ 4	.750	1/ 5	0	0	4	0	0	17	.630
MCCOY, TEYON	20	2/ 5	.400	1/ 4	.250	1/ 2	.500	0/ 0	3	1	5	1	0	6	.300
BURDITT, ALBERT	12	1/ 2	.500	0/ 0	.000	0/ 0	.000	1/ 5	0	1	0	0	1	2	.167
WATSON, TONY	1	0/ 0	.000	0/ 0	.000	0/ 0	.000	0/ 0	0	0	0	0	0	0	.000
Totals	200	27/65	.415	5/17	.294	17/20	.850	12/35	10	10	22	6	2	76	.380

St. John's (84)　Coach: Lou Carnesecca

	Min.	Total FG/FGA	Pct.	3–Pt. FG/FGA	Pct.	FT/FTA	Pct.	Reb. O/T	A	TO	PF	S	Blk	TP	PPM
SEALY, MALIK	40	8/18	.444	0/ 0	.000	3/ 5	.600	0/12	2	3	3	2	2	19	.475
SINGLETON, BILLY	38	7/ 9	.778	0/ 0	.000	7/ 9	.778	4/ 5	2	0	2	0	0	21	.553
WERDANN, ROBERT	33	6/ 9	.667	0/ 0	.000	1/ 2	.500	1/ 6	0	2	3	1	2	13	.394
BUCHANAN, JASON	38	4/ 8	.500	1/ 3	.333	5/ 7	.714	0/ 5	11	5	1	1	0	14	.368
SPROLING, CHUCKY	38	6/ 6	1.000	1/ 1	1.000	1/ 3	.333	2/ 5	6	2	5	0	0	14	.368
MUTO, SEAN	2	0/ 0	.000	0/ 0	.000	0/ 0	.000	0/ 0	0	0	1	0	0	0	.000
CAIN, DAVID	4	0/ 0	.000	0/ 0	.000	2/ 6	.333	0/ 0	0	2	0	0	0	2	.500
SCOTT, SHAWNELLE	7	0/ 1	.000	0/ 0	.000	1/ 2	.500	1/ 1	0	0	2	0	0	1	.143
Totals	200	31/51	.608	2/ 4	.500	20/34	.588	8/34	21	14	17	4	4	84	.420

Team Rebounds: St. John's 1; Texas 1. Deadball Rebounds: St. John's 3; Texas 1. Disqualified: St. John's—Sproling; Texas—McCoy. Technical Fouls: None.

	1st Half	2nd Half	Final
Texas	36	40	76
St. John's	45	39	84

U. Conn. (66)　Coach: Jim Calhoun

	Min.	Total FG / FGA	Pct.	3–Pt. FG / FGA	Pct.	FT / FTA	Pct.	Reb. O / T	A	TO	PF	S	Blk	TP	PPM
BURRELL, SCOTT	35	3/ 6	.500	1/ 4	.250	2/ 3	.667	1/ 8	2	4	3	7	2	9	.257
WALKER, TORAINO	19	1/ 4	.250	0/ 0	.000	0/ 2	.000	1/ 4	2	2	3	1	0	2	.105
SELLERS, ROD	30	5/ 6	.833	0/ 0	.000	8/11	.727	4/ 7	1	3	2	0	1	18	.600
PIKIELL, STEVE	26	1/ 1	1.000	1/ 1	1.000	0/ 2	.000	0/ 1	1	0	0	2	0	3	.115
SMITH, CHRIS	39	7/14	.500	1/ 3	.333	5/ 6	.833	1/ 3	3	2	2	0	1	20	.513
DEPRIEST, LYMAN	24	3/ 4	.750	0/ 0	.000	0/ 0	.000	1/ 3	1	2	2	3	0	6	.250
GWYNN, JOHN	18	4/12	.333	0/ 1	.000	0/ 0	.000	1/ 3	0	3	1	1	0	8	.444
CYRULIK, DAN	5	0/ 2	.000	0/ 0	.000	0/ 0	.000	0/ 1	0	0	0	0	0	0	.000
ELLISON, SHAWN	1	0/ 0	.000	0/ 0	.000	0/ 0	.000	0/ 0	0	0	0	0	0	0	.000
KATZ, GILAD	1	0/ 1	.000	0/ 1	.000	0/ 0	.000	0/ 0	0	0	0	0	0	0	.000
SUHR, MARC	1	0/ 0	.000	0/ 0	.000	0/ 0	.000	0/ 0	0	0	0	0	0	0	.000
MACKLIN, OLIVER	1	0/ 0	.000	0/ 0	.000	0/ 0	.000	0/ 0	0	0	0	0	0	0	.000
Totals	200	24/50	.480	3/10	.300	15/24	.625	9/30	10	16	13	14	4	66	.330

Xavier (Ohio) (50)　Coach: Pete Gillen

	Min.	Total FG / FGA	Pct.	3–Pt. FG / FGA	Pct.	FT / FTA	Pct.	Reb. O / T	A	TO	PF	S	Blk	TP	PPM
DAVENPORT, MICHAEL	35	3/13	.231	2/ 9	.222	0/ 0	.000	1/ 2	3	2	0	3	0	8	.229
WILLIAMS, AARON	23	0/ 1	.000	0/ 0	.000	0/ 0	.000	0/ 1	1	3	1	1	0	0	.000
GRANT, BRIAN	35	5/10	.500	0/ 0	.000	6/ 7	.857	7/12	0	1	4	0	1	16	.457
WALKER, JAMAL	6	0/ 3	.000	0/ 0	.000	0/ 0	.000	1/ 2	1	1	0	0	0	0	.000
GLADDEN, JAMIE	38	3/11	.273	1/ 6	.167	0/ 1	.000	0/ 2	2	6	3	2	0	7	.184
BRANTLEY, MAURICE	29	3/ 8	.375	0/ 1	.000	0/ 1	.000	2/ 5	4	4	5	0	0	6	.207
WILSON, DWAYNE	4	0/ 0	.000	0/ 0	.000	0/ 2	.000	1/ 2	0	0	2	0	0	0	.000
EDWARDS, ERIK	4	1/ 1	1.000	0/ 0	.000	0/ 0	.000	1/ 1	0	1	1	0	0	2	.500
PARKER, COLIN	11	2/ 7	.286	1/ 2	.500	0/ 0	.000	1/ 3	0	2	0	1	0	5	.455
POYNTER, MARK	2	1/ 1	1.000	0/ 0	.000	0/ 0	.000	0/ 1	0	0	0	0	0	2	1.000
WALKER, TYRICE	6	1/ 2	.500	0/ 0	.000	0/ 0	.000	0/ 0	0	1	1	0	0	2	.333
KNOP, ERIC	1	0/ 0	.000	0/ 0	.000	0/ 0	.000	0/ 0	0	0	0	0	0	0	.000
ROSE, DEWAUN	4	1/ 1	1.000	0/ 0	.000	0/ 0	.000	0/ 0	0	0	1	0	0	2	.500
WINSTON, WALT	2	0/ 0	.000	0/ 0	.000	0/ 0	.000	0/ 0	0	0	1	0	0	0	.000
Totals	200	20/58	.345	4/18	.222	6/11	.545	14/31	11	21	19	7	1	50	.250

Team Rebounds: U. Conn. 4; Xavier (Ohio) 6. Deadball Rebounds: U. Conn. 6; Xavier (Ohio) 1. Disqualified: Xavier (Ohio)—Brantley. Technical Fouls: None.

	1st Half	2nd Half	Final
U. Conn.	36	30	66
Xavier (Ohio)	24	26	50

Iowa (70)   Coach: Tom Davis

	Min.	Total FG / FGA	Pct.	3–Pt. FG / FGA	Pct.	FT / FTA	Pct.	Reb. O / T	A	TO	PF	S	Blk	TP	PPM
DAVIS, RODELL	21	5/ 9	.556	0/ 0	.000	1/ 2	.500	2/ 3	0	5	4	1	0	11	.524
STREET, CHRIS	25	2/ 2	1.000	0/ 0	.000	1/ 3	.333	0/ 4	1	3	4	0	0	5	.200
WINTERS, JAMES	18	1/ 3	.333	0/ 0	.000	0/ 1	.000	1/ 4	1	0	2	0	0	2	.111
SKINNER, TROY	25	1/ 5	.200	1/ 5	.200	4/ 5	.800	0/ 0	0	4	0	0	0	7	.280
MOSES, JAMES	23	10/14	.714	3/ 4	.750	0/ 0	.000	0/ 0	0	2	5	1	0	23	1.000
EARL, ACIE	32	6/ 9	.667	0/ 0	.000	3/ 5	.600	2/ 6	1	2	4	2	4	15	.469
SMITH, KEVIN	19	0/ 6	.000	0/ 1	.000	1/ 2	.500	1/ 2	6	3	0	2	0	1	.053
BARNES, VAL	31	2/ 5	.400	0/ 2	.000	0/ 0	.000	1/ 2	3	2	2	1	0	4	.129
WEBB, JAY	6	0/ 0	.000	0/ 0	.000	2/ 2	1.000	0/ 0	0	0	1	0	0	2	.333
Totals	200	27/53	.509	4/12	.333	12/20	.600	7/21	15	22	26	7	4	70	.350

Duke (85)   Coach: Mike Krzyzewski

	Min.	Total FG / FGA	Pct.	3–Pt. FG / FGA	Pct.	FT / FTA	Pct.	Reb. O / T	A	TO	PF	S	Blk	TP	PPM
KOUBEK, GREG	16	4/ 8	.500	1/ 4	.250	0/ 0	.000	3/ 3	1	2	2	0	0	9	.563
HILL, GRANT	30	6/11	.545	0/ 0	.000	2/ 3	.667	5/ 9	3	3	2	6	0	14	.467
LAETTNER, CHRISTIAN	31	5/ 7	.714	1/ 1	1.000	8/ 9	.889	1/ 4	2	2	4	2	0	19	.613
HURLEY, BOBBY	35	1/ 6	.167	0/ 5	.000	2/ 2	1.000	0/ 2	8	1	3	1	0	4	.114
HILL, THOMAS	26	6/10	.600	0/ 0	.000	5/ 7	.714	4/ 5	0	2	3	0	1	17	.654
MCCAFFREY, BILL	27	4/ 9	.444	0/ 0	.000	2/ 4	.500	0/ 3	2	2	1	3	0	10	.370
LANG, ANTONIO	7	0/ 0	.000	0/ 0	.000	1/ 2	.500	0/ 2	0	1	2	0	0	1	.143
DAVIS, BRIAN	22	3/ 6	.500	0/ 0	.000	2/ 2	1.000	0/ 5	2	2	0	0	0	8	.364
PALMER, CRAWFORD	2	1/ 1	1.000	0/ 0	.000	0/ 0	.000	0/ 0	0	0	1	0	0	2	1.000
BUCKLEY, CLAY	1	0/ 0	.000	0/ 0	.000	0/ 0	.000	0/ 2	0	0	0	0	0	0	.000
CLARK, MARTY	2	0/ 0	.000	0/ 0	.000	1/ 4	.250	0/ 0	1	0	0	0	0	1	.500
AST. CHRISTIAN	1	0/ 0	.000	0/ 0	.000	0/ 0	.000	0/ 0	0	0	0	0	0	0	.000
Totals	200	30/58	.517	2/10	.200	23/33	.697	13/35	19	15	18	12	1	85	.425

Team Rebounds: Duke 0; Iowa 8. Deadball Rebounds: Duke 6; Iowa 2. Team Turnovers: Iowa 1. Disqualified: Iowa—Moses. Technical Fouls: Duke—Davis.

	1st Half	2nd Half	Final
Iowa	29	41	70
Duke	44	41	85

REGIONAL SEMIFINAL EAST

N. Carolina (93)   Coach: Dean Smith

	Min.	Total FG/FGA	Pct.	3-Pt. FG/FGA	Pct.	FT/FTA	Pct.	Reb. O/T	A	TO	PF	S	Blk	TP	PPM
FOX, RICK	24	3/10	.300	0/ 2	.000	0/ 0	.000	2/ 6	0	2	4	3	2	6	.250
CHILCUTT, PETE	24	8/ 9	.889	0/ 0	.000	2/ 2	1.000	4/ 5	2	1	0	2	0	18	.750
MONTROSS, ERIC	18	5/ 7	.714	0/ 0	.000	7/ 8	.875	2/ 6	0	1	3	0	3	17	.944
DAVIS, HUBERT	29	5/ 6	.833	5/ 5	1.000	3/ 3	1.000	0/ 4	1	3	1	1	0	18	.621
RICE, KING	25	4/ 6	.667	1/ 2	.500	3/ 3	1.000	0/ 3	6	0	2	1	0	12	.480
LYNCH, GEORGE	30	5/11	.455	0/ 0	.000	0/ 1	.000	1/ 7	0	2	3	0	1	10	.333
RODL, HENRIK	9	1/ 2	.500	0/ 0	.000	0/ 0	.000	0/ 0	1	1	0	1	0	2	.222
PHELPS, DERRICK	13	2/ 2	1.000	0/ 0	.000	0/ 0	.000	0/ 0	4	1	1	1	0	4	.308
ROZIER, CLIFFORD	4	0/ 2	.000	0/ 0	.000	0/ 0	.000	0/ 0	1	0	0	0	1	0	.000
REESE, BRIAN	12	1/ 4	.250	0/ 0	.000	1/ 2	.500	0/ 0	0	0	0	0	0	3	.250
SULLIVAN, PAT	4	0/ 0	.000	0/ 0	.000	0/ 2	.000	0/ 1	1	0	0	0	0	0	.000
HARRIS, KENNY	2	0/ 1	.000	0/ 0	.000	0/ 0	.000	0/ 0	0	0	0	0	0	0	.000
CHERRY, SCOTT	2	0/ 1	.000	0/ 0	.000	0/ 0	.000	1/ 1	0	0	0	0	0	0	.000
SALVADORI, KEVIN	2	1/ 3	.333	0/ 0	.000	0/ 0	.000	2/ 2	0	0	0	0	1	2	1.000
WENSTROM, MATT	2	0/ 2	.000	0/ 0	.000	1/ 2	.500	3/ 3	0	1	0	0	0	1	.500
Totals	200	35/66	.530	6/ 9	.667	17/23	.739	15/38	16	12	14	9	8	93	.465

Eastern Mich. (67)   Coach: Ben Braun

	Min.	Total FG/FGA	Pct.	3-Pt. FG/FGA	Pct.	FT/FTA	Pct.	Reb. O/T	A	TO	PF	S	Blk	TP	PPM
HALLAS, KORY	31	4/ 9	.444	0/ 0	.000	1/ 2	.500	1/ 2	2	2	3	1	0	9	.290
THOMAS, CARL	33	10/16	.625	5/10	.500	2/ 2	1.000	1/ 5	2	3	3	1	2	27	.818
KENNEDY, MARCUS	37	8/14	.571	0/ 0	.000	3/ 6	.500	4/ 6	1	2	4	1	3	19	.514
THOMAS, CHARLES	37	3/11	.273	2/ 9	.222	0/ 0	.000	2/ 5	6	2	2	3	1	8	.216
NEELY, LORENZO	33	0/ 4	.000	0/ 0	.000	0/ 0	.000	0/ 4	5	4	0	1	0	0	.000
BOYKIN, MIKE	7	1/ 2	.500	0/ 0	.000	0/ 0	.000	1/ 3	0	0	0	0	0	2	.286
LEWIS, ROGER	10	0/ 1	.000	0/ 1	.000	0/ 0	.000	0/ 0	1	0	3	0	0	0	.000
FELDER, KAHLIL	7	0/ 0	.000	0/ 0	.000	0/ 0	.000	0/ 0	1	3	0	0	0	0	.000
FRASOR, JOE	1	1/ 1	1.000	0/ 0	.000	0/ 0	.000	1/ 1	0	0	0	0	0	2	2.000
PANGAS, PETE	1	0/ 0	.000	0/ 0	.000	0/ 0	.000	0/ 0	0	0	0	0	0	0	.000
NICKLEBERRY, VON	1	0/ 2	.000	0/ 0	.000	0/ 0	.000	0/ 0	0	0	1	0	0	0	.000
PEARSON, FENORRIS	2	0/ 1	.000	0/ 0	.000	0/ 0	.000	0/ 0	0	0	0	0	0	0	.000
Totals	200	27/61	.443	7/20	.350	6/10	.600	10/26	18	16	16	7	6	67	.335

Team Rebounds: N. Carolina 2; Eastern Mich. 4. Deadball Rebounds: N. Carolina 3; Eastern Mich. 2. Disqualified: None. Technical Fouls: None.

	1st Half	2nd Half	Final
N. Carolina	47	46	93
Eastern Mich.	42	25	67

Oklahoma State (63)　Coach: Eddie Sutton

	Min.	Total FG / FGA	Pct.	3–Pt. FG / FGA	Pct.	FT / FTA	Pct.	Reb. O / T	A	TO	PF	S	Blk	TP	PPM
POTTER, JOHN	26	4/ 6	.667	2/ 3	.667	2/ 2	1.000	0/ 4	1	2	5	0	0	12	.462
HOUSTON, BYRON	44	6/18	.333	1/ 2	.500	1/ 2	.500	2/ 7	2	2	4	1	1	14	.318
PITTMAN, JOHNNY	28	1/ 5	.200	0/ 0	.000	0/ 0	.000	5/ 9	0	2	4	1	2	2	.071
ALEXANDER, DARWYN	20	0/ 1	.000	0/ 1	.000	0/ 0	.000	0/ 1	2	1	0	0	0	0	.000
SUTTON, SEAN	35	2/11	.182	2/ 9	.222	0/ 0	.000	3/ 4	5	4	0	1	0	6	.171
WILLIAMS, COREY	33	7/12	.583	3/ 6	.500	0/ 0	.000	0/ 2	3	2	2	0	0	17	.515
HATCHER, CORNELL	18	1/ 4	.250	0/ 0	.000	1/ 2	.500	2/ 4	1	2	1	0	0	3	.167
SAHLSTROM, MATTIAS	17	3/ 3	1.000	0/ 0	.000	0/ 1	.000	2/ 4	1	0	3	0	0	6	.353
JONES, EARL	1	0/ 0	.000	0/ 0	.000	0/ 0	.000	0/ 0	0	0	0	0	0	0	.000
PHILPOTT, MIKE	1	0/ 0	.000	0/ 0	.000	0/ 0	.000	0/ 0	0	0	0	0	0	0	.000
BROWN, MILTON	1	0/ 0	.000	0/ 0	.000	0/ 0	.000	0/ 0	0	0	0	0	0	0	.000
BURBANK, DENNIS	1	1/ 1	1.000	1/ 1	1.000	0/ 0	.000	0/ 0	0	0	0	0	0	3	3.000
Totals	225	25/61	.410	9/22	.409	4/ 7	.571	14/35	15	15	19	3	3	63	.280

Temple (72)　Coach: John Chaney

	Min.	Total FG / FGA	Pct.	3–Pt. FG / FGA	Pct.	FT / FTA	Pct.	Reb. O / T	A	TO	PF	S	Blk	TP	PPM
KILGORE, MIK	45	6/12	.500	0/ 3	.000	5/ 6	.833	1/ 5	4	2	1	0	0	17	.378
STRICKLAND, MARK	45	3/ 5	.600	0/ 0	.000	0/ 2	.000	2/ 6	0	2	4	1	8	6	.133
HODGE, DONALD	41	3/ 5	.600	0/ 0	.000	6/ 8	.750	2/ 5	2	2	2	0	0	12	.293
CARSTARPHEN, VIC	40	2/ 7	.286	1/ 4	.250	2/ 2	1.000	0/ 2	3	1	2	3	1	7	.175
MACON, MARK	44	11/21	.524	1/ 2	.500	3/ 3	1.000	0/ 3	0	0	5	3	0	26	.591
HARDEN, MICHAEL	6	0/ 1	.000	0/ 0	.000	2/ 4	.500	0/ 0	0	1	0	1	0	2	.333
SPEARS, JAMES	4	1/ 1	1.000	0/ 0	.000	0/ 0	.000	1/ 2	0	0	0	0	0	2	.500
Totals	225	26/52	.500	2/ 9	.222	18/25	.720	6/23	9	8	14	8	9	72	.320

Team Rebounds: Temple 6; Oklahoma State 3. Deadball Rebounds: Temple 4; Oklahoma State 2. Disqualified: Temple—Macon; Oklahoma State—Potter. Technical Fouls: None.

	1st Half	2nd Half	1 OT	Final
Oklahoma State	30	23	10	63
Temple	36	17	19	72

REGIONAL SEMIFINAL SOUTHEAST

Arkansas (93)   Coach: Nolan Richardson

	Min.	Total FG/FGA	Pct.	3-Pt. FG/FGA	Pct.	FT/FTA	Pct.	Reb. O/T	A	TO	PF	S	Blk	TP	PPM
DAY, TODD	36	14/24	.583	2/ 5	.400	1/ 1	1.000	2/ 7	1	0	1	2	0	31	.861
MORRIS, ISAIAH	21	2/ 7	.286	0/ 0	.000	0/ 0	.000	3/ 7	0	0	1	0	0	4	.190
MILLER, OLIVER	19	7/ 9	.778	0/ 0	.000	1/ 2	.500	3/ 7	0	4	2	1	2	15	.789
MAYBERRY, LEE	32	6/12	.500	3/ 7	.429	1/ 2	.500	0/ 3	4	0	1	4	0	16	.500
BOWERS, ARLYN	26	1/ 8	.125	1/ 4	.250	4/ 4	1.000	0/ 0	6	3	3	1	0	7	.269
MURRY, ERNIE	16	0/ 3	.000	0/ 2	.000	0/ 0	.000	1/ 4	3	2	0	0	0	0	.000
HUERY, RON	24	4/ 8	.500	1/ 1	1.000	0/ 0	.000	0/ 2	2	1	1	2	0	9	.375
FLETCHER, CLYDE	13	3/ 5	.600	0/ 0	.000	0/ 0	.000	5/ 6	0	1	0	0	0	6	.462
WALLACE, ROOSEVELT	13	2/ 9	.222	1/ 1	1.000	0/ 0	.000	5/ 8	1	2	1	0	0	5	.385
Totals	200	39/85	.459	8/20	.400	7/ 9	.778	19/44	17	13	10	10	2	93	.465

Alabama (70)   Coach: Wimp Sanderson

	Min.	Total FG/FGA	Pct.	3-Pt. FG/FGA	Pct.	FT/FTA	Pct.	Reb. O/T	A	TO	PF	S	Blk	TP	PPM
SPREWELL, LATRELL	34	5/11	.455	0/ 0	.000	0/ 0	.000	1/ 4	4	6	3	0	2	10	.294
CHEATUM, MELVIN	38	6/11	.545	0/ 0	.000	1/ 2	.500	0/12	0	2	1	3	0	13	.342
HORRY, ROBERT	37	7/15	.467	1/ 3	.333	3/ 4	.750	6/11	1	5	2	1	3	18	.486
WAITES, GARY	35	1/ 4	.250	0/ 1	.000	0/ 0	.000	0/ 3	4	5	2	1	0	2	.057
LANCASTER, BRYANT	5	0/ 1	.000	0/ 1	.000	0/ 0	.000	0/ 1	1	0	0	0	0	0	.000
JONES, MARCUS	7	1/ 1	1.000	0/ 0	.000	0/ 0	.000	0/ 0	2	2	2	0	0	2	.286
ROBINSON, JAMES	34	7/15	.467	3/ 5	.600	4/ 6	.667	1/ 2	0	4	1	0	1	21	.618
CAMPBELL, MARCUS	1	0/ 0	.000	0/ 0	.000	0/ 0	.000	0/ 1	1	0	0	0	0	0	.000
WEBB, MARCUS	9	2/ 4	.500	0/ 0	.000	0/ 1	.000	2/ 2	0	2	3	0	0	4	.444
Totals	200	29/62	.468	4/10	.400	8/13	.615	10/36	13	26	14	5	6	70	.350

Team Rebounds: Arkansas 1; Alabama 3. Deadball Rebounds: Arkansas 1; Alabama 1. Disqualified: None.
Technical Fouls: Arkansas—bench.

	1st Half	2nd Half	Final
Arkansas	40	53	93
Alabama	37	33	70

Kansas (83)   Coach: Roy Williams

	Min.	Total FG/FGA	Pct.	3–Pt. FG/FGA	Pct.	FT/FTA	Pct.	Reb. O/T	A	TO	PF	S	Blk	TP	PPM
JAMISON, ALONZO	26	7/10	.700	0/ 0	.000	0/ 0	.000	7/10	3	2	2	1	0	14	.538
MADDOX, MIKE	24	2/ 4	.500	0/ 1	.000	0/ 1	.000	2/ 2	5	1	3	0	0	4	.167
RANDALL, MARK	29	4/ 9	.444	0/ 0	.000	0/ 3	.000	5/ 6	6	2	4	2	0	8	.276
BROWN, TERRY	25	7/16	.438	4/ 9	.444	5/ 6	.833	1/ 6	1	0	1	1	0	23	.920
JORDAN, ADONIS	35	3/10	.300	2/ 5	.400	3/ 4	.750	0/ 2	1	2	3	2	0	11	.314
RICHEY, PATRICK	5	0/ 1	.000	0/ 1	.000	0/ 0	.000	0/ 0	0	1	0	0	0	0	.000
WOODBERRY, STEVE	11	0/ 0	.000	0/ 0	.000	0/ 0	.000	0/ 2	1	1	1	0	0	0	.000
TUNSTALL, SEAN	25	4/ 9	.444	2/ 4	.500	5/ 6	.833	0/ 3	1	0	0	1	1	15	.600
WAGNER, KIRK	5	0/ 0	.000	0/ 0	.000	0/ 0	.000	0/ 1	0	1	0	0	0	0	.000
SCOTT, RICHARD	15	4/ 9	.444	0/ 0	.000	0/ 2	.000	1/ 3	0	0	2	0	0	8	.533
Totals	200	31/68	.456	8/20	.400	13/22	.591	16/35	18	9	17	7	1	83	.415

Indiana (65)   Coach: Bob Knight

	Min.	Total FG/FGA	Pct.	3–Pt. FG/FGA	Pct.	FT/FTA	Pct.	Reb. O/T	A	TO	PF	S	Blk	TP	PPM
ANDERSON, ERIC	36	3/ 8	.375	0/ 0	.000	0/ 0	.000	1/ 4	0	1	4	0	1	6	.167
CHEANEY, CALBERT	36	8/14	.571	3/ 6	.500	4/ 5	.800	0/ 6	1	0	4	1	1	23	.639
NOVER, MATT	7	0/ 4	.000	0/ 0	.000	0/ 0	.000	2/ 3	0	1	0	0	1	0	.000
GRAHAM, GREG	10	1/ 4	.250	0/ 1	.000	0/ 1	.000	0/ 1	1	0	1	0	0	2	.200
MEEKS, JAMAL	33	1/ 2	.500	0/ 0	.000	0/ 0	.000	1/ 1	4	5	1	0	0	2	.061
JONES, LYNDON	8	0/ 1	.000	0/ 0	.000	1/ 2	.500	0/ 2	0	2	1	0	0	1	.125
REYNOLDS, CHRIS	26	3/ 3	1.000	0/ 0	.000	5/ 5	1.000	1/ 5	1	3	2	2	0	11	.423
BAILEY, DAMON	31	8/14	.571	2/ 5	.400	2/ 4	.500	3/ 5	2	2	5	1	3	20	.645
KNIGHT, PAT	6	0/ 1	.000	0/ 0	.000	0/ 0	.000	0/ 1	1	1	1	0	0	0	.000
GRAHAM, PAT	7	0/ 2	.000	0/ 0	.000	0/ 0	.000	1/ 1	1	2	0	0	0	0	.000
Totals	200	24/53	.453	5/12	.417	12/17	.706	9/29	11	17	19	4	6	65	.325

Team Rebounds: Kansas 7; Indiana 4. Deadball Rebounds: Kansas 3; Indiana 2. Disqualified: Indiana—Bailey.
Technical Fouls: None.

	1st Half	2nd Half	Final
Kansas	49	34	83
Indiana	27	38	65

REGIONAL SEMIFINAL WEST

UNLV (83) Coach: Jerry Tarkanian

	Min.	Total FG / FGA	Pct.	3-Pt. FG / FGA	Pct.	FT / FTA	Pct.	Reb. O/T	A	TO	PF	S	Blk	TP	PPM
JOHNSON, LARRY	33	10/13	.769	0/ 1	.000	3/ 4	.750	6/13	1	1	2	4	1	23	.697
AUGMON, STACEY	31	6/ 9	.667	2/ 3	.667	1/ 1	1.000	0/ 3	3	1	4	3	0	15	.484
ACKLES, GEORGE	21	6/ 8	.750	0/ 0	.000	0/ 0	.000	1/ 3	0	1	1	0	2	12	.571
HUNT, ANDERSON	33	4/ 9	.444	3/ 7	.429	1/ 2	.500	0/ 2	0	2	1	0	0	12	.364
ANTHONY, GREG	34	2/ 6	.333	0/ 0	.000	2/ 4	.500	1/ 3	10	1	2	1	0	6	.176
SPENCER, ELMORE	26	6/14	.429	0/ 0	.000	3/ 9	.333	3/ 5	0	1	1	0	2	15	.577
GRAY, EVRIC	11	0/ 2	.000	0/ 1	.000	0/ 0	.000	0/ 1	1	1	1	1	0	0	.000
BICE, TRAVIS	6	0/ 0	.000	0/ 0	.000	0/ 0	.000	0/ 0	0	0	0	0	0	0	.000
WALDMAN, H	5	0/ 0	.000	0/ 0	.000	0/ 0	.000	0/ 2	0	1	1	0	0	0	.000
Totals	200	34/61	.557	5/12	.417	10/20	.500	11/32	15	9	13	9	5	83	.415

Utah (66) Coach: Rick Majerus

	Min.	Total FG / FGA	Pct.	3-Pt. FG / FGA	Pct.	FT / FTA	Pct.	Reb. O/T	A	TO	PF	S	Blk	TP	PPM
GRANT, JOSH	32	7/12	.583	1/ 3	.333	2/ 2	1.000	4/10	3	6	3	1	1	17	.531
MCGRATH, M'KAY	14	1/ 1	1.000	0/ 0	.000	0/ 0	.000	1/ 3	0	3	4	0	0	2	.143
WATTS, WALTER	22	4/ 6	.667	0/ 0	.000	3/ 3	1.000	1/ 5	0	1	0	0	1	11	.500
TATE, TYRONE	27	2/ 4	.500	0/ 0	.000	3/ 3	1.000	1/ 1	7	2	1	0	0	7	.259
WILSON, BYRON	23	3/11	.273	1/ 3	.333	2/ 3	.667	1/ 3	2	2	2	0	0	9	.391
SOTO, JIMMY	25	4/ 5	.800	3/ 3	1.000	1/ 1	1.000	0/ 3	1	1	3	0	0	12	.480
RYDALCH, CRAIG	16	1/ 6	.167	0/ 3	.000	1/ 1	1.000	0/ 0	0	1	1	0	0	3	.188
DIXON, PHIL	15	1/ 7	.143	1/ 4	.250	0/ 0	.000	0/ 1	1	1	1	1	0	3	.200
AFEAKI, PAUL	16	1/ 2	.500	0/ 0	.000	0/ 0	.000	1/ 3	0	0	2	0	1	2	.125
HOWARD, BARRY	2	0/ 0	.000	0/ 0	.000	0/ 0	.000	1/ 1	0	0	0	0	0	0	.000
CAIN, LARRY	2	0/ 1	.000	0/ 0	.000	0/ 0	.000	1/ 2	0	0	1	1	0	0	.000
MOONEY, SEAN	2	0/ 1	.000	0/ 0	.000	0/ 0	.000	0/ 1	0	0	0	0	0	0	.000
MCKINNEY, RALPH	2	0/ 1	.000	0/ 0	.000	0/ 0	.000	0/ 0	0	0	0	0	0	0	.000
WILLIAMS, ANTHONY	2	0/ 2	.000	0/ 0	.000	0/ 0	.000	0/ 0	0	0	0	0	0	0	.000
Totals	200	24/59	.407	6/16	.375	12/13	.923	11/33	14	18	20	3	3	66	.330

Team Rebounds: UNLV 2; Utah 1. Deadball Rebounds: UNLV 3; Utah 0. Team Turnovers: Utah 1. Disqualified: None. Technical Fouls: None.

	1st Half	2nd Half	Final
UNLV	41	42	83
Utah	35	31	66

Seton Hall (81)   Coach: P. J. Carlesimo

	Min.	Total FG/FGA	Pct.	3-Pt. FG/FGA	Pct.	FT/FTA	Pct.	Reb. O/T	A	TO	PF	S	Blk	TP	PPM
WINCHESTER, GORDON	31	5/8	.625	0/0	.000	1/2	.500	4/6	0	2	3	2	0	11	.355
KARNISHOVAS, ARTURAS	19	4/8	.500	3/4	.750	0/0	.000	2/4	0	4	4	0	0	11	.579
AVENT, ANTHONY	31	6/13	.462	0/0	.000	3/6	.500	1/4	1	0	3	0	1	15	.484
TAYLOR, OLIVER	16	1/5	.200	0/1	.000	4/4	1.000	1/1	2	1	1	0	0	6	.375
DEHERE, TERRY	39	8/14	.571	2/8	.250	10/11	.909	1/6	1	2	1	1	0	28	.718
CAVER, BRYAN	25	2/4	.500	0/0	.000	1/2	.500	0/3	6	0	2	2	1	5	.200
WALKER, JERRY	31	2/4	.500	0/0	.000	1/2	.500	2/4	0	2	4	3	0	5	.161
DAVIS, CHRIS	1	0/0	.000	0/0	.000	0/0	.000	0/0	0	0	0	0	0	0	.000
BARNEA, ASSAF	7	0/0	.000	0/0	.000	0/0	.000	0/0	1	1	1	0	0	0	.000
Totals	200	28/56	.500	5/13	.385	20/27	.741	11/28	11	12	19	8	2	81	.405

Arizona (77)   Coach: Lute Olson

	Min.	Total FG/FGA	Pct.	3-Pt. FG/FGA	Pct.	FT/FTA	Pct.	Reb. O/T	A	TO	PF	S	Blk	TP	PPM
WILLIAMS, BRIAN	33	8/14	.571	0/0	.000	5/5	1.000	7/10	0	4	1	0	1	21	.636
MILLS, CHRIS	31	9/12	.750	2/3	.667	0/0	.000	3/5	2	3	2	1	0	20	.645
ROOKS, SEAN	27	5/13	.385	0/0	.000	2/2	1.000	1/5	2	2	1	1	1	12	.444
OTHICK, MATT	31	4/9	.444	2/6	.333	1/2	.500	0/0	3	0	3	0	0	11	.355
MUEHLEBACH, MATT	32	1/3	.333	1/1	1.000	1/2	.500	0/0	5	1	5	1	0	4	.125
REEVES, KHALID	17	1/5	.200	1/3	.333	1/2	.500	0/2	1	3	4	0	0	4	.235
WOMACK, WAYNE	12	1/1	1.000	0/0	.000	1/3	.333	2/4	1	1	0	0	1	3	.250
STOKES, ED	17	1/4	.250	0/0	.000	0/0	.000	1/4	1	0	4	3	1	2	.118
Totals	200	30/61	.492	6/13	.462	11/16	.688	14/30	15	14	20	6	4	77	.385

Team Rebounds: Seton Hall 4; Arizona 2. Deadball Rebounds: Seton Hall 4; Arizona 0. Disqualified: Arizona—Muehlebach. Technical Fouls: None.

	1st Half	2nd Half	Final
Seton Hall	37	44	81
Arizona	37	40	77

REGIONAL SEMIFINAL MIDWEST

Ohio State (74) Coach: Randy Ayers

	Min.	Total FG/FGA	Pct.	3-Pt. FG/FGA	Pct.	FT/FTA	Pct.	Reb. O/T	A	TO	PF	S	Blk	TP	PPM
JACKSON, JIM	32	7/15	.467	0/ 2	.000	5/ 8	.625	2/ 4	5	3	1	1	2	19	.594
LEE, TREG	24	3/ 8	.375	0/ 0	.000	0/ 0	.000	3/ 4	0	3	3	1	0	6	.250
CARTER, PERRY	20	4/ 7	.571	0/ 0	.000	1/ 3	.333	5/ 7	0	3	4	1	1	9	.450
BAKER, MARK	32	5/10	.500	0/ 1	.000	3/ 4	.750	0/ 0	4	5	3	1	1	13	.406
BROWN, JAMAAL	32	6/ 8	.750	1/ 1	1.000	1/ 2	.500	1/ 3	5	3	0	3	0	14	.438
ROBINSON, BILL	14	0/ 1	.000	0/ 0	.000	0/ 0	.000	1/ 2	0	1	2	0	1	0	.000
JENT, CHRIS	27	1/ 6	.167	1/ 5	.200	0/ 0	.000	1/ 4	2	0	4	0	0	3	.111
SKELTON, JAMIE	9	4/ 5	.800	1/ 1	1.000	0/ 0	.000	2/ 2	1	3	1	2	0	9	1.000
DAVIS, ALEX	10	0/ 2	.000	0/ 1	.000	1/ 2	.500	1/ 1	1	0	1	0	0	1	.100
Totals	200	30/62	.484	3/11	.273	11/19	.611	16/27	18	21	19	9	5	74	.370

St. John's (91) Coach: Lou Carnesecca

	Min.	Total FG/FGA	Pct.	3-Pt. FG/FGA	Pct.	FT/FTA	Pct.	Reb. O/T	A	TO	PF	S	Blk	TP	PPM
SEALY, MALIK	32	10/17	.588	0/ 0	.000	2/ 2	1.000	3/ 5	2	7	4	1	0	22	.688
SINGLETON, BILLY	35	4/ 7	.571	0/ 0	.000	6/ 7	.857	3/ 8	5	3	2	1	0	14	.400
WERDANN, ROBERT	33	8/ 9	.889	0/ 0	.000	5/ 7	.714	3/ 6	1	7	3	1	4	21	.636
BUCHANAN, JASON	38	4/ 7	.571	1/ 1	1.000	5/ 6	.833	0/ 4	9	1	1	6	0	14	.368
SPROLING, CHUCKY	40	6/10	.600	2/ 4	.500	1/ 2	.500	1/ 4	3	4	3	4	0	15	.375
MUTO, SEAN	3	0/ 1	.000	0/ 0	.000	0/ 0	.000	0/ 0	0	0	0	0	0	0	.000
CAIN, DAVID	9	1/ 2	.500	0/ 0	.000	1/ 2	.500	0/ 0	2	0	0	1	0	3	.333
SCOTT, SHAWNELLE	10	1/ 1	1.000	0/ 0	.000	0/ 0	.000	0/ 0	0	0	0	0	0	2	.200
Totals	200	34/54	.630	3/ 5	.600	20/26	.769	10/27	22	22	13	14	4	91	.455

Team Rebounds: St. John's 2; Ohio State 1. Deadball Rebounds: St. John's 5; Ohio State 4. Disqualified: None.
Technical Fouls: None.

	1st Half	2nd Half	Final
Ohio State	24	50	74
St. John's	43	48	91

U. Conn. (67)   Coach: Jim Calhoun

	Min.	Total FG / FGA	Pct.	3–Pt. FG / FGA	Pct.	FT / FTA	Pct.	Reb. O / T	A	TO	PF	S	Blk	TP	PPM
BURRELL, SCOTT	32	4/10	.400	1/ 3	.333	2/ 5	.400	0/ 3	2	2	5	3	0	11	.344
WALKER, TORAINO	10	2/ 3	.667	0/ 0	.000	1/ 2	.500	2/ 2	0	3	4	0	0	5	.500
SELLERS, ROD	27	2/ 5	.400	0/ 0	.000	2/ 2	1.000	4/ 7	2	3	5	1	1	6	.222
SMITH, CHRIS	40	5/18	.278	3/ 9	.333	3/ 4	.750	0/ 1	3	2	2	1	0	16	.400
PIKIELL, STEVE	15	1/ 3	.333	1/ 1	1.000	0/ 0	.000	2/ 3	2	1	3	0	0	3	.200
GWYNN, JOHN	28	6/13	.462	4/ 6	.667	0/ 0	.000	0/ 3	4	2	3	1	0	16	.571
DEPRIEST, LYMAN	30	0/ 1	.000	0/ 0	.000	0/ 0	.000	0/ 0	3	3	2	1	0	0	.000
CYRULIK, DAN	15	3/ 5	.600	0/ 1	.000	1/ 3	.333	2/ 5	1	1	2	0	0	7	.467
SUHR, MARC	2	1/ 2	.500	0/ 0	.000	0/ 0	.000	2/ 2	0	0	0	0	0	2	1.000
MACKLIN, OLIVER	1	0/ 0	.000	0/ 0	.000	1/ 2	.500	1/ 1	0	1	0	0	0	1	1.000
Totals	200	24/60	.400	9/20	.450	10/18	.556	13/27	14	18	26	7	1	67	.335

Duke (81)   Coach: Mike Krzyzewski

	Min.	Total FG / FGA	Pct.	3–Pt. FG / FGA	Pct.	FT / FTA	Pct.	Reb. O / T	A	TO	PF	S	Blk	TP	PPM
KOUBEK, GREG	30	6/10	.600	3/ 5	.600	3/ 4	.750	2/ 5	2	2	2	0	0	18	.600
HILL, GRANT	16	0/ 2	.000	0/ 0	.000	3/ 4	.750	0/ 5	2	4	4	1	1	3	.188
LAETTNER, CHRISTIAN	29	7/13	.538	0/ 1	.000	5/ 7	.714	1/ 4	1	3	2	0	3	19	.655
HURLEY, BOBBY	38	3/ 7	.429	2/ 4	.500	4/ 5	.800	0/ 2	7	0	0	1	0	12	.316
HILL, THOMAS	22	4/ 5	.800	2/ 2	1.000	3/ 3	1.000	0/ 1	1	3	4	2	1	13	.591
DAVIS, BRIAN	23	0/ 1	.000	0/ 0	.000	5/ 6	.833	2/ 5	1	3	3	1	0	5	.217
MCCAFFREY, BILL	26	3/ 5	.600	0/ 0	.000	1/ 2	.500	0/ 4	2	4	0	0	0	7	.269
PALMER, CRAWFORD	9	1/ 1	1.000	0/ 0	.000	0/ 0	.000	0/ 1	0	0	1	0	0	2	.222
LANG, ANTONIO	4	0/ 0	.000	0/ 0	.000	0/ 0	.000	0/ 0	0	2	2	0	0	0	.000
CLARK, MARTY	2	1/ 1	1.000	0/ 0	.000	0/ 0	.000	1/ 1	0	0	1	0	0	2	1.000
BUCKLEY, CLAY	1	0/ 0	.000	0/ 0	.000	0/ 2	.000	0/ 0	0	0	0	0	0	0	.000
Totals	200	25/45	.556	7/12	.583	24/33	.727	6/28	16	21	19	5	5	81	.405

Team Rebounds: Duke 1; U. Conn. 5. Deadball Rebounds: Duke 6; U. Conn. 6. Disqualified: U. Conn.—Burrell, Sellers.
Technical Fouls: U. Conn.—Sellers.

	1st Half	2nd Half	Final
U. Conn.	27	40	67
Duke	44	37	81

REGIONAL FINAL EAST

N. Carolina (75)   Coach: Dean Smith

	Min.	Total FG/FGA	Pct.	3-Pt. FG/FGA	Pct.	FT/FTA	Pct.	Reb. O/T	A	TO	PF	S	Blk	TP	PPM
FOX, RICK	32	8/16	.500	2/7	.286	1/1	1.000	2/7	5	1	3	0	1	19	.594
CHILCUTT, PETE	32	3/10	.300	0/1	.000	1/2	.500	4/9	0	2	1	1	2	7	.219
MONTROSS, ERIC	15	0/3	.000	0/0	.000	1/2	.500	0/2	0	0	3	0	2	1	.067
DAVIS, HUBERT	30	7/13	.538	2/6	.333	3/3	1.000	0/3	2	0	1	0	0	19	.633
RICE, KING	32	2/4	.500	2/2	1.000	6/6	1.000	0/2	7	1	0	1	0	12	.375
LYNCH, GEORGE	30	5/9	.556	0/0	.000	0/0	.000	3/8	0	1	3	0	1	10	.333
RODL, HENRIK	7	2/3	.667	1/1	1.000	0/0	.000	0/0	0	0	1	0	0	5	.714
PHELPS, DERRICK	8	0/1	.000	0/0	.000	0/0	.000	1/2	0	1	0	0	0	0	.000
ROZIER, CLIFFORD	1	0/1	.000	0/0	.000	0/0	.000	0/0	1	0	0	0	0	0	.000
REESE, BRIAN	10	1/1	1.000	0/0	.000	0/0	.000	0/2	0	1	0	0	0	2	.200
SULLIVAN, PAT	3	0/0	.000	0/0	.000	0/0	.000	0/0	0	0	0	0	0	0	.000
Totals	200	28/61	.459	7/17	.412	12/14	.857	10/35	15	7	12	2	6	75	.375

Temple (72)   Coach: John Chaney

	Min.	Total FG/FGA	Pct.	3-Pt. FG/FGA	Pct.	FT/FTA	Pct.	Reb. O/T	A	TO	PF	S	Blk	TP	PPM
KILGORE, MIK	40	7/15	.467	3/6	.500	1/5	.200	1/5	4	2	4	0	3	18	.450
STRICKLAND, MARK	37	3/7	.429	0/0	.000	3/6	1.000	3/6	1	1	2	0	3	8	.216
HODGE, DONALD	39	3/7	.429	0/0	.000	1/2	.500	2/6	0	1	1	0	1	7	.179
CARSTARPHEN, VIC	38	3/11	.273	2/9	.222	0/0	.000	0/3	5	1	5	1	0	8	.211
MACON, MARK	38	12/23	.522	4/9	.444	3/3	1.000	4/9	1	0	3	2	0	31	.816
HARDEN, MICHAEL	5	0/0	.000	0/0	.000	0/0	.000	0/1	1	1	1	0	0	0	.000
SPEARS, JAMES	3	0/2	.000	0/0	.000	0/0	.000	0/1	0	0	0	0	0	0	.000
Totals	200	28/65	.431	9/24	.375	7/12	.583	10/31	12	6	16	3	7	72	.360

Team Rebounds: N. Carolina 5; Temple 4. Deadball Rebounds: N. Carolina 1; Temple 1. Disqualified: Temple—Carstarphen. Technical Fouls: None.

	1st Half	2nd Half	Final
N. Carolina	35	40	75
Temple	30	42	72

REGIONAL FINAL SOUTHEAST

Arkansas (81)   Coach: Nolan Richardson

	Min.	Total FG/FGA	Pct.	3–Pt. FG/FGA	Pct.	FT/FTA	Pct.	Reb. O/T	A	TO	PF	S	Blk	TP	PPM
DAY, TODD	34	8/19	.421	4/8	.500	6/7	.857	3/4	1	3	4	2	3	26	.765
MORRIS, ISAIAH	15	5/6	.833	0/0	.000	1/1	1.000	3/5	0	2	3	1	0	11	.733
MILLER, OLIVER	34	7/11	.636	0/0	.000	2/3	.667	5/9	1	3	3	0	2	16	.471
MAYBERRY, LEE	38	3/9	.333	0/4	.000	1/2	.500	0/6	4	1	3	0	0	7	.184
BOWERS, ARLYN	20	1/4	.250	1/1	1.000	0/0	.000	0/0	3	2	3	0	0	3	.150
WALLACE, ROOSEVELT	11	1/3	.333	0/1	.000	0/0	.000	2/2	1	2	2	0	0	2	.182
HUERY, RON	18	1/7	.143	0/0	.000	0/0	.000	1/1	4	2	2	0	0	2	.111
MURRY, ERNIE	25	6/13	.462	2/5	.400	0/2	.000	3/4	2	1	5	1	1	14	.560
FLETCHER, CLYDE	5	0/1	.000	0/0	.000	0/0	.000	0/0	0	0	0	0	0	0	.000
Totals	200	32/73	.438	7/19	.368	10/15	.667	17/31	16	16	25	4	6	81	.405

Kansas (93)   Coach: Roy Williams

	Min.	Total FG/FGA	Pct.	3–Pt. FG/FGA	Pct.	FT/FTA	Pct.	Reb. O/T	A	TO	PF	S	Blk	TP	PPM
JAMISON, ALONZO	28	11/14	.786	1/1	1.000	3/5	.600	4/9	2	1	3	1	0	26	.929
MADDOX, MIKE	22	3/4	.750	0/0	.000	2/2	1.000	2/4	1	1	2	0	0	8	.364
RANDALL, MARK	27	4/5	.800	0/0	.000	2/4	.500	1/2	3	4	4	1	0	10	.370
BROWN, TERRY	26	5/12	.417	1/5	.200	0/0	.000	2/3	1	1	4	2	0	11	.423
JORDAN, ADONIS	34	3/9	.333	0/3	.000	8/10	.800	2/6	3	4	3	1	0	14	.412
WOODBERRY, STEVE	16	1/4	.250	0/0	.000	4/4	1.000	0/4	1	0	0	1	1	6	.375
TUNSTALL, SEAN	18	3/7	.429	1/3	.333	4/4	1.000	0/3	1	1	0	0	0	11	.611
SCOTT, RICHARD	16	1/5	.200	0/0	.000	1/2	.500	3/3	0	1	2	0	0	3	.188
WAGNER, KIRK	5	1/1	1.000	0/0	.000	2/2	1.000	0/0	0	0	0	0	0	4	.800
JOHANNING, DAVID	3	0/0	.000	0/0	.000	0/0	.000	0/0	0	0	0	0	0	0	.000
RICHEY, PATRICK	5	0/1	.000	0/0	.000	0/0	.000	1/1	0	0	0	0	0	0	.000
Totals	200	32/62	.516	3/12	.250	26/33	.788	15/35	12	14	18	6	1	93	.465

Team Rebounds: Kansas 6; Arkansas 7. Deadball Rebounds: Kansas 3; Arkansas 1. Team Turnovers: Kansas—1. Disqualified: Arkansas—Murry. Technical Fouls: None.

	1st Half	2nd Half	Final
Arkansas	47	34	81
Kansas	35	58	93

REGIONAL FINAL WEST

UNLV (77)   Coach: Jerry Tarkanian

	Min.	Total FG / FGA	Pct.	3–Pt. FG / FGA	Pct.	FT / FTA	Pct.	Reb. O / T	A	TO	PF	S	Blk	TP	PPM
JOHNSON, LARRY	37	13/19	.684	2/ 3	.667	2/ 4	.500	2/ 6	0	0	3	3	0	30	.811
AUGMON, STACEY	36	6/10	.600	1/ 1	1.000	0/ 1	.000	2/ 5	4	1	3	4	2	13	.361
ACKLES, GEORGE	30	3/ 6	.500	0/ 0	.000	0/ 0	.000	1/ 5	0	2	3	1	3	6	.200
HUNT, ANDERSON	37	5/16	.313	3/11	.273	0/ 1	.000	1/ 3	1	1	1	1	0	13	.351
ANTHONY, GREG	35	3/ 8	.375	0/ 1	.000	0/ 0	.000	0/ 5	11	3	5	5	0	6	.171
SPENCER, ELMORE	10	0/ 1	.000	0/ 0	.000	3/ 4	.750	1/ 1	1	1	0	0	1	3	.300
GRAY, EVRIC	7	1/ 2	.500	0/ 0	.000	2/ 2	1.000	3/ 4	0	1	2	0	0	4	.571
BICE, TRAVIS	4	0/ 1	.000	0/ 0	.000	0/ 0	.000	1/ 1	0	0	0	0	0	0	.000
WALDMAN, H	2	0/ 0	.000	0/ 0	.000	2/ 2	1.000	0/ 0	0	0	0	0	0	2	1.000
RICE, DAVE	1	0/ 0	.000	0/ 0	.000	0/ 0	.000	0/ 0	0	0	0	0	0	0	.000
LOVE, MELVIN	1	0/ 0	.000	0/ 0	.000	0/ 0	.000	0/ 0	0	0	0	0	0	0	.000
Totals	200	31/63	.492	6/16	.375	9/14	.643	11/30	17	9	15	14	6	77	.385

Seton Hall (65)   Coach: P. J. Carlesimo

	Min.	Total FG / FGA	Pct.	3–Pt. FG / FGA	Pct.	FT / FTA	Pct.	Reb. O / T	A	TO	PF	S	Blk	TP	PPM
WINCHESTER, GORDON	30	3/ 6	.500	0/ 0	.000	2/ 3	.667	6/ 8	2	2	2	0	0	8	.267
KARNISHOVAS, ARTURAS	26	2/ 6	.333	2/ 3	.667	2/ 2	1.000	2/ 4	1	3	4	0	0	8	.308
AVENT, ANTHONY	35	5/10	.500	0/ 0	.000	3/ 4	.750	3/ 8	2	4	3	0	2	13	.371
TAYLOR, OLIVER	26	3/11	.273	1/ 4	.250	2/ 2	1.000	0/ 4	2	4	3	0	0	9	.346
DEHERE, TERRY	36	5/15	.333	2/ 5	.400	3/ 3	1.000	1/ 3	1	2	1	2	2	15	.417
CAVER, BRYAN	16	1/ 5	.200	0/ 1	.000	0/ 0	.000	0/ 2	1	2	1	0	0	2	.125
WALKER, JERRY	25	3/ 4	.750	0/ 0	.000	1/ 2	.500	2/ 4	1	1	3	2	0	7	.280
DAVIS, CHRIS	2	0/ 0	.000	0/ 0	.000	0/ 0	.000	0/ 0	0	0	0	0	0	0	.000
BARNEA, ASSAF	2	0/ 0	.000	0/ 0	.000	0/ 0	.000	0/ 0	0	0	0	0	0	0	.000
CRIST, DARYL	2	1/ 1	1.000	1/ 1	1.000	0/ 0	.000	0/ 0	0	0	1	0	0	3	1.500
Totals	200	23/58	.397	6/14	.429	13/16	.813	14/33	10	18	18	4	4	65	.325

Team Rebounds: UNLV 1; Seton Hall 3. Deadball Rebounds: UNLV 4; Seton Hall 4. Disqualified: None.
Technical Fouls: None.

	1st Half	2nd Half	Final
UNLV	39	38	77
Seton Hall	36	29	65

REGIONAL FINAL MIDWEST

St. John's (61)   Coach: Lou Carnesecca

	Min.	Total FG / FGA	Pct.	3–Pt. FG / FGA	Pct.	FT / FTA	Pct.	Reb. O / T	A	TO	PF	S	Blk	TP	PPM
SEALY, MALIK	29	8/19	.421	1/ 2	.500	2/ 4	.500	1/ 6	1	4	2	2	1	19	.655
SINGLETON, BILLY	32	4/ 6	.667	0/ 1	.000	0/ 0	.000	1/ 5	0	8	3	3	0	8	.250
WERDANN, ROBERT	12	2/ 2	1.000	0/ 0	.000	0/ 0	.000	2/ 7	0	1	1	0	0	4	.333
BUCHANAN, JASON	27	6/11	.545	3/ 3	1.000	0/ 0	.000	0/ 0	7	6	5	0	0	15	.556
SPROLING, CHUCKY	37	2/ 9	.222	2/ 3	.667	0/ 0	.000	2/ 3	3	3	2	0	0	6	.162
SCOTT, SHAWNELLE	17	0/ 1	.000	0/ 0	.000	0/ 0	.000	1/ 2	0	0	4	1	0	0	.000
CAIN, DAVID	15	1/ 3	.333	0/ 0	.000	0/ 0	.000	0/ 0	3	2	1	0	0	2	.133
MUTO, SEAN	16	0/ 2	.000	0/ 0	.000	2/ 2	1.000	1/ 3	0	2	4	0	0	2	.125
MULLIN, TERENCE	4	0/ 0	.000	0/ 0	.000	0/ 0	.000	0/ 0	0	0	0	0	0	0	.000
BECKETT, CARL	5	1/ 2	.500	1/ 1	1.000	0/ 0	.000	0/ 1	0	0	0	1	0	3	.600
LUYK, SERGIO	6	1/ 2	.500	0/ 0	.000	0/ 0	.000	2/ 3	1	0	0	2	0	2	.333
Totals	200	25/57	.439	7/10	.700	4/ 6	.667	10/30	15	26	22	9	1	61	.305

Duke (78)   Coach: Mike Krzyzewski

	Min.	Total FG / FGA	Pct.	3–Pt. FG / FGA	Pct.	FT / FTA	Pct.	Reb. O / T	A	TO	PF	S	Blk	TP	PPM
KOUBEK, GREG	22	3/ 6	.500	1/ 3	.333	0/ 0	.000	1/ 2	1	1	2	1	0	7	.318
HILL, GRANT	23	3/ 6	.500	0/ 0	.000	6/ 8	.750	0/ 2	1	2	0	2	0	12	.522
LAETTNER, CHRISTIAN	29	5/ 6	.833	0/ 1	.000	9/ 9	1.000	1/ 5	3	3	0	4	0	19	.655
HURLEY, BOBBY	36	6/10	.600	4/ 7	.571	4/ 6	.667	2/ 7	4	1	2	4	0	20	.556
HILL, THOMAS	26	1/ 4	.250	0/ 2	.000	2/ 2	1.000	1/ 2	3	2	3	2	3	4	.154
DAVIS, BRIAN	20	1/ 4	.250	0/ 0	.000	2/ 3	.667	0/ 3	1	2	2	0	0	4	.200
MCCAFFREY, BILL	23	3/ 9	.333	0/ 0	.000	0/ 0	.000	0/ 2	1	3	0	1	1	6	.261
PALMER, CRAWFORD	9	2/ 2	1.000	0/ 0	.000	0/ 0	.000	0/ 1	0	1	0	1	0	4	.444
LANG, ANTONIO	7	0/ 0	.000	0/ 0	.000	0/ 0	.000	0/ 0	1	2	0	1	0	0	.000
CLARK, MARTY	3	1/ 1	1.000	0/ 0	.000	0/ 0	.000	0/ 0	0	1	0	0	0	2	.667
BUCKLEY, CLAY	1	0/ 0	.000	0/ 0	.000	0/ 0	.000	0/ 0	0	0	0	1	0	0	.000
AST, CHRISTIAN	1	0/ 0	.000	0/ 0	.000	0/ 0	.000	0/ 0	0	0	1	0	0	0	.000
Totals	200	25/48	.521	5/13	.385	23/28	.821	5/24	15	18	10	17	4	78	.390

Team Rebounds: Duke 2; St. John's 1. Deadball Rebounds: Duke 3; St. John's 2. Disqualified: St. John's—Buchanan. Technical Fouls: None.

	1st Half	2nd Half	Final
St. John's	27	34	61
Duke	40	38	78

FINAL FOUR

N. Carolina (73)   Coach: Dean Smith

	Min.	Total FG / FGA	Pct.	3–Pt. FG / FGA	Pct.	FT / FTA	Pct.	Reb. O / T	A	TO	PF	S	Blk	TP	PPM
LYNCH, GEORGE	30	5/ 8	.625	0/ 0	.000	3/ 6	.500	0/ 5	2	4	5	2	0	13	.433
FOX, RICK	29	5/22	.227	0/ 7	.000	3/ 3	1.000	5/ 9	7	4	5	0	0	13	.448
CHILCUTT, PETE	27	2/ 8	.250	0/ 1	.000	0/ 0	.000	6/11	1	0	3	2	2	4	.148
RICE, KING	30	1/ 6	.167	0/ 3	.000	3/ 4	.750	0/ 0	3	3	2	0	0	5	.167
DAVIS, HUBERT	31	9/16	.563	2/ 4	.500	5/ 5	1.000	4/ 5	1	2	0	1	0	25	.806
MONTROSS, ERIC	19	3/ 4	.750	0/ 0	.000	0/ 1	.000	0/ 3	1	0	4	1	1	6	.316
SULLIVAN, PAT	0	0/ 0	.000	0/ 0	.000	0/ 0	.000	0/ 0	0	0	3	1	0	0	-
HARRIS, KENNY	2	0/ 2	.000	0/ 2	.000	0/ 0	.000	0/ 0	0	0	0	1	0	0	.000
RODL, HENRIK	8	0/ 1	.000	0/ 0	.000	0/ 0	.000	1/ 2	0	2	1	1	0	0	.000
PHELPS, DERRICK	10	1/ 1	1.000	0/ 0	.000	0/ 1	.000	0/ 1	1	0	4	1	0	2	.200
REESE, BRIAN	11	2/ 5	.400	1/ 1	1.000	0/ 3	.000	1/ 2	0	0	0	1	0	5	.455
ROZIER, CLIFFORD	3	0/ 0	.000	0/ 0	.000	0/ 0	.000	0/ 0	0	0	0	0	0	0	.000
CHERRY, SCOTT	0	0/ 0	.000	0/ 0	.000	0/ 0	.000	0/ 0	0	0	0	0	0	0	-
SALVADORI, KEVIN	0	0/ 0	.000	0/ 0	.000	0/ 0	.000	0/ 0	0	0	0	0	0	0	-
WENSTROM, MATT	0	0/ 0	.000	0/ 0	.000	0/ 0	.000	0/ 0	0	0	0	0	0	0	-
Totals	200	28/73	.384	3/18	.167	14/23	.609	17/38	16	15	27	11	4	73	.365

Kansas (79)   Coach: Roy Williams

	Min.	Total FG / FGA	Pct.	3–Pt. FG / FGA	Pct.	FT / FTA	Pct.	Reb. O / T	A	TO	PF	S	Blk	TP	PPM
JAMISON, ALONZO	25	4/ 8	.500	0/ 0	.000	1/ 3	.333	3/11	2	2	4	0	1	9	.360
MADDOX, MIKE	27	4/10	.400	0/ 0	.000	2/ 4	1.000	2/ 4	2	3	3	1	0	10	.370
RANDALL, MARK	34	6/11	.545	0/ 0	.000	4/ 6	.667	4/11	4	1	1	0	0	16	.471
BROWN, TERRY	24	1/10	.100	1/ 6	.167	0/ 0	.000	0/ 4	1	1	2	1	0	3	.125
JORDAN, ADONIS	36	4/11	.364	2/ 6	.333	6/13	.462	2/ 4	7	5	2	2	0	16	.444
RICHEY, PATRICK	10	1/ 1	1.000	0/ 0	.000	2/ 2	1.000	0/ 1	0	2	2	0	0	4	.400
WOODBERRY, STEVE	6	0/ 0	.000	0/ 0	.000	2/ 2	1.000	1/ 1	0	0	1	0	0	2	.333
TUNSTALL, SEAN	20	1/ 5	.200	1/ 2	.500	2/ 5	.400	1/ 2	1	2	2	1	0	5	.250
WAGNER, KIRK	2	0/ 1	.000	0/ 0	.000	0/ 0	.000	0/ 1	0	0	0	0	0	0	.000
SCOTT, RICHARD	16	6/ 9	.667	0/ 0	.000	2/ 3	.667	3/ 6	0	2	3	0	0	14	.875
JOHANNING, DAVID	0	0/ 0	.000	0/ 0	.000	0/ 0	.000	0/ 1	0	0	0	0	0	0	-
Totals	200	27/66	.409	4/14	.286	21/36	.583	16/46	17	18	20	5	1	79	.395

Team Rebounds: Kansas 5; N. Carolina 4. Deadball Rebounds: Kansas 10; N. Carolina 5. Disqualified: N. Carolina—Lynch, Fox. Technical Fouls: N. Carolina—Coach Smith 2.
Players with 0 min. played less than 1 min. each.

	1st Half	2nd Half	Final
N. Carolina	34	39	73
Kansas	43	36	79

UNLV (77) Coach: Jerry Tarkanian

	Min.	Total FG/FGA	Pct.	3-Pt. FG/FGA	Pct.	FT/FTA	Pct.	Reb. O/T	A	TO	PF	S	Blk	TP	PPM
JOHNSON, LARRY	39	5/10	.500	0/ 2	.000	3/ 4	.750	5/13	2	3	3	1	2	13	.333
AUGMON, STACEY	39	3/10	.300	0/ 0	.000	0/ 1	.000	5/ 8	2	4	2	2	1	6	.154
ACKLES, GEORGE	25	3/ 6	.500	0/ 0	.000	1/ 2	.500	2/ 5	0	0	4	0	1	7	.280
HUNT, ANDERSON	39	11/20	.550	4/11	.364	3/ 5	.600	1/ 4	2	1	0	1	0	29	.744
ANTHONY, GREG	35	8/18	.444	2/ 2	1.000	1/ 1	1.000	3/ 5	6	1	5	3	0	19	.543
GRAY, EVRIC	14	1/ 2	.500	0/ 0	.000	0/ 0	.000	0/ 1	0	3	2	0	0	2	.143
SPENCER, ELMORE	9	0/ 2	.000	0/ 0	.000	1/ 2	.500	1/ 3	1	0	2	0	0	1	.111
Totals	200	31/68	.456	6/15	.400	9/15	.600	17/39	13	12	18	7	4	77	.385

Duke (79) Coach: Mike Krzyzewski

	Min.	Total FG/FGA	Pct.	3-Pt. FG/FGA	Pct.	FT/FTA	Pct.	Reb. O/T	A	TO	PF	S	Blk	TP	PPM
KOUBEK, GREG	22	1/ 6	.167	0/ 3	.000	0/ 0	.000	0/ 1	3	1	1	0	1	2	.091
HILL, GRANT	33	5/ 8	.625	0/ 0	.000	1/ 1	1.000	0/ 5	5	5	2	1	0	11	.333
LAETTNER, CHRISTIAN	40	9/14	.643	1/ 1	1.000	9/11	.818	3/ 7	2	4	2	1	1	28	.700
HURLEY, BOBBY	40	4/ 7	.571	3/ 4	.750	1/ 1	1.000	0/ 2	7	3	3	2	0	12	.300
HILL, THOMAS	22	2/ 6	.333	0/ 0	.000	2/ 2	1.000	0/ 2	1	0	2	1	1	6	.273
MCCAFFREY, BILL	14	2/ 3	.667	0/ 0	.000	1/ 2	.500	0/ 0	2	0	1	0	0	5	.357
LANG, ANTONIO	2	0/ 0	.000	0/ 0	.000	0/ 0	.000	0/ 0	0	0	0	0	1	0	.000
DAVIS, BRIAN	21	6/12	.500	0/ 0	.000	3/ 4	.750	1/ 4	1	1	1	1	0	15	.714
PALMER, CRAWFORD	6	0/ 0	.000	0/ 0	.000	0/ 0	.000	0/ 1	0	0	1	0	0	0	.000
Totals	200	29/56	.518	4/ 8	.500	17/21	.810	4/22	21	14	13	6	4	79	.395

Team Rebounds: Duke 4; UNLV 1. Deadball Rebounds: Duke 3; UNLV 5. Disqualified: UNLV—Anthony.
Technical Fouls: UNLV—Johnson.

	1st Half	2nd Half	Final
UNLV	43	34	77
Duke	41	38	79

NATIONAL CHAMPIONSHIP

Duke (72) Coach: Mike Krzyzewski

	Min.	Total FG / FGA	Pct.	3–Pt. FG / FGA	Pct.	FT / FTA	Pct.	Reb. O / T	A	TO	PF	S	Blk	TP	PPM
KOUBEK, GREG	17	2/ 4	.500	1/ 2	.500	0/ 0	.000	2/ 4	0	2	1	1	0	5	.294
HILL, GRANT	28	4/ 6	.667	0/ 0	.000	2/ 8	.250	0/ 8	3	2	1	2	2	10	.357
LAETTNER, CHRISTIAN	32	3/ 8	.375	0/ 0	.000	12/12	1.000	4/10	0	4	3	1	0	18	.563
HURLEY, BOBBY	40	3/ 5	.600	2/ 4	.500	4/ 4	1.000	0/ 1	9	3	1	2	0	12	.300
HILL, THOMAS	23	1/ 5	.200	1/ 1	1.000	0/ 0	.000	0/ 4	1	1	2	0	0	3	.130
MCCAFFREY, BILL	26	6/ 8	.750	2/ 3	.667	2/ 2	1.000	0/ 1	0	4	1	0	0	16	.615
LANG, ANTONIO	1	0/ 0	.000	0/ 0	.000	0/ 0	.000	0/ 0	0	0	0	0	0	0	.000
DAVIS, BRIAN	24	4/ 5	.800	0/ 0	.000	0/ 2	.000	0/ 2	1	1	4	0	0	8	.333
PALMER, CRAWFORD	9	0/ 0	.000	0/ 0	.000	0/ 0	.000	0/ 0	0	1	0	0	0	0	.000
Totals	200	23/41	.561	6/10	.600	20/28	.714	6/30	14	18	13	6	2	72	.360

Kansas (65) Coach: Roy Williams

	Min.	Total FG / FGA	Pct.	3–Pt. FG / FGA	Pct.	FT / FTA	Pct.	Reb. O / T	A	TO	PF	S	Blk	TP	PPM
JAMISON, ALONZO	29	1/10	.100	0/ 2	.000	0/ 0	.000	2/ 4	5	1	4	4	0	2	.069
MADDOX, MIKE	19	2/ 4	.500	0/ 0	.000	0/ 0	.000	1/ 3	4	2	3	0	1	4	.211
RANDALL, MARK	33	7/ 9	.778	1/ 1	1.000	3/ 6	.500	3/10	2	3	4	1	0	18	.545
BROWN, TERRY	31	6/15	.400	4/11	.364	0/ 0	.000	1/ 4	1	2	1	3	0	16	.516
JORDAN, ADONIS	34	4/ 6	.667	2/ 2	1.000	1/ 2	.500	0/ 0	3	3	0	1	0	11	.324
RICHEY, PATRICK	4	0/ 1	.000	0/ 1	.000	0/ 0	.000	0/ 1	0	0	0	0	0	0	.000
WOODBERRY, STEVE	18	1/ 4	.250	0/ 0	.000	0/ 0	.000	2/ 4	0	1	4	1	0	2	.111
TUNSTALL, SEAN	11	1/ 5	.200	0/ 1	.000	0/ 0	.000	1/ 1	0	1	3	0	0	2	.182
WAGNER, KIRK	3	1/ 1	1.000	0/ 0	.000	0/ 0	.000	1/ 1	0	0	0	0	0	2	.667
SCOTT, RICHARD	15	3/ 9	.333	0/ 0	.000	0/ 0	.000	2/ 2	0	1	1	0	1	6	.400
JOHANNING, DAVID	3	1/ 1	1.000	0/ 0	.000	0/ 0	.000	1/ 2	1	0	1	0	0	2	.667
Totals	200	27/65	.415	7/18	.389	4/ 8	.500	14/32	16	14	21	10	2	65	.325

Team Rebounds: Duke 1; Kansas 0. Deadball Rebounds: Duke 2; Kansas 3. Disqualified: None.
Technical Fouls: None.

	1st Half	2nd Half	Final
Duke	42	30	72
Kansas	34	31	65

1991 FINAL FOUR TEAMS
(Composite Tourney Statistics)

N. CAROLINA

Player	Gms	Min	FG/FGA	Pct	FG3/FG3A	Pct	FT/FTA	Pct	Reb	Reb PG	A	APG	TO	PF	BLK	S	TP	PPG	PPM
HUBERT DAVIS	5	142	32/55	.582	13/23	.565	19/20	.950	16	3.20	13	2.60	7	12	3	4	96	19.20	.676
RICK FOX	5	143	28/68	.412	6/25	.240	6/6	1.000	30	6.00	23	4.60	13	15	1	9	68	13.60	.476
GEORGE LYNCH	5	146	28/45	.622	0/0	.000	8/13	.615	37	7.40	2	.40	10	14	3	5	64	12.80	.438
PETE CHILCUTT	5	130	23/45	.511	0/3	.000	6/9	.667	34	6.80	4	.80	7	7	5	8	52	10.40	.400
KING RICE	5	138	13/29	.448	4/9	.444	15/17	.882	7	1.40	31	6.20	12	6	0	5	45	9.00	.326
ERIC MONTROSS	5	82	12/24	.500	0/0	.000	9/12	.750	21	4.20	4	.80	2	13	8	2	33	6.60	.402
BRIAN REESE	5	51	7/15	.467	1/1	1.000	1/6	.167	8	1.60	0	.00	2	6	1	1	16	3.20	.314
DERRICK PHELPS	5	54	6/10	.600	0/0	.000	3/5	.600	9	1.80	12	2.40	4	5	0	4	15	3.00	.278
HENRIK RODL	5	46	6/9	.667	1/1	1.000	0/5	.000	4	.80	6	1.20	7	3	1	3	13	2.60	.283
CLIFFORD ROZIER	5	22	4/12	.333	0/0	.000	3/5	.600	4	.80	2	.40	3	3	3	0	11	2.20	.500
KEVIN SALVADORI	4	7	2/5	.400	0/0	.000	4/6	.667	2	.50	0	.00	1	0	2	0	8	2.00	1.143
MATT WENSTROM	4	7	1/5	.200	0/0	.000	1/2	.500	6	1.50	0	.00	2	2	0	0	3	.75	.429
KENNY HARRIS	4	9	0/4	.000	0/2	.000	2/2	1.000	1	.25	1	.25	0	1	0	1	2	.50	.222
SCOTT CHERRY	4	7	0/1	.000	0/0	.000	0/0	.000	2	.50	1	.25	1	0	0	1	0	.00	.000
PAT SULLIVAN	5	16	0/1	.000	0/0	.000	0/2	.000	2	.40	1	.20	0	3	0	1	0	.00	.000

KANSAS

Player	Gms	Min	FG/FGA	Pct	FG3/FG3A	Pct	FT/FTA	Pct	Reb	Reb PG	A	APG	TO	PF	BLK	S	TP	PPG	PPM
TERRY BROWN	6	155	26/75	.347	14/45	.311	11/14	.786	22	3.67	5	.83	6	12	1	7	77	12.83	.497
ADONIS JORDAN	6	210	23/53	.434	11/24	.458	20/31	.645	19	3.17	21	3.50	20	10	0	11	77	12.83	.367
ALONZO JAMISON	6	159	31/54	.574	1/3	.333	6/14	.429	45	7.50	20	3.33	11	21	1	10	69	11.50	.434
MARK RANDALL	6	194	28/53	.528	1/1	1.000	11/23	.478	44	7.33	21	3.50	12	19	0	5	68	11.33	.351
MIKE MADDOX	6	139	21/39	.538	0/1	.000	4/5	.800	21	3.50	18	3.00	9	19	1	1	46	7.67	.331
SEAN TUNSTALL	6	105	13/32	.406	6/14	.429	11/15	.733	15	2.50	3	.50	7	6	1	2	43	7.17	.420
RICHARD SCOTT	6	84	17/38	.447	0/1	.000	5/11	.455	18	3.00	0	.00	7	14	2	0	39	6.50	.464
STEVE WOODBERRY	6	89	4/14	.286	0/1	.000	7/8	.875	19	3.17	4	.67	6	10	1	5	15	2.50	.169
KIRK WAGNER	6	23	2/5	.400	0/0	.000	6/6	1.000	4	.67	0	.00	3	0	0	0	10	1.67	.435
PATRICK RICHEY	5	31	2/5	.400	0/2	.000	2/2	1.000	3	.60	0	.00	3	3	0	0	6	1.20	.194
DAVID JOHANNING	5	11	1/2	.500	0/0	.000	0/0	.000	4	.80	1	.20	0	1	0	0	2	.40	.182

UNLV

Player	Gms	Min	FG/FGA	Pct	FG3/FG3A	Pct	FT/FTA	Pct	Reb	Reb PG	A	APG	TO	PF	BLK	S	TP	PPG	PPM
LARRY JOHNSON	5	179	44/72	.611	3/13	.231	18/23	.783	51	10.20	11	2.20	10	10	5	12	109	21.80	.609
ANDERSON HUNT	5	176	29/66	.439	12/38	.316	6/11	.545	13	2.60	4	.80	9	4	0	6	76	15.20	.432
GREG ANTHONY	5	173	24/57	.421	4/9	.444	14/17	.824	18	3.60	40	8.00	8	13	0	11	66	13.20	.382
STACEY AUGMON	5	174	27/50	.540	5/9	.556	4/8	.500	32	6.40	12	2.40	9	12	4	10	63	12.60	.362
GEORGE ACKLES	5	103	15/25	.600	0/0	.000	1/2	.500	17	3.40	0	.00	5	8	8	2	31	6.20	.301
ELMORE SPENCER	5	93	8/29	.276	0/1	.000	10/20	.500	18	3.60	5	1.00	4	9	15	0	26	5.20	.280
EVRIC GRAY	5	49	7/17	.412	1/1	1.000	5/6	.833	14	2.80	2	.40	6	8	0	3	19	3.80	.388
TRAVIS BICE	3	21	1/3	.333	1/2	.500	0/0	.000	3	1.00	0	.00	0	0	0	0	3	1.00	.143
CHRIS JETER	2	2	1/2	.500	1/1	1.000	0/0	.000	1	.50	2	1.00	0	0	0	1	2	1.00	1.000
H. WALDMAN	4	18	0/1	.000	0/1	.000	2/2	1.000	2	.50	0	.00	2	2	0	0	2	.50	.111
MELVIN LOVE	3	6	0/1	.000	0/0	.000	1/2	.500	3	1.00	2	.50	0	1	0	0	1	.33	.167
DAVE RICE	3	6	0/2	.000	0/1	.000	0/0	.000	0	.00	0	.00	0	0	0	0	0	.00	.000

DUKE

Player	Gms	Min	FG/FGA	Pct	FG3/FG3A	Pct	FT/FTA	Pct	Reb	Reb PG	A	APG	TO	PF	BLK	S	TP	PPG	PPM
CHRISTIAN LAETTNER	6	190	37/60	.617	2/4	.500	49/54	.907	34	5.67	11	1.83	17	14	5	9	125	20.83	.658
BOBBY HURLEY	6	219	19/40	.475	12/28	.429	15/18	.833	16	2.67	43	7.17	10	14	0	11	65	10.83	.297
THOMAS HILL	6	150	22/44	.500	4/6	.667	13/15	.867	17	2.83	9	1.50	8	16	6	9	61	10.17	.407
BILL MCCAFFREY	6	140	25/45	.556	3/4	.750	8/12	.667	11	1.83	7	1.17	14	4	1	4	61	10.17	.436
GRANT HILL	6	156	22/40	.550	0/0	.000	15/27	.556	34	5.67	18	3.00	19	9	4	15	59	9.83	.378
BRIAN DAVIS	6	137	20/37	.541	0/0	.000	15/21	.714	28	4.67	8	1.33	12	13	0	2	55	9.17	.401
GREG KOUBEK	6	118	16/38	.421	6/18	.333	3/4	.750	16	2.67	8	1.33	8	11	1	2	41	6.83	.347
CRAWFORD PALMER	6	37	6/6	1.000	0/0	.000	0/0	.000	3	.50	0	.00	2	4	0	1	12	2.00	.324
ANTONIO LANG	6	34	4/5	.800	0/0	.000	1/2	.500	9	1.00	2	.33	5	6	2	1	9	1.50	.265
MARTY CLARK	4	10	2/3	.667	0/1	.000	1/4	.250	2	.50	2	.50	1	1	0	0	5	1.25	.500
CHRISTIAN AST	3	3	1/1	1.000	0/0	.000	0/0	.000	0	.00	0	.00	0	1	0	0	2	.67	.667
CLAY BUCKLEY	4	6	1/1	1.000	0/0	.000	0/2	.000	4	1.00	0	.00	1	0	0	1	2	.50	.333

✪ FINAL FOUR TEAM RECORDS ✪

KANSAS

Results (Final Record 27–8)

Arizona State	L		68–70
Northern Arizona	W		84–57
Marquette	W		108–71
SMU	W		80–60
Kentucky	L		71–88
Rider	W		103–51
Texas-San Antonio	W		101–69
Hawaii Loa	W		111–58
Pepperdine	W		88–62
N.C. State	W		105–94
Oklahoma	L		82–88
Md.-Baltimore Cty.	W		97–46
Oklahoma State	L	OT	73–78
Miami (FL)	W		73–60
Missouri	W		91–64
Wichita State	W		84–50
Colorado	W		95–62
Kansas State	W		78–69
Iowa State	W		85–78
Nebraska	W		85–77
Oklahoma State	W		79–69
Missouri	W		74–70
Kansas State	W		69–67
Colorado	L		71–79
Oklahoma	W		109–87
Iowa State	W		88–57
Nebraska	L		75–85
#Colorado	W		82–76
#Nebraska	L		83–87
*New Orleans	W		55–49
*Pittsburgh	W		77–66
*Indiana	W		83–65
*Arkansas	W		93–81
*North Carolina	W		79–73
*Duke	L		65–72

\# Big 8 Tournament
* NCAA Tournament

PLAYERS' SEASON RECORDS

KANSAS

Player	Games	Total FG/FGA	Pct.	3 Pt. FG/FGA	Pct.	FT/FTA	Pct.	Reb.	RebPG	A	APG	TO	PF-D	BLK	S	TP	PPG
TERRY BROWN	35	191/442	.432	111/277	.401	68/95	.716	125	3.6	21	0.6	48	61-0	1	43	561	16.0
MARK RANDALL	35	205/319	.643	1/4	.250	113/178	.635	216	6.2	80	2.3	88	101-3	6	33	524	15.0
ADONIS JORDAN	34	138/272	.507	47/115	.409	101/132	.765	102	3.0	154	4.5	88	79-1	1	50	424	12.5
ALONZO JAMISON	35	141/237	.595	2/4	.500	80/161	.497	225	6.4	127	3.6	111	107-7	15	80	364	10.4
MIKE MADDOX	34	110/209	.526	0/1	.000	30/65	.462	109	3.2	97	2.9	61	99-2	11	31	250	7.4
RICHARD SCOTT	35	85/151	.563	0/2	.000	35/86	.407	92	2.6	15	0.4	38	74-0	7	14	205	5.9
SEAN TURNSTALL	35	68/164	.415	14/42	.333	50/68	.735	91	2.6	41	1.2	53	61-2	4	23	200	5.7
PATRICK RICHEY	32	49/108	.454	17/41	.415	19/27	.704	62	1.9	35	1.1	20	43-1	6	15	134	4.2
STEVE WOODBERRY	35	35/69	.507	5/11	.455	29/37	.784	67	1.9	53	1.5	45	39-0	10	23	104	3.0
KIRK WAGNER	28	29/52	.558	—	—	23/28	.821	45	1.6	9	0.3	21	30-0	1	7	81	2.9
DAVID JOHANNING	30	21/37	.568	—	—	13/25	.520	43	1.4	8	0.3	11	26-0	15	1	55	1.8
MACOLM NASH	20	11/25	.440	0/1	.000	13/20	.650	24	1.2	4	0.2	16	16-0	1	2	35	1.8
DOUG ELSTUN	13	3/12	.250	2/6	.333	1/2	.500	5	0.4	4	0.3	4	4-0	0	3	9	0.7
TEAM								116				2					
Kansas Totals	35	1086/2097	.518	199/504	.395	575/924	.622	1322	37.8	648	18.5	606	741-16	78	325	2946	84.2
Opponent Totals	35	870/2015	.432	150/437	.343	545/826	.660	1218	34.8	439	12.5	721	772-29	112	262	2435	69.6

NORTH CAROLINA

Results (Final Record 29–6)

San Diego State	W		99–63
Jacksonville	W		104–61
South Carolina	L		74–76
Iowa State	W		118–93
U. Conn.	W		79–64
Kentucky	W		84–81
Alabama	W		95–79
Purdue	W		86–74
DePaul	W		90–75
Stanford	W		71–60
Cornell	W		108–64
Notre Dame	W		82–47
Maryland	W		105–73
Virginia	W	2OT	89–86
Duke	L		60–74
Wake Forest	W		91–81
Georgia Tech	L		86–88
Clemson	W		90–77
N.C. State	L		91–97
N.C. State	W		92–70
Virginia	W		77–58
Wake Forest	W		85–70
Maryland	W		87–75
The Citadel	W		118–50
Clemson	W		73–57
Georgia Tech	W		91–74
Duke	L		77–83
#Clemson	W		67–59
#Virginia	W		76–71
#Duke	W		96–74
*Northeastern	W		101–66
*Villanova	W		84–69
*Eastern Michigan	W		93–67
*Temple	W		75–72
*Kansas	L		73–79

\# ACC Tournament
* NCAA Tournament

PLAYERS' SEASON RECORDS

NORTH CAROLINA

Player	Games	Total FG/FGA	Pct.	3 Pt. FG/FGA	Pct.	FT/FTA	Pct.	Reb.	RebPG	A	APG	TO	PF-D	BLK	S	TP	PPG
RICK FOX	35	206/455	.453	67/196	.342	111/138	.804	232	6.6	131	3.7	102	103-3	17	70	590	16.9
HUBERT DAVIS	35	161/309	.521	64/131	.489	81/97	.835	85	2.4	66	1.9	37	35-0	9	30	467	13.3
GEORGE LYNCH	35	172/329	.523	7/10	.700	85/135	.630	258	7.4	41	1.2	86	91-2	15	49	436	12.5
PETE CHILCUTT	35	175/325	.538	5/19	.263	65/85	.765	231	6.6	47	1.3	60	38-0	35	41	420	12.0
KING RICE	35	91/199	.457	26/63	.413	79/109	.725	62	1.8	207	5.9	76	51-0	1	38	287	8.2
ERIC MONTROSS	35	81/138	.587	—	—	41/67	.612	148	4.2	11	0.3	32	79-0	30	6	203	5.8
CLIFFORD ROZIER	34	64/136	.471	—	—	39/69	.565	101	3.0	18	0.5	30	41-1	17	12	167	4.9
BRIAN REESE	33	56/105	.533	3/5	.600	18/33	.545	54	1.6	18	0.5	20	14-0	2	9	133	4.0
HENRIK RODL	35	46/81	.568	12/27	.444	23/37	.622	53	1.5	62	1.8	36	39-0	6	13	127	3.6
DERRICK PHELPS	30	25/51	.490	2/9	.222	16/21	.762	33	1.1	58	1.9	40	30-0	3	27	68	2.3
KEVIN SALVADORI	31	18/35	.514	—	—	12/19	.632	27	0.9	0	0.0	5	13-0	8	1	48	1.5
SCOTT CHERRY	20	10/14	.714	1/1	1.000	9/13	.692	8	0.4	11	0.6	5	2-0	1	5	30	1.5
KENNY HARRIS	27	14/42	.333	4/17	.235	8/11	.727	21	0.8	12	0.4	18	14-0	0	7	40	1.5
PAT SULLIVAN	34	10/23	.435	1/5	.200	13/20	.650	22	0.6	18	0.5	10	18-0	1	6	34	1.0
MATT WENSTROM	24	5/15	.333	—	—	7/12	.583	21	0.9	0	0.0	6	6-0	3	1	17	0.7
TEAM								99				3					
North Carolina Totals	35	1134/2257	.502	192/483	.398	607/866	.701	1455	41.6	699	20.0	566	574-6	148	315	3067	87.6
Opponent Totals	35	974/2329	.418	197/622	.317	362/568	.637	1225	35.0	519	14.8	635	708-21	—	270	2507	71.6

UNLV

Results (Final Record 34–1)

Alabama-Birmingham	W	109–68
Nevada-Reno	W	131–81
Michigan State	W	95–75
Princeton	W	69–35
Florida State	W	101–69
Pacific	W	92–72
James Madison	W	89–65
Cal State Fullerton	W	98–67
San Jose State	W	95–63
Utah State	W	124–93
Fresno State	W	117–91
UC Irvine	W	117–76
Long Beach State	W	114–63
UC Santa Barbara	W	88–71
Louisville	W	97–85
Utah State	W	126–83
San Jose State	W	88–64
Rutgers	W	115–73
Fresno State	W	113–64
Arkansas	W	112–105
UC Santa Barbara	W	98–71
New Mexico State	W	86–74
Long Beach State	W	122–75
Pacific	W	80–59
UC Irvine	W	114–86
New Mexico State	W	86–74
Cal State Fullerton	W	104–83
#Long Beach State	W	49–29
#UC Santa Barbara	W	95–67
#Fresno State	W	98–74
*Montana	W	99–65
*Georgetown	W	62–54
*Utah	W	83–66
*Seton Hall	W	77–65
*Duke	L	77–79

\# Big West Tournament
* NCAA Tournament

PLAYERS' SEASON RECORDS
UNLV

Player	Games	Total FG/FGA	Pct.	3 Pt. FG/FGA	Pct.	FT/FTA	Pct.	Reb.	RebPG	A	APG	TO	PF-D	BLK	S	TP	PPG
LARRY JOHNSON	35	308/ 465	.662	17/ 48	.354	162/198	.818	380	10.9	104	3.0	78	79- 0	36	74	795	22.7
ANDERSON HUNT	33	218/ 455	.479	105/263	.399	28/ 42	.667	53	1.6	95	2.9	45	46- 0	3	46	569	17.2
STACEY AUGMON	35	220/ 375	.587	38/ 81	.469	101/139	.727	255	7.3	125	3.6	62	76- 0	28	78	579	16.5
GREG ANTHONY	35	141/ 309	.456	45/114	.395	79/102	.775	89	2.5	310	8.9	68	68- 1	14	84	406	11.6
GEORGE ACKLES	35	125/ 232	.539	1/ 1	1.000	37/ 63	.587	201	5.7	28	0.8	47	69- 1	77	36	288	8.2
EVRIC GRAY	35	90/ 181	.497	18/ 42	.429	40/ 66	.606	128	3.7	50	1.4	43	68- 1	14	14	238	6.8
ELMORE SPENCER	31	82/ 157	.522	—	—	33/ 70	.471	124	4.0	38	1.2	55	62- 2	76	22	197	6.4
TRAVIS BICE	31	48/ 107	.449	42/ 90	.467	8/ 11	.727	20	0.6	22	0.7	15	34- 0	2	11	146	4.7
MELVIN LOVE	19	18/ 27	.667	—	—	12/ 30	.400	35	1.8	0	0.0	10	23- 0	2	1	48	2.5
BOBBY JOYCE	16	16/ 34	.471	0/ 2	.000	5/ 15	.333	31	1.9	5	0.3	11	11- 0	5	3	37	2.3
H WALDMAN	31	21/ 41	.512	11/ 24	.458	12/ 20	.600	31	1.0	71	2.3	44	45- 0	2	22	65	2.1
DAVE RICE	22	14/ 33	.424	5/ 15	.333	6/ 7	.857	24	1.1	13	0.6	2	14- 0	0	3	39	1.8
CHRIS JETER	15	4/ 19	.211	0/ 1	.000	5/ 7	.714	13	0.9	2	0.1	5	8- 0	7	4	13	0.9
BRYAN EMERZIAN	11	0/ 6	.000	0/ 1	.000	—	—	1	0.1	0	0.0	3	1- 0	0	1	0	0.0
TEAM								104									
UNLV Totals	35	1305/2441	.535	282/682	.413	528/770	.686	1489	42.5	863	24.7	488	604- 5	266	399	3420	97.7
Opponent Totals	35	893/2235	.400	211/563	.375	487/699	.697	1218	34.8	497	14.2	690	634-17	89	188	2484	71.0

DUKE

Results (Final Record 32–7)

Marquette	W	87–74
Boston College	W	100–76
Arkansas	L	88–98
Notre Dame	W	85–77
East Carolina	W	125–82
N.C.-Charlotte	W	111–94
Georgetown	L	74–79
Michigan	W	75–68
Harvard	W	103–61
Oklahoma	W	90–85
Lehigh	W	97–67
Boston U.	W	109–55
Virginia	L	64–81
Georgia Tech	W	98–57
Maryland	W	94–78
Wake Forest	W	89–67
The Citadel	W	83–50
North Carolina	W	74–60
N.C. State	L	89–95
Clemson	W	99–70
Georgia Tech	W	77–75
Notre Dame	W	90–77
Virginia	W	86–74
Maryland	W	101–81
Louisiana State	W	88–70
Davidson	W	74–39
Wake Forest	L	77–86
N.C. State	W	72–65
Arizona	L	96–103
Clemson	W	79–62
North Carolina	W	83–77
#N.C. State	W	93–72
#North Carolina	L	74–96
*Northeast La.	W	102–73
*Iowa	W	85–70
*U. Conn.	W	81–67
*St. John's	W	78–61
*UNLV	W	79–77
*Kansas	W	72–65

#ACC Tournament
*NCAA Tournament

PLAYERS' SEASON RECORDS

Duke

Player	Games	Total FG/FGA	Pct.	3 Pt. FG/FGA	Pct.	FT/FTA	Pct.	Reb.	RebPG	A	APG	TO	PF-D	BLK	S	TP	PPG
CHRISTIAN LAETTNER	39	271/ 471	.575	18/ 53	.340	211/ 263	.802	340	8.7	76	1.9	121	111–1	44	75	771	19.8
BILL McCAFFREY	38	167/ 347	.481	24/ 70	.343	84/ 100	.832	69	1.8	71	1.9	67	50– 0	4	34	442	11.6
THOMAS HILL	39	164/ 297	.552	21/ 52	.404	101/ 136	.743	142	3.6	51	1.3	55	67– 1	15	59	450	11.5
BOBBY HURLEY	39	141/ 333	.423	76/188	.404	83/ 114	.728	93	2.4	289	7.4	151	100– 4	3	51	441	11.3
GRANT HILL	36	160/ 310	.516	1/ 2	.500	81/ 133	.609	183	5.1	79	2.2	74	79– 1	30	51	402	11.2
BRIAN DAVIS	39	104/ 228	.456	1/ 5	.200	89/ 122	.730	158	4.1	63	1.6	60	83– 2	8	39	298	7.6
GREG KOUBEK	38	77/ 177	.435	32/ 76	.421	39/ 48	.813	110	2.9	33	0.9	29	67– 2	3	21	225	5.9
ANTONIO LANG	36	57/ 94	.606	—	—	40/ 76	.526	92	2.6	7	0.2	25	55– 1	28	14	154	4.3
CRAWFORD PALMER	38	51/ 79	.646	—	—	33/ 40	.825	77	2.0	10	0.3	28	69– 1	19	11	135	3.6
MARTY CLARK	23	13/ 29	.448	2/ 9	.222	20/ 32	.625	17	0.7	8	0.3	25	15– 0	2	5	48	2.1
CHRISTIAN AST	17	12/ 18	.667	1/ 4	.250	3/ 4	.750	10	0.6	0	0.0	6	7– 0	3	0	28	1.6
CLAY BUCKLEY	19	10/ 18	.556	—	—	7/ 20	.350	20	1.1	2	0.1	4	12– 0	1	2	27	1.4
TEAM								103									
Duke Totals	39	1227/2401	.511	176/459	.383	791/1089	.726	1414	36.3	689	17.7	645	715–13	160	362	3421	87.7
Opponent Totals	39	1087/2445	.445	165/474	.348	525/ 792	.663	1327	34.0	528	13.5	779	865–	111	299	2864	73.4

✪ 1991 INDIVIDUAL RECORDS ✪

Most points in a single game
1	BRIAN PENNY, COASTAL CARO. (vs. INDIANA)	34
2	JOEY WRIGHT, TEXAS (vs. ST. JOHN'S)	32
3	MARK MACON, TEMPLE (vs. N. CAROLINA)	31
3	TODD DAY, ARKANSAS (vs. ALABAMA)	31
3	KENNY ANDERSON, GEORGIA TECH (vs. DEPAUL)	31

Most total points in the tournament
1	CHRISTIAN LAETTNER, DUKE	125
2	LARRY JOHNSON, UNLV	109
3	TERRY DEHERE, SETON HALL	97
4	MARK MACON, TEMPLE	96
4	HUBERT DAVIS, N. CAROLINA	96

Highest scoring average (minimum 2 games)
1	KENNY ANDERSON, GEORGIA TECH (56-2)	28.00
2	TERRY DEHERE, SETON HALL (97-4)	24.25
3	MARK MACON, TEMPLE (96-4)	24.00
4	STEVE SMITH, MICHIGAN STATE (47-2)	23.50
5	JOSH GRANT, UTAH (68-3)	22.67

Most field goals in a single game
1	TODD DAY, ARKANSAS (vs. ALABAMA)	14
2	CHRIS KING, WAKE FOREST (vs. ALABAMA)	13
2	BRIAN PENNY, COASTAL CARO. (vs. INDIANA)	13
2	LARRY JOHNSON, UNLV (vs. SETON HALL)	13
5	3 tied for fifth place.	12

Most total field goals in the tournament
1	LARRY JOHNSON, UNLV	44
2	CHRISTIAN LAETTNER, DUKE	37
3	MARK MACON, TEMPLE	36
4	MALIK SEALY, ST. JOHN'S	34
4	TERRY DEHERE, SETON HALL	34

Most field goal attempts in a single game
1	KENNY ANDERSON, GEORGIA TECH (vs. OHIO STATE)	28
2	HAROLD MINER, USC (vs. FLORIDA STATE)	27
3	TODD DAY, ARKANSAS (vs. ALABAMA)	24
3	CHUCK LIGHTENING, TOWSON STATE (vs. OHIO STATE)	24
5	4 tied for fifth place.	23

Most total field goal attempts in tournament
1	TERRY BROWN, KANSAS	75
2	MARK MACON, TEMPLE	74
3	LARRY JOHNSON, UNLV	72
4	MALIK SEALY, ST. JOHN'S	70
5	RICK FOX, N. CAROLINA	68

Highest field goal percentage in a single game (minimum 10 attempts)
1	BRIAN PENNY, COASTAL CARO. (vs. INDIANA) (13-15)	.867
2	MATT OTHICK, ARIZONA (vs. ST. FRANCIS-PA.) (8-10)	.800
3	ALONZO JAMISON, KANSAS (vs. ARKANSAS) (11-14)	.786
3	CALBERT CHEANEY, INDIANA (vs. FLORIDA STATE) (11-14)	.786
5	LARRY JOHNSON, UNLV (vs. UTAH) (10-13)	.769

Highest field goal percentage in the tournament (minimum 20 attempts)
1	ROBERT WERDANN, ST. JOHN'S (20-26)	.769
2	OLIVER MILLER, ARKANSAS (29-41)	.707
3	BILLY SINGLETON, ST. JOHN'S (18-27)	.667
4	ISAAC AUSTIN, ARIZONA STATE (16-24)	.667
5	LANCE MILLER, VILLANOVA (14-21)	.667

Most 3-pt. field goals in a single game
1	CHRIS FLEMING, RICHMOND (vs. TEMPLE)	7
2	MIGJEN BAKALLI, N.C. STATE (vs. SOUTHERN MISS.)	6
3	10 tied for third place.	5

Most total 3-pt. field goals in the tournament
1	TERRY BROWN, KANSAS	14
2	HUBERT DAVIS, N. CAROLINA	13
3	BOBBY HURLEY, DUKE	12
3	ANDERSON HUNT, UNLV	12
3	TERRY DEHERE, SETON HALL	12

Most 3-pt. field goals attempted in a single game
1	MARSHALL WILSON, GEORGIA (vs. PITTSBURGH)	13
2	TERRY BROWN, KANSAS (vs. PITTSBURGH)	12
2	JODY PATTON, GEORGIA (vs. PITTSBURGH)	12
2	HAROLD MINER, USC (vs. FLORIDA STATE)	12
2	SCOTT DRAUD, VANDERBILT (vs. GEORGETOWN)	12

Most total 3-pt. field goals attempted in the tournament
1	TERRY BROWN, KANSAS	45
2	ANDERSON HUNT, UNLV	38
3	BOBBY HURLEY, DUKE	28
3	TERRY DEHERE, SETON HALL	28
5	RICK FOX, N. CAROLINA	25

Highest 3-pt. field goal percentage in a single game (minimum 4 attempts)

1	MIGJEN BAKALLI, N.C. STATE (vs. SOUTHERN MISS.) (6-6)	1.000
2	HUBERT DAVIS, N. CAROLINA (vs. EASTERN MICH.) (5-5)	1.000
3	CHUCK MURPHY, DEPAUL (vs. GEORGIA TECH) (4-4)	1.000
3	TROY SKINNER, IOWA (vs. EAST TENN. STATE) (4-4)	1.000
5	2 tied for fifth place.	.833

Highest 3-pt. field goal percentage in the tournament (minimum 8 attempts)

1	CHRIS FLEMING, RICHMOND (9-13)	.692
2	JIMMY SOTO, UTAH (5-8)	.625
2	JOHN HILVERT, ST. FRANCIS-PA. (5-8)	.625
4	JASON BUCHANAN, ST. JOHN'S (8-13)	.615
5	CHUCKY SPROLING, ST. JOHN'S (6-10)	.600

Most free throws in a single game

1	CHRISTIAN LAETTNER, DUKE (vs. KANSAS)	12
2	5 tied for second place.	10

Most total free throws in the tournament

1	CHRISTIAN LAETTNER, DUKE	49
2	BILLY SINGLETON, ST. JOHN'S	20
2	ADONIS JORDAN, KANSAS	20
4	MIK KILGORE, TEMPLE	19
4	HUBERT DAVIS, N. CAROLINA	19

Most free throws attempted in a single game

1	WALTER WATTS, UTAH (vs. MICHIGAN STATE)	16
2	ACIE EARL, IOWA (vs. EAST TENN. STATE)	14
3	ADONIS JORDAN, KANSAS (vs. N. CAROLINA)	13
3	CHUCK LIGHTENING, TOWSON STATE (vs. OHIO STATE)	13
5	5 tied for fifth place.	12

Most free throws attempted in the tournament

1	CHRISTIAN LAETTNER, DUKE	54
2	ADONIS JORDAN, KANSAS	31
3	GRANT HILL, DUKE	27
4	WALTER WATTS, UTAH	25
5	2 tied for fifth place.	24

Highest free throw percentage in a single game (minimum 7 attempts)

1	CHRISTIAN LAETTNER, DUKE (vs. KANSAS) (12-12)	1.000
2	JOEY WRIGHT, TEXAS (vs. ST. JOHN'S) (10-10)	1.000
3	CHRISTIAN LAETTNER, DUKE (vs. ST. JOHN'S) (9-9)	1.000
3	RODNEY MONROE, N.C. STATE (vs. OKLAHOMA STATE) (9-9)	1.000
5	4 tied for fifth place.	1.000

Highest free throw percentage in the tournament (minimum 15 attempts)

1	RODNEY MONROE, N.C. STATE (17-17)	1.000
2	HUBERT DAVIS, N. CAROLINA (19-20)	.950
3	CHRISTIAN LAETTNER, DUKE (49-54)	.907
4	KING RICE, N. CAROLINA (15-17)	.882
4	JOSH GRANT, UTAH (15-17)	.882

Most rebounds in a single game

1	MALCOLM MACKEY, GEORGIA TECH (vs. OHIO STATE)	19
2	PERRY CARTER, OHIO STATE (vs. GEORGIA TECH)	18
3	BYRON HOUSTON, OKLAHOMA STATE (vs. NEW MEXICO)	17
3	GUILLERMO MYERS, TEXAS (vs. ST. PETER'S)	17
5	3 tied for fifth place.	16

Most total rebounds in the tournament

1	LARRY JOHNSON, UNLV	51
2	ALONZO JAMISON, KANSAS	45
3	MARK RANDALL, KANSAS	44
4	GEORGE LYNCH, N. CAROLINA	37
5	2 tied for fifth place.	36

Most rebounds per game (minimum 2 games)

1	MALCOLM MACKEY, GEORGIA TECH (27-2)	13.50
2	GUILLERMO MYERS, TEXAS (26-2)	13.00
2	CHAD GALLAGHER, CREIGHTON (26-2)	13.00
4	BYRON HOUSTON, OKLAHOMA STATE (36-3)	12.00
4	PERRY CARTER, OHIO STATE (36-3)	12.00

Most assists in a single game

1	KEITH JENNINGS, EAST TENN. STATE (vs. IOWA)	13
2	GREG ANTHONY, UNLV (vs. SETON HALL)	11
2	CHRIS CORCHIANI, N.C. STATE (vs. SOUTHERN MISS.)	11
2	JASON BUCHANAN, ST. JOHN'S (vs. TEXAS)	11
2	ERNIE MURRY, ARKANSAS (vs. GEORGIA STATE)	11

Most total assists in the tournament

1	BOBBY HURLEY, DUKE	43
2	GREG ANTHONY, UNLV	40
3	JASON BUCHANAN, ST. JOHN'S	32
4	KING RICE, N. CAROLINA	31
5	2 tied for fifth place.	23

Most assists per game (minimum 2 appearances)

1	CHRIS CORCHIANI, N.C. STATE (17-2)	8.50
2	GREG ANTHONY, UNLV (40-5)	8.00
3	JASON BUCHANAN, ST. JOHN'S (32-4)	8.00
4	LATRELL WRIGHTSELL, CREIGHTON (16-2)	8.00
5	GARY WAITES, ALABAMA (23-3)	7.67

Most turnovers in a single game

1	BILLY SINGLETON, ST. JOHN'S (vs. DUKE)	8
1	PHILLIP LUCKYDO, GEORGIA STATE (vs. ARKANSAS)	8
3	6 tied for third place.	7

Most total turnovers in the tournament

1	ADONIS JORDAN, KANSAS	20
2	GRANT HILL, DUKE	19
3	CHRISTIAN LAETTNER, DUKE	17
4	MALIK SEALY, ST. JOHN'S	16
5	2 tied for fifth place.	14

Most shots blocked in a single game

1	SHAWN BRADLEY, BRIGHAM YOUNG (vs. VIRGINIA)	10
2	MARK STRICKLAND, TEMPLE (vs. OKLAHOMA STATE)	8
3	ELMORE SPENCER, UNLV (vs. GEORGETOWN)	6
3	ELMORE SPENCER, UNLV (vs. MONTANA)	6
3	ZAVIAN SMITH, GEORGIA STATE (vs. ARKANSAS)	6

Most total shots blocked in the tournament

1	MARK STRICKLAND, TEMPLE	15
1	ELMORE SPENCER, UNLV	15
3	SHAWN BRADLEY, BRIGHAM YOUNG	12
4	OLIVER MILLER, ARKANSAS	9
5	3 tied for fifth place.	8

Most steals in a single game

1	SCOTT BURRELL, U. CONN. (vs. XAVIER [OHIO])	7
2	JASON BUCHANAN, ST. JOHN'S (vs. OHIO STATE)	6
2	GRANT HILL, DUKE (vs. IOWA)	6
2	MONROE BROWN, PENN STATE (vs. UCLA)	6
5	7 tied for fifth place.	5

Most total steals in the tournament

1	GRANT HILL, DUKE	15
2	LARRY JOHNSON, UNLV	12
3	5 tied for third place.	11

❂ 1991 TEAM RECORDS ❂

Most points in a single game

1	ARKANSAS (vs. GEORGIA STATE)	117
2	N.C. STATE (vs. SOUTHERN MISS.)	114
3	DUKE (vs. NORTHEAST LA.)	102

Most total points in the tournament

1	DUKE	497
2	KANSAS	452
3	N. CAROLINA	426

Highest scoring average (minimum 2 games)

1	ARKANSAS (388-4)	97.00
2	N.C. STATE (178-2)	89.00
3	N. CAROLINA (426-5)	85.20

Most field goals in a single game

1	DUKE (vs. NORTHEAST LA.)	43
2	ARKANSAS (vs. GEORGIA STATE)	40
3	2 tied for third place.	39

Most total field goals in the tournament

1	DUKE	175
2	KANSAS	168
3	N. CAROLINA	162

Most field goals attempted in a single game

1	ARKANSAS (vs. ALABAMA)	85
2	ARKANSAS (vs. GEORGIA STATE)	82
3	SOUTHERN MISS. (vs. N.C. STATE)	77

Most total field goals attempted in the tournament

1	KANSAS	370
2	N. CAROLINA	328
3	UNLV	325

Highest field goal percentage in a single game

1	TEMPLE (vs. PURDUE) (30-46)	.652
2	ST. JOHN'S (vs. OHIO STATE) (34-54)	.630
3	ST. JOHN'S (vs. TEXAS) (31-51)	.608

Highest field goal percentage in a tournament (minimum 2 games)

1	DUKE (175-320)	.547
2	ST. JOHN'S (114-212)	.538
3	WAKE FOREST (63-123)	.512

Most 3-pt. field goals in a single game

1	ST. FRANCIS-PA. (vs. ARIZONA)	13
2	RICHMOND (vs. TEMPLE)	12
2	N.C. STATE (vs. SOUTHERN MISS.)	12

Most total 3-pt. field goals in the tournament

1	KANSAS	33
2	ARKANSAS	31
3	DUKE	27

Most 3-pt. field goals attempted in a single game

1	RICHMOND (vs. TEMPLE)	28
2	GEORGIA (vs. PITTSBURGH)	27
3	EAST TENN. STATE (vs. IOWA)	25
3	ST. FRANCIS-PA. (vs. ARIZONA)	25
3	N.C. STATE (vs. SOUTHERN MISS.)	25

Most total 3-pt. field goals attempted in the tournament

1	KANSAS	91
2	ARKANSAS	78
3	UNLV	73

Highest 3-pt. field goal percentage in a single game (minimum 10 attempts)

1	ST. JOHN'S (vs. DUKE) (7-10)	.700
1	IOWA (vs. EAST TENN. STATE) (7-10)	.700
3	2 tied for third place.	.600

Highest 3-pt. field goal percentage in the tournament (minimum 20 attempts)

1	ST. JOHN'S (16-27)	.593
2	WIS.-GREEN BAY (11-20)	.550
3	ST. FRANCIS-PA. (13-25)	.520

Most free throws in a single game

1	ARKANSAS (vs. GEORGIA STATE)	31
2	ARIZONA (vs. BRIGHAM YOUNG)	30
3	XAVIER (OHIO) (vs. NEBRASKA)	29

Most total free throws in the tournament

1	DUKE	120
2	KANSAS	83
3	N. CAROLINA	77

Most free throws attempted in a single game

1	UTAH (vs. MICHIGAN STATE)	46
2	ARKANSAS (vs. GEORGIA STATE)	42
3	XAVIER (OHIO) (vs. NEBRASKA)	40

Most total free throws attempted in the tournament

1	DUKE	159
2	KANSAS	129
3	N. CAROLINA	110

Highest free throw percentage in a single game
1 VILLANOVA (vs. N. CAROLINA) (12-12) 1.000
2 WIS.-GREEN BAY (vs. MICHIGAN STATE)
  (7-7) 1.000
3 RUTGERS (vs. ARIZONA ST.) (15-16) .938

Highest free throw percentage in the tournament (minimum 2 games)
1 VILLANOVA (26-27) .963
2 N.C. STATE (45-50) .900
3 OKLAHOMA STATE (53-65) .815

Fewest free throws in a single game
1 OKLAHOMA STATE (vs. TEMPLE) 4
1 ST. JOHN'S (vs. DUKE) 4
1 KANSAS (vs. DUKE) 4

Lowest free throw percentage in a single game
1 ST. PETER'S (vs. TEXAS) (8-17) .471
2 DEPAUL (vs. GEORGIA TECH) (9-19) .474
3 KANSAS (vs. DUKE) (4-8) .500

Lowest free throw percentage in the tournament (minimum 2 games)
1 OHIO STATE (48-85) .565
2 U. CONN. (38-66) .576
3 WAKE FOREST (27-46) .587

Most rebounds in a single game
1 ARKANSAS (vs. GEORGIA STATE) 53
2 OHIO STATE (vs. GEORGIA TECH) 50
3 KANSAS (vs. N. CAROLINA) 46

Most rebounds per game (minimum 2 games)
1 ARKANSAS (169-4) 42.25
2 OHIO STATE (121-3) 40.33
3 TEXAS (76-2) 38.00

Most assists in a single game
1 ARKANSAS (vs. GEORGIA STATE) 32
2 WAKE FOREST (vs. ALABAMA) 27
2 N. CAROLINA (vs. VILLANOVA) 27

Most assists per game (minimum 2 games)
1 ARKANSAS (89-4) 22.25
2 WAKE FOREST (43-2) 21.50
3 ALABAMA (60-3) 20.00

Most turnovers in a single game
1 GEORGIA STATE (vs. ARKANSAS) 32
2 ST. JOHN'S (vs. DUKE) 26
2 ALABAMA (vs. ARKANSAS) 26

Most turnovers per game (minimum 2 games)
1 IOWA (44-2) 22.00
2 VILLANOVA (37-2) 18.50
3 XAVIER (OHIO) (36-2) 18.00

Most shots blocked in a single game
1 BRIGHAM YOUNG (vs. VIRGINIA) 13
2 SETON HALL (vs. CREIGHTON) 10
3 BRIGHAM YOUNG (vs. ARIZONA) 9
3 UNLV (vs. MONTANA) 9
3 TEMPLE (vs. OKLAHOMA STATE) 9

Most shots blocked per game (minimum 2 games)
1 BRIGHAM YOUNG (22-2) 11.00
2 GEORGETOWN (13-2) 6.50
3 UNLV (32-5) 6.40

Most steals in a single game
1 DUKE (vs. ST. JOHN'S) 17
1 SETON HALL (vs. PEPPERDINE) 17
3 ARKANSAS (vs. GEORGIA STATE) 16

Most steals per game
1 U. CONN. (30-3) 10.00
2 SETON HALL (37-4) 9.25
2 ARKANSAS (37-4) 9.25

○ 1991 ALL-STARS ○

(Composite Tourney Statistics)

EAST REGIONAL

Player	School	Gms	Min	FG/FGA	Pct	FG3/FG3A	Pct	FT/FTA	Pct	Reb	Reb PG	A	APG	TO	PF	BLK	S	TP	PPG	PPM
HUBERT DAVIS	N. CAROLINA	5	142	32/55	.582	13/23	.565	19/20	.950	16	3.20	13	2.60	7	3	1	4	96	19.20	.676
RICK FOX	N. CAROLINA	5	143	28/68	.412	6/25	.240	6/6	1.000	30	6.00	23	4.60	13	15	4	9	68	13.60	.476
MIK KILGORE	TEMPLE	4	159	26/49	.531	7/15	.467	19/24	.792	21	5.25	16	4.00	6	9	0	1	78	19.50	.491
*MARK MACON	TEMPLE	4	156	36/74	.486	8/17	.471	16/19	.842	18	4.50	7	1.75	4	13	4	8	96	24.00	.615
CARL THOMAS	EASTERN MICH.	3	110	17/33	.515	10/23	.435	6/9	.667	15	5.00	8	2.67	9	7	2	1	50	16.67	.455

SOUTHEAST REGIONAL

Player	School	Gms	Min	FG/FGA	Pct	FG3/FG3A	Pct	FT/FTA	Pct	Reb	Reb PG	A	APG	TO	PF	BLK	S	TP	PPG	PPM
TERRY BROWN	KANSAS	6	155	26/75	.347	14/45	.311	11/14	.786	22	3.67	5	.83	6	12	1	7	77	12.83	.497
TODD DAY	ARKANSAS	4	122	31/66	.470	10/23	.435	14/17	.824	23	5.75	5	1.25	10	13	4	11	86	21.50	.705
*ALONZO JAMISON	KANSAS	6	159	31/54	.574	1/3	.333	6/14	.429	45	7.50	20	3.33	11	21	1	10	69	11.50	.434
ADONIS JORDAN	KANSAS	6	210	23/53	.434	11/24	.458	20/31	.645	19	3.17	21	3.50	20	10	0	11	77	12.83	.367
OLIVER MILLER	ARKANSAS	4	101	29/41	.707	0/1	.000	12/20	.600	31	7.75	6	1.50	11	11	9	3	70	17.50	.693

WEST REGIONAL

Player	School	Gms	Min	FG/FGA	Pct	FG3/FG3A	Pct	FT/FTA	Pct	Reb	Reb PG	A	APG	TO	PF	BLK	S	TP	PPG	PPM
GREG ANTHONY	UNLV	5	173	24/57	.421	4/9	.444	14/17	.824	18	3.60	40	8.00	8	13	0	11	66	13.20	.382
STACEY AUGMON	UNLV	5	174	27/50	.540	5/9	.556	4/8	.500	32	6.40	12	2.40	9	10	4	10	63	12.60	.362
TERRY DEHERE	SETON HALL	4	142	34/64	.531	12/28	.429	17/20	.850	16	4.00	4	1.00	9	5	2	8	97	24.25	.683
*LARRY JOHNSON	UNLV	5	179	44/72	.611	3/13	.231	18/23	.783	51	10.20	11	2.20	10	10	5	12	109	21.80	.609
BRIAN WILLIAMS	ARIZONA	3	90	19/37	.514	0/0	.000	11/13	.846	27	9.00	1	.33	6	6	5	2	49	16.33	.544

*Most Outstanding Player

MIDWEST REGIONAL

Player	School	Gms	Min	FG/FGA	Pct	FG3/FG3A	Pct	FT/FTA	Pct	Reb	Reb PG	A	APG	TO	PF	BLK	S	TP	PPG	PPM
JASON BUCHANAN	ST. JOHN'S	4	142	19/37	.514	8/13	.615	17/21	.810	13	3.25	32	8.00	13	9	0	10	63	15.75	.444
THOMAS HILL	DUKE	6	150	22/44	.500	4/6	.667	13/15	.867	17	2.83	9	1.50	8	16	6	9	61	10.17	.407
*#BOBBY HURLEY	DUKE	6	219	19/40	.475	12/28	.429	15/18	.833	16	2.67	43	7.17	10	14	0	11	65	10.83	.297
#CHRISTIAN LAETTNER	DUKE	6	190	37/60	.617	2/4	.500	49/54	.907	34	5.67	11	1.83	17	14	5	9	125	20.83	.658
MALIK SEALY	ST. JOHN'S	4	141	34/70	.486	1/2	.500	10/17	.588	31	7.75	9	2.25	16	11	4	9	79	19.75	.560

ALL-TOURNAMENT

Player	School	Gms	Min	FG/FGA	Pct	FG3/FG3A	Pct	FT/FTA	Pct	Reb	Reb PG	A	APG	TO	PF	BLK	S	TP	PPG	PPM
ANDERSON HUNT	UNLV	5	176	29/66	.439	12/38	.316	6/11	.545	13	2.60	4	.80	9	4	0	6	76	15.20	.432
BOBBY HURLEY	DUKE	6	219	19/40	.475	12/28	.429	15/18	.833	16	2.67	43	7.17	10	14	0	11	65	10.83	.297
*CHRISTIAN LAETTNER	DUKE	6	190	37/60	.617	2/4	.500	49/54	.907	34	5.67	11	1.83	17	14	5	9	125	20.83	.658
BILL MCCAFFREY	DUKE	6	140	25/45	.556	3/4	.750	8/12	.667	11	1.83	7	1.17	14	14	1	4	61	10.17	.436
MARK RANDALL	KANSAS	6	194	28/53	.528	1/1	1.000	11/23	.478	44	7.33	21	3.50	12	19	0	5	68	11.33	.351

*Most Outstanding Player
#Also All-Tournament All Star

PART II

The Conferences

Every conference represented in the tournament in the last dozen years is listed, along with independents. Schools changing conference affiliation during this period are listed by affiliation at the time of their tournament appearances. Thus, some schools are listed in more than one conference. Schools are listed alphabetically under each conference name. Next to the school names are the years they appeared in the tournament, and, in parentheses, their finishes in the regional final round and beyond. To the right are the composite tournament records for each school and each conference. Following are the abbreviations used in this section:

App	Number of Appearances
W	Games Won
L	Games Lost
Ch.	Championships
2nd	2nd Place
F-4	Final Four Appearances
F-8	Round of 8 (Regional Final) Appearances

NOTE:
F-8 in the left-hand column (Conference/School/Years) indicates that the team lost in the Round of 8.
F-8 in the right-hand column (Tournament Totals) indicates appearances (both wins and losses) in the Round of 8.

CONFERENCE AFFILIATIONS AND RECORDS—1980-1991

AMERICAN SOUTH

	App	W	L	Ch.	2nd	F-4	F-8
LOUISIANA TECH—1989, 1991	2	1	2	0	0	0	0
NEW ORLEANS—1991	1	0	1	0	0	0	0
TOTAL	3	1	3	0	0	0	0

ATLANTIC 10

	App	W	L	Ch.	2nd	F-4	F-8
PENN STATE—1991	1	1	1	0	0	0	0
PITTSBURGH—1981, 1982	2	1	2	0	0	0	0
RHODE ISLAND—1988	1	2	1	0	0	0	0
RUTGERS—1983, 1989, 1991	3	1	3	0	0	0	0
ST. JOSEPH'S—1986	1	1	1	0	0	0	0
TEMPLE—1984, 1985, 1986, 1987, 88 (F-8), 1990, 91 (F-8)	7	10	7	0	0	0	2
VILLANOVA—1980	1	1	1	0	0	0	0
WEST VIRGINIA—1982, 1983, 1984, 1986, 1987, 1989	6	3	6	0	0	0	0
TOTAL	22	20	22	0	0	0	2

ATLANTIC COAST

	App	W	L	Ch.	2nd	F-4	F-8
CLEMSON—80 (F-8), 1987, 1989, 1990	4	6	4	0	0	0	1
DUKE—80 (F-8), 1984, 1985, 86 (2), 1987, 88 (F-4), 89 (F-4), 90 (2), 91 (Ch.)	9	29	8	1	2	2	6
GEORGIA TECH—85 (F-8), 1986, 1987, 1988, 1989, 90 (F-4), 1991	7	11	7	0	0	1	2
MARYLAND—1980, 1981, 1983, 1984, 1985, 1986, 1988	7	8	7	0	0	0	0
N. CAROLINA—1980, 81 (2), 82 (Ch.), 83 (F-8), 1984, 85 (F-8), 1986, 87 (F-8), 88 (F-8), 1989, 1990, 91 (F-4)	12	31	11	1	1	1	7
N.C. STATE—1980, 1982, 83 (Ch.), 85 (F-8), 86 (F-8), 1987, 1988, 1989, 1991	9	15	8	1	0	0	3
VIRGINIA—81 (F-4), 1982, 83 (F-8), 84 (F-4), 1986, 1987, 89 (F-8), 1990, 1991	9	15	9	0	0	2	4
WAKE FOREST—1981, 1982, 84 (F-8), 1991	4	4	4	0	0	0	1
TOTAL	61	119	58	3	3	6	24

BIG EAST

	App	W	L	Ch.	2nd	F-4	F-8
BOSTON COLLEGE—1981, 82 (F-8), 1983, 1985	4	8	4	0	0	0	1
GEORGETOWN—80 (F-8), 1981, 82 (2), 1983, 84 (Ch.), 85 (2), 1986, 87 (F-8), 1988, 89 (F-8), 1990, 1991	12	27	11	1	2	0	6
PITTSBURGH—1985, 1987, 1988, 1989, 1991	5	3	5	0	0	0	0
PROVIDENCE—87 (F-4), 1989, 1990	3	4	3	0	0	1	1
SETON HALL—1988, 89 (2), 91 (F-8)	3	9	3	0	1	0	2
ST. JOHN'S—1980, 1982, 1983, 1984, 85 (F-4), 1986, 1987, 1988, 1990, 91 (F-8)	10	12	10	0	0	1	2
SYRACUSE—1980, 1983, 1984, 1985, 1986, 87 (2), 1988, 89 (F-8), 1990, 1991	10	16	10	0	1	0	2
U. CONN.—90 (F-8), 1991	2	5	2	0	0	0	1
VILLANOVA—1981, 82 (F-8), 83 (F-8), 1984, 85 (Ch.), 1986, 88 (F-8), 1990, 1991	9	17	8	1	0	0	4
TOTAL	58	101	56	2	4	2	19

BIG EIGHT

	App	W	L	Ch.	2nd	F-4	F-8
IOWA STATE—1985, 1986, 1988, 1989	4	2	4	0	0	0	0
KANSAS—1981, 1984, 1985, 86 (F-4), 1987, 88 (Ch.), 1990, 91 (2)	8	22	7	1	1	1	3
KANSAS STATE—1980, 81 (F-8), 1982, 1987, 88 (F-8), 1989, 1990	7	10	7	0	0	0	2
MISSOURI—1980, 1981, 1982, 1983, 1986, 1987, 1988, 1989, 1990	9	5	9	0	0	0	0
NEBRASKA—1986, 1991	2	0	2	0	0	0	0
OKLAHOMA—1983, 1984, 85 (F-8), 1986, 1987, 88 (2), 1989, 1990	8	15	8	0	1	0	2
OKLAHOMA STATE—1983, 1991	2	2	2	0	0	0	0
TOTAL	40	56	39	1	2	1	7

BIG SKY

	App	W	L	Ch.	2nd	F-4	F-8
BOISE STATE—1988	1	0	1	0	0	0	0
IDAHO—1981, 1982, 1989, 1990	4	1	4	0	0	0	0
IDAHO STATE—1987	1	0	1	0	0	0	0
MONTANA—1991	1	0	1	0	0	0	0
MONTANA ST.—1986	1	0	1	0	0	0	0
NEVADA-RENO—1984, 1985	2	0	2	0	0	0	0
WEBER STATE—1980, 1983	2	0	2	0	0	0	0
TOTAL	12	1	12	0	0	0	0

BIG SOUTH

	App	W	L	Ch.	2nd	F-4	F-8
COASTAL CARO.—1991	1	0	1	0	0	0	0
TOTAL	1	0	1	0	0	0	0

BIG TEN

	App	W	L	Ch.	2nd	F-4	F-8
ILLINOIS—1981, 1983, 84 (F-8), 1985, 1986, 1987, 1988, 89 (F-4), 1990	9	11	9	0	0	1	2
INDIANA—1980, 81 (Ch.), 1982, 1983, 84 (F-8), 1986, 87 (Ch.), 1988, 1989, 1990, 1991	11	20	9	2	0	0	3
IOWA—80 (F-4), 1981, 1982, 1983, 1985, 1986, 87 (F-8), 1988, 1989, 1991	10	14	11	0	0	1	2
MICHIGAN—1985, 1986, 1987, 1988, 89 (Ch.), 1990	6	12	5	1	0	0	1
MICHIGAN STATE—1985, 1986, 1990, 1991	4	5	4	0	0	0	0
MINNESOTA—1982, 1989, 90 (F-8)	3	6	3	0	0	0	1
OHIO STATE—1980, 1982, 1983, 1985, 1987, 1990, 1991	7	7	7	0	0	0	0
PURDUE—80 (F-4), 1983, 1984, 1985, 1986, 1987, 1988, 1990, 1991	9	10	9	0	0	1	1
TOTAL	59	85	57	3	0	3	10

BIG WEST

	App	W	L	Ch.	2nd	F-4	F-8
FRESNO STATE—1981, 1982, 1984	3	1	3	0	0	0	0
NEW MEXICO STATE—1990, 1991	2	0	2	0	0	0	0
SAN JOSE STATE—1980	1	0	1	0	0	0	0
UC SANTA BARB.—1988, 1990	2	1	2	0	0	0	0
UNLV—1983, 1984, 1985, 1986, 87 (F-4), 1988, 89 (F-8), 90 (Ch.), 91 (F-4)	9	23	8	1	0	2	4
UTAH STATE—1980, 1983, 1988	3	0	3	0	0	0	0
TOTAL	20	25	19	1	0	2	4

COLONIAL ATHLETIC

	App	W	L	Ch.	2nd	F-4	F-8
GEORGE MASON—1989	1	0	1	0	0	0	0
JAMES MADISON—1981, 1982, 1983	3	3	3	0	0	0	0
NAVY—1985, 86 (F-8), 1987	3	4	3	0	0	0	1
RICHMOND—1984, 1986, 1988, 1990, 1991	5	5	5	0	0	0	0
TOTAL	12	12	12	0	0	0	1

EAST COAST

	App	W	L	Ch.	2nd	F-4	F-8
DREXEL—1986	1	0	1	0	0	0	0
RIDER—1984	1	0	1	0	0	0	0
TOWSON STATE—1990, 1991	2	0	2	0	0	0	0
TOTAL	4	0	4	0	0	0	0

INDEPENDENT*

	App	W	L	Ch.	2nd	F-4	F-8
DAYTON—84 (F-8), 1985	2	3	2	0	0	0	1
DEPAUL—1980, 1981, 1982, 1984, 1985, 1986, 1987, 1988, 1989, 1991	10	7	10	0	0	0	0
IONA—1980	1	1	1	0	0	0	0
LA SALLE—1980, 1983	2	1	2	0	0	0	0
LIU—1981	1	0	1	0	0	0	0
MARQUETTE—1980, 1982, 1983	3	1	3	0	0	0	0
NEW ORLEANS—1987	1	1	1	0	0	0	0
NOTRE DAME—1980, 1981, 1985, 1986, 1987, 1988, 1989, 1990	8	5	8	0	0	0	0
OLD DOMINION—1980	1	0	1	0	0	0	0
S'WESTERN LA.—1983	1	0	1	0	0	0	0
ST. JOSEPH'S—81 (F-8), 1982	2	3	2	0	0	0	1
TOTAL	32	22	32	0	0	0	2

IVY LEAGUE

	App	W	L	Ch.	2nd	F-4	F-8
BROWN—1986	1	0	1	0	0	0	0
CORNELL—1988	1	0	1	0	0	0	0
PENNSYLVANIA—1980, 1982, 1985, 1987	4	1	4	0	0	0	0
PRINCETON—1981, 1983, 1984, 1989, 1990, 1991	6	3	6	0	0	0	0
TOTAL	12	4	12	0	0	0	0

METRO

	App	W	L	Ch.	2nd	F-4	F-8
CREIGHTON—1981, 1989, 1991	3	1	3	0	0	0	0
FLORIDA STATE—1980, 1988, 1989, 1991	4	2	4	0	0	0	0
LOUISVILLE—80 (Ch.), 1981, 82 (F-4), 83 (F-4), 1984, 86 (Ch.), 1988, 1989, 1990	9	24	7	2	0	2	4
MEMPHIS STATE—1982, 1983, 1984, 85 (F-4), 1986, 1988, 1989	7	10	7	0	0	1	1
S. CAROLINA—1989	1	0	1	0	0	0	0
SOUTHERN MISS.—1990, 1991	2	0	2	0	0	0	0
VIRGINIA TECH—1980, 1985, 1986	3	1	3	0	0	0	0
TOTAL	29	38	27	2	0	3	5

METRO ATLANTIC

	App	W	L	Ch.	2nd	F-4	F-8
FAIRFIELD—1986, 1987	2	0	2	0	0	0	0
IONA—1984, 1985	2	0	2	0	0	0	0
LA SALLE—1988, 1989, 1990	3	1	3	0	0	0	0
ST. PETER'S—1991	1	0	1	0	0	0	0
TOTAL	8	1	8	0	0	0	0

MID-AMERICAN

	App	W	L	Ch.	2nd	F-4	F-8
BALL STATE—1981, 1986, 1989, 1990	4	3	4	0	0	0	0
CENTRAL MICH.—1987	1	0	1	0	0	0	0
EASTERN MICH.—1988, 1991	2	2	2	0	0	0	0
MIAMI (OHIO)—1984, 1985, 1986	3	0	3	0	0	0	0
NORTHERN ILL.—1982	1	0	1	0	0	0	0
OHIO—1983, 1985	2	1	2	0	0	0	0
TOLEDO—1980	1	0	1	0	0	0	0
TOTAL	14	6	14	0	0	0	0

MID-CONTINENT

	App	W	L	Ch.	2nd	F-4	F-8
CLEVELAND STATE—1986	1	2	1	0	0	0	0
NORTHERN ILL.—1991	1	0	1	0	0	0	0
NORTHERN IOWA—1990	1	1	1	0	0	0	0
SW MISSOURI STATE—1987, 1988, 1989, 1990	4	1	4	0	0	0	0
WIS.-GREEN BAY—1991	1	0	1	0	0	0	0
TOTAL	8	4	8	0	0	0	0

MID-EASTERN ATHLETIC

	App	W	L	Ch.	2nd	F-4	F-8
COPPIN STATE—1990	1	0	1	0	0	0	0
HOWARD—1981	1	0	1	0	0	0	0
N.C. A&T—1982, 1983, 1984, 1985, 1986, 1987, 1988	7	0	7	0	0	0	0
S. CAROLINA STATE—1989	1	0	1	0	0	0	0
TOTAL	10	0	10	0	0	0	0

MIDWESTERN COLLEGIATE

	App	W	L	Ch.	2nd	F-4	F-8
DAYTON—1990	1	1	1	0	0	0	0
EVANSVILLE—1982, 1989	2	1	2	0	0	0	0
LOYOLA-CHICAGO—1985	1	2	1	0	0	0	0
ORAL ROBERTS—1984	1	0	1	0	0	0	0
XAVIER (OHIO)—1983, 1986, 1987, 1988, 1989, 1990, 1991	7	4	7	0	0	0	0
TOTAL	12	8	12	0	0	0	0

MISSOURI VALLEY

	App	W	L	Ch.	2nd	F-4	F-8
BRADLEY—1980, 1986, 1988	3	1	3	0	0	0	0
ILLINOIS STATE—1983, 1984, 1985, 1990	4	2	4	0	0	0	0
TULSA—1982, 1984, 1985, 1986, 1987	5	0	5	0	0	0	0
WICHITA STATE—81 (F-8), 1985, 1987, 1988	4	3	4	0	0	0	1
TOTAL	16	6	16	0	0	0	1

NORTH ATLANTIC

	App	W	L	Ch.	2nd	F-4	F-8
BOSTON UNIV.—1983, 1988, 1990	3	0	3	0	0	0	0
HOLY CROSS—1980	1	0	1	0	0	0	0
NORTHEASTERN—1981, 1982, 1984, 1985, 1986, 1987, 1991	7	3	7	0	0	0	0
SIENA—1989	1	1	1	0	0	0	0
TOTAL	12	4	12	0	0	0	0

NORTHEAST

	App	W	L	Ch.	2nd	F-4	F-8
F. DICKINSON—1985, 1988	2	0	2	0	0	0	0
LIU—1984	1	0	1	0	0	0	0
MARIST—1986, 1987	2	0	2	0	0	0	0
ROBERT MORRIS—1982, 1983, 1989, 1990	4	1	4	0	0	0	0
ST. FRANCIS-PA.—1991	1	0	1	0	0	0	0
TOTAL	10	1	10	0	0	0	0

OHIO VALLEY

	App	W	L	Ch.	2nd	F-4	F-8
AKRON—1986	1	0	1	0	0	0	0
AUSTIN PEAY—1987	1	1	1	0	0	0	0
MIDDLE TENN. STATE—1982, 1985, 1987, 1989	4	2	4	0	0	0	0
MOREHEAD STATE—1983, 1984	2	1	2	0	0	0	0
MURRAY STATE—1988, 1990, 1991	3	1	3	0	0	0	0
WESTERN KY.—1980, 1981	2	0	2	0	0	0	0
TOTAL	13	5	13	0	0	0	0

PACIFIC-10

	App	W	L	Ch.	2nd	F-4	F-8
ARIZONA—1985, 1986, 1987, 88 (F-4), 1989, 1990, 1991	7	9	7	0	0	1	1
ARIZONA STATE—1980, 1981, 1991	3	2	3	0	0	0	0
CALIFORNIA—1990	1	1	1	0	0	0	0
OREGON STATE—1980, 1981, 82 (F-8), 1984, 1985, 1988, 1989, 1990	8	2	8	0	0	0	1
STANFORD—1989	1	0	1	0	0	0	0
UCLA—80 (2), 1981, 1983, 1987, 1989, 1990, 1991	7	9	7	0	1	0	1
USC—1982, 1985, 1991	3	0	3	0	0	0	0
WASHINGTON—1984, 1985, 1986	3	2	3	0	0	0	0
WASHINGTON STATE—1980, 1983	2	1	2	0	0	0	0
TOTAL	35	26	35	0	1	1	3

PATRIOT

	App	W	L	Ch.	2nd	F-4	F-8
BUCKNELL—1987, 1989	2	0	2	0	0	0	0
LEHIGH—1985, 1988	2	0	2	0	0	0	0
TOTAL	4	0	4	0	0	0	0

SOUTHEASTERN

	App	W	L	Ch.	2nd	F-4	F-8
ALABAMA—1982, 1983, 1984, 1985, 1986, 1987, 1989, 1990, 1991	9	11	9	0	0	0	0
AUBURN—1984, 1985, 86 (F-8), 1987, 1988	5	7	5	0	0	0	1
FLORIDA—1987, 1988, 1989	3	3	3	0	0	0	0
GEORGIA—83 (F-4), 1985, 1987, 1990, 1991	5	4	5	0	0	1	1
KENTUCKY—1980, 1981, 1982, 83 (F-8), 84 (F-4), 1985, 86 (F-8), 1987, 1988	9	13	9	0	0	1	3
LOUISIANA STATE—80 (F-8), 81 (F-4), 1984, 1985, 86 (F-4), 87 (F-8), 1988, 1989, 1990, 1991	10	13	11	0	0	2	4
MISSISSIPPI—1981	1	0	1	0	0	0	0
MISSISSIPPI STATE—1991	1	0	1	0	0	0	0
TENNESSEE—1980, 1981, 1982, 1983, 1989	5	4	5	0	0	0	0
VANDERBILT—1988, 1989, 1991	3	2	3	0	0	0	0
TOTAL	51	57	52	0	0	4	9

SOUTHERN

	App	W	L	Ch.	2nd	F-4	F-8
DAVIDSON—1986	1	0	1	0	0	0	0
EAST TENN. STATE—1989, 1990, 1991	3	0	3	0	0	0	0
FURMAN—1980	1	0	1	0	0	0	0
MARSHALL—1984, 1985, 1987	3	0	3	0	0	0	0
TENN.-CHATT.—1981, 1982, 1983, 1988	4	1	4	0	0	0	0
TOTAL	12	1	12	0	0	0	0

SOUTHLAND

	App	W	L	Ch.	2nd	F-4	F-8
LAMAR—1980, 1981, 1983	3	4	3	0	0	0	0
LOUISIANA TECH—1984, 1985, 1987	3	3	3	0	0	0	0
MCNEESE STATE—1989	1	0	1	0	0	0	0
NORTH TEXAS—1988	1	0	1	0	0	0	0
NORTHEAST LA.—1986, 1990, 1991	3	0	3	0	0	0	0
S'WESTERN LA.—1982	1	0	1	0	0	0	0
TOTAL	12	7	12	0	0	0	0

SOUTHWEST

	App	W	L	Ch.	2nd	F-4	F-8
ARKANSAS—1980, 1981, 1982, 1983, 1984, 1985, 1988, 1989, 90 (F-4), 91 (F-8)	10	12	10	0	0	1	2
BAYLOR—1988	1	0	1	0	0	0	0
HOUSTON—1981, 82 (F-4), 83 (2), 84 (2), 1987, 1990	6	12	6	0	2	1	3
SMU—1984, 1985, 1988	3	3	3	0	0	0	0
TCU—1987	1	1	1	0	0	0	0
TEXAS—1989, 90 (F-8), 1991	3	5	3	0	0	0	1
TEXAS A&M—1980, 1987	2	2	2	0	0	0	0
TEXAS TECH—1985, 1986	2	0	2	0	0	0	0
TOTAL	28	35	28	0	2	2	6

SOUTHWESTERN ATHLETIC

	App	W	L	Ch.	2nd	F-4	F-8
ALCORN STATE—1980, 1982, 1983, 1984	4	3	4	0	0	0	0
MISS. VALLEY STATE—1986	1	0	1	0	0	0	0
SOUTHERN-B.R.—1981, 1985, 1987, 1988, 1989	5	0	5	0	0	0	0
TEXAS SOUTHERN—1990	1	0	1	0	0	0	0
TOTAL	11	3	11	0	0	0	0

SUN BELT

	App	W	L	Ch.	2nd	F-4	F-8
ALA.-BIRMINGHAM—1981, 82 (F-8), 1983, 1984, 1985, 1986, 1987, 1990	8	6	8	0	0	0	1
JACKSONVILLE—1986	1	0	1	0	0	0	0
N.C.-CHARLOTTE—1988	1	0	1	0	0	0	0
OLD DOMINION—1982, 1985, 1986	3	1	3	0	0	0	0
SOUTH ALABAMA—1980, 1989, 1991	3	1	3	0	0	0	0
SOUTH FLORIDA—1990	1	0	1	0	0	0	0
VA. COMMONWEALTH—1980, 1981, 1983, 1984, 1985	5	4	5	0	0	0	0
WESTERN KY.—1986, 1987	2	2	2	0	0	0	0
TOTAL	24	14	24	0	0	0	1

TRANS AMERICA ATHLETIC

	App	W	L	Ch.	2nd	F-4	F-8
ARK-LITTLE ROCK—1986, 1989, 1990	3	1	3	0	0	0	0
GA. SOUTHERN—1983, 1987	2	0	2	0	0	0	0
GEORGIA STATE—1991	1	0	1	0	0	0	0
HOUSTON BAPTIST—1984	1	0	1	0	0	0	0
MERCER—1981, 1985	2	0	2	0	0	0	0
NORTHEAST LA.—1982	1	0	1	0	0	0	0
TEXAS-SAN ANT.—1988	1	0	1	0	0	0	0
TOTAL	11	1	11	0	0	0	0

WEST COAST

	App	W	L	Ch.	2nd	F-4	F-8
LOYOLA MYMT.—1980, 1988, 1989, 90 (F-8)	4	4	4	0	0	0	1
PEPPERDINE—1982, 1983, 1985, 1986, 1991	5	1	5	0	0	0	0
SAN DIEGO—1984, 1987	2	0	2	0	0	0	0
SAN FRANCISCO—1981, 1982	2	0	2	0	0	0	0
SANTA CLARA—1987	1	0	1	0	0	0	0
ST. MARY'S—1989	1	0	1	0	0	0	0
TOTAL	15	5	15	0	0	0	1

WESTERN ATHLETIC

	App	W	L	Ch.	2nd	F-4	F-8
BRIGHAM YOUNG—1980, 81 (F-8), 1984, 1987, 1988, 1990, 1991	7	6	7	0	0	0	1
COLORADO STATE—1989, 1990	2	1	2	0	0	0	0
NEW MEXICO—1991	1	0	1	0	0	0	0
SAN DIEGO ST.—1985	1	0	1	0	0	0	0
UTAH—1981, 1983, 1986, 1991	4	5	4	0	0	0	0
UTEP—1984, 1985, 1986, 1987, 1988, 1989, 1990	7	3	7	0	0	0	0
WYOMING—1981, 1982, 1987, 1988	4	4	4	0	0	0	0
TOTAL	26	19	26	0	0	0	1

*Includes ECAC affiliation.

CONFERENCE
BRAGGING RIGHTS

The numbers show it and it's useless to argue; the ACC is number 1 across the board. Numbers two and three—the Big East and the Big Ten—also rank in the top three in every single category. The dominance of these Big Three conferences is incontrovertible: eight of the last twelve tournaments have been won by ACC, Big Ten, and Big East teams; over half the total Final Four and Regional Final teams during this same period have come from the Big Three conferences (with a quarter coming from the ACC alone); and since 1980, each of the three top leagues has sent an average of five teams to the tournament every year (and the field didn't even expand to 64 until 1985)!

In each of the following benchmark stats, every conference appearing in the tournament in the last dozen years has been compared and ranked. Numbers in parentheses are the conference's totals in each specific category.

The Overall Ranking is based on the conference's comparative position in each of the six key categories. Results are calculated by adding the numeric ranking for each category (unranked = 11) and comparing the totals with all the other conferences.

THE TOP 10 CONFERENCES—1980–1991

Appearances

1. Atlantic Coast (61)
2. Big Ten (59)
3. Big East (58)*
4. Southeastern (51)
5. Big Eight (40)
6. Pac-Ten (35)
7. Metro (29)
8. Southwest (28)
9. Western Athletic (25)
10. Sun Belt (24)

*Villanova joined the Big East in 1981; Pittsburgh in 1983. If the appearances of Pitt in 1981 and 1982 and Villanova in 1980 were included, the Big East would tie the ACC for total tournament appearances since 1980.

Wins

1. Atlantic Coast (119)
2. Big East (101)
3. Big Ten (85)
4. Southeastern (57)
5. Big Eight (56)
6. Metro (38)
7. Southwest (35)
8. Pac-Ten (26)
9. Big West (25)
10. Atlantic Ten (20)

Won-Lost (min. 40 games)

1. Atlantic Coast (119–58, .672)
2. Big East (101–56, .643)
3. Big Ten (85–57, .599)
4. Big Eight (56–39, .589)
5. Metro (38–27, .585)
6. Big West (25–19, .568)
7. Southwest (35–28, .556)
8. Southeastern (57–52, .523)
9. Atlantic 10 (20–22, .476)
10. Pac-Ten (26–35, .426)

Regional Final Appearances

1. Atlantic Coast (24)
2. Big East (19)
3. Big Ten (10)
4. Southeastern (9)
5. Big Eight (7)
6. Southwest (6)
7. Metro (5)
8. Big West (4)
9. Pac-Ten (3)
10. Atlantic Ten (2)

Final Four Appearances

1. Atlantic Coast (12)
2. Big East (8)
3. Big Ten (6)
4. Metro (5)
5. Big Eight (4)
5. Southwest (4)
5. Southeastern (4)
8. Big West (3)
9. Pac-Ten (2)

Championships

1. Atlantic Coast (3)
1. Big Ten (3)
3. Big East (2)
3. Metro (2)
5. Big Eight (1)
5. Big West (1)

OVERALL RANKING*

1. Atlantic Coast (6)
2. Big East (14)
3. Big Ten (15)
4. Big Eight (29)
5. Metro (32)
6. Southeastern (36)
7. Southwest (44)
8. Pac-Ten (47)
8. Big West (47)
10. Atlantic Ten (62)

*Overall ranking based on composite of six categories. Results calculated by adding numerical position for each category (unranked = 11).

CONFERENCE UPDATE—1991–92

An unprecedented reshaping of the college sports map is currently taking place. The wholesale realignment of conferences, driven largely by television marketing decisions and changes in NCAA Division I conference eligibility regulations, won't affect everybody (the Big Eight and the Pac-Ten, among other major conferences, are standing pat), but a number of schools and leagues are responding to the pressure of economic competition by changing their loyalties.

Even the Big Three basketball conferences are adding one school each to their lineups: The upstart, twelve-year-old Big East, whose geographic boundaries have always been clearly defined by the Boston to Washington northeast corridor, is now reaching *south* of ACC/SEC territory to bring in Miami. The Big Ten, founded almost a hundred years ago, will for the first time extend itself beyond the midwest when Penn State (formerly of the Atlantic 10) becomes Big Ten member number 11 for the 1992–93 season. Only the ACC remains true to its historic boundaries, spreading just one state south by bringing Florida State (previously of the Metro Conference) into the fold. In all three cases, the newcomers have been taken aboard to beef up their new conferences' strength (and potential revenue) in *football*! So for the time being (even though Florida State and Penn State made the 1991 NCAA tournament field), the new members will have to get used to some Big Time hoopsmania before they can challenge the Tar Heels, Hoosiers, and Hoyas for league honors.

Outside the Big Three conferences, the real action is largely about the scramble for a bigger piece of the TV money pie. In today's game, television is essential for a league's success: the more exposure a conference gets, the more powerful it is, almost automatically. As Dick Tarrant, the mastermind of CAA standout Richmond's tournament upsets of the SEC's Auburn in '84, the Big Ten's Indiana in '88, and the Big East's Syracuse in '91, so aptly put it, "TV is very important to kids." Tarrant says blue-chip recruits "usually drop us to go to a conference with glitter . . . to the ACC team, the Big East team, or the SEC team." To deal with this reality, even the most well established conferences compete to present the most attractive package to CBS, NBC, ABC, ESPN, SportsChannel, MSG, Raycom, Home Team Sports, HSE, Creative Sports Marketing, JP Sports, KBL, NESN, Pass Sports, Prime Network, SportSouth, SPI Sports Productions, et al.

For the leagues ranking just below the Big Three, a single step can mean a big jump in network exposure. For example, the SEC, playing Pac-Man with the SWC's Arkansas and the Metro's South Carolina, will immediately challenge the ACC/Big East/Big Ten triumvirate as the nation's top basketball conference. Seriously, can a network executive with any sense of self-preservation ignore a matchup between Kentucky and Arkansas? With LSU (powered by the nation's premier big man, Shaquille O'Neal) and Alabama also in the SEC mix, the league is as tough, as competitive, and as telegenic as any in the country.

Even more significant changes will reshape the Metro, the nation's number 5 conference of the last dozen years. Not only is Florida State defecting to the ACC and South Carolina splitting for the SEC, the Metro is also losing Cincinnati and Memphis State to the new Great Midwest Conference. By last spring, things looked pretty bleak for the incredible shrinking Metro. With only four of the conference's original eight members remaining on board, it appeared that the Metro was in danger of disappearing altogether. The once-powerful league no longer even qualified for an automatic tournament bid (NCAA bylaws require that a conference must be "a member of the Association for the five preceding years, be composed entirely of institutions that have been members of Division I during the eight preceding academic years and have at least *six* member institutions that have held continuous membership in the conference for the five preceding years"). Even if the Metro was able to replace its defecting members, it was looking at five years of at-large exile. But a hastily formed "Special NCAA Committee" amended the regulation with a new waiver provision, the upshot of which is that the revamped Metro, with longtime members Louisville, Southern Mississippi, Virginia Tech, and Tulane (itself considering a move to the SWC as early as the 1992–93 season) joined by North Carolina-Charlotte, Virginia Commonwealth, and South Florida (all formerly of the Sun Belt Conference), will lose its automatic bid for only one year, 1992.

The Sun Belt, on the other hand, has disappeared entirely. After the eight-team league lost three schools to the Metro, Old Dominion to the Colonial Athletic Association, and Alabama-Birmingham to the Great Midwest, the three remaining Sun Belt schools merged into the fledgling American South Conference, which only started competing in 1987–88.

Of course, there's more. Southeast Missouri's heading downstream to the Ohio Valley. Navy's jumping the CAA ship for the Patriot Conference. Liberty's the latest word in the Big South. And most significantly, you can forget all the conference "Bigs," now there's finally a "Great"—the Great Midwest . . . brand new for '91–'92. It's so great that it's redefined the boundaries of the old industrial heartland, which now stretch from Alabama to Wisconsin. Its six teams come from all over the conference map: Alabama-Birmingham is from the Sun Belt, Cincinnati and Memphis State from the Metro, Marquette and St. Louis from the Midwestern Collegiate Conference (MCC), and DePaul is a defector from the dwindling ranks of the independents. Even though the Great Midwest won't qualify for an automatic tourney bid for five years, it already has its assurance of success: a syndication deal. Which isn't too bad at all, considering that in the past dozen years, the six teams of the Great Midwest have a composite tournament record that would have ranked them no better than tenth on the overall conference list.

The revamped Metro, the merged American South, the improved SEC, the brand-new Great Midwest—all have something to prove this year. But despite all the changes in the lineup of conferences, one thing hasn't changed: the ACC is king until someone proves otherwise.

PART III

All-Time Tournament Records

COMPLETE SCHOOL-BY-SCHOOL RECORDS

Coaches are listed alphabetically under each school name. Next to the coaches' names are the years they coached in the tournament, and, in parentheses, their finishes in the regional final round and beyond. To the right are the composite tournament records for each coach and each school. Following are the abbreviations used in this section:

Yrs	Number of Years
W	Games Won
L	Games Lost
Ch.	Championships
2nd	2nd Place
F-4	Final Four Appearances
F-8	Round of 8 (Regional Final) Appearances

NOTE:
F-8 in the left-hand column (School/Coach/Years) indicates that the team lost in the Round of 8.
F-8 in the right-hand column (Tournament Totals) indicates appearances (both wins and losses) in the Round of 8.

ALL-TIME RECORDS—SCHOOL BY SCHOOL

	Yrs	W	L	Ch.	2nd	F-4	F-8
AIR FORCE							
Spear, Bob—1960, 1962	2	0	2	0	0	0	0
TOTAL	2	0	2	0	0	0	0
AKRON							
Huggins, Bob—1986	1	0	1	0	0	0	0
TOTAL	1	0	1	0	0	0	0
ALA.-BIRMINGHAM							
Bartow, Gene—1981, 82 (F-8), 1983, 1984, 1985, 1986, 1987, 1990	8	6	8	0	0	0	1
TOTAL	8	6	8	0	0	0	1
ALABAMA							
Newton, C. M.—1975, 1976	2	1	2	0	0	0	0
Sanderson, Wimp—1982, 1983, 1984, 1985, 1986, 1987, 1989, 1990, 1991	9	11	9	0	0	0	0
TOTAL	11	12	11	0	0	0	0
ALCORN STATE							
Whitney, Davey—1980, 1982, 1983, 1984	4	3	4	0	0	0	0
TOTAL	4	3	4	0	0	0	0
APPALACHIAN STATE							
Cremins, Bobby—1979	1	0	1	0	0	0	0
TOTAL	1	0	1	0	0	0	0
ARIZONA							
Enke, Fred—1951	1	0	1	0	0	0	0
Olson, Lute—1985, 1986, 1987, 88 (F-4), 1989, 1990, 1991	7	9	7	0	0	1	1
Snowden, Fred—76 (F-8), 1977	2	2	2	0	0	0	1
TOTAL	10	11	10	0	0	1	2
ARIZONA STATE							
Frieder, Bill—1991	1	1	1	0	0	0	0
Wulk, Ned—1958, 61 (F-8), 1962, 63, (F-8), 1964, 1973, 75 (F-8), 1980, 1981	9	8	10	0	0	0	3
TOTAL	10	9	11	0	0	0	3
ARK-LITTLE ROCK							
Newell, Mike—1986, 1989, 1990	3	1	3	0	0	0	0
TOTAL	3	1	3	0	0	0	0
ARKANSAS							
Lambert, Eugene—45 (F-4), 49 (F-8)	2	2	2	0	0	1	2
Richardson, Nolan—1988, 1989, 90 (F-4), 91 (F-8)	4	8	4	0	0	1	2
Rose, Glen—41 (F-4), 1958	2	1	3	0	0	1	1
Sutton, Eddie—1977, 78 (F-4), 79 (F-8), 1980, 1981, 1982,	9	10	9	0	0	1	2

AUBURN

	Yrs	W	L	Ch.	2nd	F-4	F-8
Smith, Sonny—1984, 1985, 86 (F-8), 1987, 1988	5	7	5	0	0	0	1
TOTAL	5	7	5	0	0	0	1

AUSTIN PEAY

	Yrs	W	L	Ch.	2nd	F-4	F-8
Kelly, Lake—1973, 1974, 1987	3	2	4	0	0	0	0
TOTAL	3	2	4	0	0	0	0

BALL STATE

	Yrs	W	L	Ch.	2nd	F-4	F-8
Brown, Al—1986	1	0	1	0	0	0	0
Hunsaker, Dick—1990	1	2	1	0	0	0	0
Majerus, Rick—1989	1	1	1	0	0	0	0
Yoder, Steve—1981	1	0	1	0	0	0	0
TOTAL	4	3	4	0	0	0	0

BAYLOR

	Yrs	W	L	Ch.	2nd	F-4	F-8
Henderson, Bill—46 (F-8), 48 (2), 50 (F-4)	3	3	5	0	1	1	3
Iba, Gene—1988	1	0	1	0	0	0	0
TOTAL	4	3	6	0	1	1	3

BOISE STATE

	Yrs	W	L	Ch.	2nd	F-4	F-8
Connor, Bus—1976	1	0	1	0	0	0	0
Dye, Bob—1988	1	0	1	0	0	0	0
TOTAL	2	0	2	0	0	0	0

BOSTON COLLEGE

	Yrs	W	L	Ch.	2nd	F-4	F-8
Cousy, Bob—67 (F-8), 1968	2	2	2	0	0	0	1
Davis, Tom—1981, 82 (F-8)	2	5	2	0	0	0	1
Martin, Donald—1958	1	0	1	0	0	0	0
Williams, Gary—1983, 1985	2	3	2	0	0	0	0
Zuffelato, Bob—1975	1	1	2	0	0	0	0
TOTAL	8	11	9	0	0	0	2

BOSTON UNIV.

	Yrs	W	L	Ch.	2nd	F-4	F-8
Jarvis, Mike—1988, 1990	2	0	2	0	0	0	0
Pitino, Rick—1983	1	0	1	0	0	0	0
Zunic, Matt—59 (F-8)	1	2	1	0	0	0	1
TOTAL	4	2	4	0	0	0	1

BOWLING GREEN

	Yrs	W	L	Ch.	2nd	F-4	F-8
Anderson, Harold—1959, 1962, 1963	3	1	4	0	0	0	0
Fitch, Bob—1968	1	0	1	0	0	0	0
TOTAL	4	1	5	0	0	0	0

BRADLEY

	Yrs	W	L	Ch.	2nd	F-4	F-8
Albeck, Stan—1988	1	0	1	0	0	0	0
Anderson, Forddy—50 (2), 54 (2)	2	6	2	0	2	0	2
Vanatta, Bob—55 (F-8)	1	2	1	0	0	0	1
Versace, Dick—1980, 1986	2	1	2	0	0	0	0
TOTAL	6	9	6	0	2	0	3

BRIGHAM YOUNG

	Yrs	W	L	Ch.	2nd	F-4	F-8
Anderson, Ladell—1984, 1987, 1988	3	2	3	0	0	0	0
Arnold, Frank—1979, 1980, 81 (F-8)	3	3	3	0	0	0	1
Reid, Roger—1990, 1991	2	1	2	0	0	0	0
Watts, Stan—50 (F-8), 51 (F-8), 1957, 1965, 1969, 1971, 1972	7	4	10	0	0	0	2
TOTAL	15	10	18	0	0	0	3

BROWN

	Yrs	W	L	Ch.	2nd	F-4	F-8
Allen, George—39 (F-8)	1	0	1	0	0	0	1
Cingiser, Mike—1986	1	0	1	0	0	0	0
TOTAL	2	0	2	0	0	0	1

BUCKNELL
Woollum, Charles—1987, 1989

	Yrs	W	L	Ch.	2nd	F-4	F-8
	2	0	2	0	0	0	0
TOTAL	2	0	2	0	0	0	0

BUTLER
Hinkle, Tony—1962

	Yrs	W	L	Ch.	2nd	F-4	F-8
	1	2	1	0	0	0	0
TOTAL	1	2	1	0	0	0	0

CAL STATE F'LERTON
Dye, Bob—78 (F-8)

	Yrs	W	L	Ch.	2nd	F-4	F-8
	1	2	1	0	0	0	1
TOTAL	1	2	1	0	0	0	1

CAL STATE LA
Miller, Bob—1974

	Yrs	W	L	Ch.	2nd	F-4	F-8
	1	0	1	0	0	0	0
TOTAL	1	0	1	0	0	0	0

CALIFORNIA
Campanelli, Lou—1990
Newell, Pete—57 (F-8), 58 (F-8), 59 (Ch.), 60 (2)
Price, Nibs—46 (F-4)

	Yrs	W	L	Ch.	2nd	F-4	F-8
	1	1	1	0	0	0	0
	4	10	3	1	1	0	4
	1	1	2	0	0	1	1
TOTAL	6	12	6	1	1	1	5

CANISIUS
Curran, Joseph—55 (F-8), 56 (F-8), 1957

	Yrs	W	L	Ch.	2nd	F-4	F-8
	3	6	3	0	0	0	2
TOTAL	3	6	3	0	0	0	2

CATHOLIC
Long, John—44 (F-8)

	Yrs	W	L	Ch.	2nd	F-4	F-8
	1	0	2	0	0	0	1
TOTAL	1	0	2	0	0	0	1

CCNY
Holman, Nat—47 (F-4), 50 (Ch.)

	Yrs	W	L	Ch.	2nd	F-4	F-8
	2	4	2	1	0	1	2
TOTAL	2	4	2	1	0	1	2

CENTRAL MICH.
Coles, Charles—1987
Parfitt, Dick—1975, 1977

	Yrs	W	L	Ch.	2nd	F-4	F-8
	1	0	1	0	0	0	0
	2	2	2	0	0	0	0
TOTAL	3	2	3	0	0	0	0

CINCINNATI
Baker, Tay—1966
Catlett, Gale—1975, 1976, 1977
Jucker, Ed—61 (Ch.), 62 (Ch.), 63 (2)
Smith, George—1958, 59 (F-4), 60 (F-4)

	Yrs	W	L	Ch.	2nd	F-4	F-8
	1	0	2	0	0	0	0
	3	2	3	0	0	0	0
	3	11	1	2	1	0	3
	3	7	3	0	0	2	2
TOTAL	10	20	9	2	1	2	5

CLEMSON
Ellis, Cliff—1987, 1989, 1990
Foster, Wm. C. (Bill)—80 (F-8)

	Yrs	W	L	Ch.	2nd	F-4	F-8
	3	3	3	0	0	0	0
	1	3	1	0	0	0	1
TOTAL	4	6	4	0	0	0	1

CLEVELAND STATE
MacKey, Kevin—1986

	Yrs	W	L	Ch.	2nd	F-4	F-8
	1	2	1	0	0	0	0
TOTAL	1	2	1	0	0	0	0

COASTAL CARO.
Bergman, Russ—1991

	Yrs	W	L	Ch.	2nd	F-4	F-8
	1	0	1	0	0	0	0
TOTAL	1	0	1	0	0	0	0

COLORADO
Cox, Frosty—40 (F-8), 42 (F-4), 46 (F-8)
Lee, Bebe—1954, 55 (F-4)
Walseth, Sox—62 (F-8), 63 (F-8), 1969

	Yrs	W	L	Ch.	2nd	F-4	F-8
	3	2	4	0	0	1	3
	2	3	3	0	0	1	1
	3	3	3	0	0	0	2
TOTAL	8	8	10	0	0	2	6

COLORADO STATE

	Yrs	W	L	Ch.	2nd	F-4	F-8
Grant, Boyd—1989, 1990	2	1	2	0	0	0	0
Strannigan, Bill—1954	1	0	2	0	0	0	0
Williams, Jim—1963, 1965, 1966, 69 (F-8)	4	2	4	0	0	0	1
TOTAL	7	3	8	0	0	0	1

COLUMBIA

	Yrs	W	L	Ch.	2nd	F-4	F-8
Ridings, Gordon—48 (F-8)	1	0	2	0	0	0	1
Rohan, Jack—1968	1	2	1	0	0	0	0
Rossini, Lou—1951	1	0	1	0	0	0	0
TOTAL	3	2	4	0	0	0	1

COPPIN STATE

	Yrs	W	L	Ch.	2nd	F-4	F-8
Mitchell, Ron—1990	1	0	1	0	0	0	0
TOTAL	1	0	1	0	0	0	0

CORNELL

	Yrs	W	L	Ch.	2nd	F-4	F-8
Dement, Mike—1988	1	0	1	0	0	0	0
Greene, Royner—1954	1	0	2	0	0	0	0
TOTAL	2	0	3	0	0	0	0

CREIGHTON

	Yrs	W	L	Ch.	2nd	F-4	F-8
Apke, Tom—1975, 1978, 1981	3	0	3	0	0	0	0
Barone, Tony—1989, 1991	2	1	2	0	0	0	0
Hickey, Eddie—41 (F-8)	1	1	1	0	0	0	1
McManus, Red—1962, 1964	2	3	3	0	0	0	0
Sutton, Eddie—1974	1	2	1	0	0	0	0
TOTAL	9	7	10	0	0	0	1

DARTMOUTH

	Yrs	W	L	Ch.	2nd	F-4	F-8
Brown, Earl—44 (2)	1	2	1	0	1	0	1
Cowles, Ozzie—41 (F-8), 42 (2), 43 (F-8)	3	4	3	0	1	0	3
Julian, Doggie—1956, 58 (F-8), 1959	3	4	3	0	0	0	1
TOTAL	7	10	7	0	2	0	5

DAVIDSON

	Yrs	W	L	Ch.	2nd	F-4	F-8
Driesell, Lefty—1966, 68 (F-8), 69 (F-8)	3	5	4	0	0	0	2
Holland, Terry—1970	1	0	1	0	0	0	0
Hussey, Bobby—1986	1	0	1	0	0	0	0
TOTAL	5	5	6	0	0	0	2

DAYTON

	Yrs	W	L	Ch.	2nd	F-4	F-8
Blackburn, Tom—1952	1	1	1	0	0	0	0
Donoher, Don—1965, 1966, 67 (2), 1969, 1970, 1974, 84 (F-8), 1985	8	11	10	0	1	0	2
O'Brien, Jim—1990	1	1	1	0	0	0	0
TOTAL	10	13	12	0	1	0	2

DEPAUL

	Yrs	W	L	Ch.	2nd	F-4	F-8
Meyer, Joey—1985, 1986, 1987, 1988, 1989, 1991	6	6	6	0	0	0	0
Meyer, Ray—43 (F-4), 1953, 1956, 1959, 1960, 1965, 1976, 78 (F-8), 79 (F-4), 1980, 1981, 1982, 1984	13	14	16	0	0	2	3
TOTAL	19	20	22	0	0	2	3

DETROIT

	Yrs	W	L	Ch.	2nd	F-4	F-8
Calihan, Robert—1962	1	0	1	0	0	0	0
Gaines, Dave Smokey—1979	1	0	1	0	0	0	0
Vitale, Dick—1977	1	1	1	0	0	0	0
TOTAL	3	1	3	0	0	0	0

DRAKE

	Yrs	W	L	Ch.	2nd	F-4	F-8
John, Maurice—69 (F-4), 70 (F-8), 71 (F-8)	3	5	3	0	0	1	3
TOTAL	3	5	3	0	0	1	3

DREXEL

	Yrs	W	L	Ch.	2nd	F-4	F-8
Burke, Eddie—1986	1	0	1	0	0	0	0
TOTAL	1	0	1	0	0	0	0

DUKE

	Yrs	W	L	Ch.	2nd	F-4	F-8
Bradley, Harold—1955	1	0	1	0	0	0	0
Bubas, Vic—60 (F-8), 63 (F-4), 64 (2), 66 (F-4)	4	11	4	0	1	2	4
Foster, Wm. E. (Bill)—78 (2), 1979, 80 (F-8)	3	6	3	0	1	0	2
Krzyzewski, Mike—1984, 1985, 86 (2), 1987, 88 (F-4), 89 (F-4), 90 (2), 91 (Ch.)	8	27	7	1	2	2	5
TOTAL	16	44	15	1	4	4	11

DUQUESNE

	Yrs	W	L	Ch.	2nd	F-4	F-8
Cinicola, John—1977	1	0	1	0	0	0	0
Davies, Chick—40 (F-4)	1	1	1	0	0	1	1
Manning, Red—1969, 1971	2	2	2	0	0	0	0
Moore, Dudey—52 (F-8)	1	1	1	0	0	0	1
TOTAL	5	4	5	0	0	1	2

EAST CAROLINA

	Yrs	W	L	Ch.	2nd	F-4	F-8
Quinn, Tom—1972	1	0	1	0	0	0	0
TOTAL	1	0	1	0	0	0	0

EAST TENN. STATE

	Yrs	W	L	Ch.	2nd	F-4	F-8
Brooks, J. Madison—1968	1	1	2	0	0	0	0
LeForce, Alan—1991	1	0	1	0	0	0	0
Robinson, Les—1989, 1990	2	0	2	0	0	0	0
TOTAL	4	1	5	0	0	0	0

EASTERN KY.

	Yrs	W	L	Ch.	2nd	F-4	F-8
Baechtold, Jim—1965	1	0	1	0	0	0	0
Byhre, Ed—1979	1	0	1	0	0	0	0
McBrayer, Paul—1953, 1959	2	0	2	0	0	0	0
Strong, Guy—1972	1	0	1	0	0	0	0
TOTAL	5	0	5	0	0	0	0

EASTERN MICH.

	Yrs	W	L	Ch.	2nd	F-4	F-8
Braun, Ben—1988, 1991	2	2	2	0	0	0	0
TOTAL	2	2	2	0	0	0	0

EVANSVILLE

	Yrs	W	L	Ch.	2nd	F-4	F-8
Crews, Jim—1989	1	1	1	0	0	0	0
Walters, Dick—1982	1	0	1	0	0	0	0
TOTAL	2	1	2	0	0	0	0

F. DICKINSON

	Yrs	W	L	Ch.	2nd	F-4	F-8
Green, Tom—1985, 1988	2	0	2	0	0	0	0
TOTAL	2	0	2	0	0	0	0

FAIRFIELD

	Yrs	W	L	Ch.	2nd	F-4	F-8
Buonaguro, Mitch—1986, 1987	2	0	2	0	0	0	0
TOTAL	2	0	2	0	0	0	0

FLORIDA

	Yrs	W	L	Ch.	2nd	F-4	F-8
Sloan, Norm—1987, 1988, 1989	3	3	3	0	0	0	0
TOTAL	3	3	3	0	0	0	0

FLORIDA STATE

	Yrs	W	L	Ch.	2nd	F-4	F-8
Durham, Hugh—1968, 72 (2), 1978	3	4	3	0	1	0	1
Kennedy, Pat—1988, 1989, 1991	3	1	3	0	0	0	0
Williams, Joe—1980	1	1	1	0	0	0	0
TOTAL	7	6	7	0	1	0	1

FORDHAM

	Yrs	W	L	Ch.	2nd	F-4	F-8
Bach, John—1953, 1954	2	0	2	0	0	0	0
Phelps, Digger—1971	1	2	1	0	0	0	0
TOTAL	3	2	3	0	0	0	0

FRESNO STATE

	Yrs	W	L	Ch.	2nd	F-4	F-8
Grant, Boyd—1981, 1982, 1984	3	1	3	0	0	0	0
TOTAL	3	1	3	0	0	0	0

FURMAN

	Yrs	W	L	Ch.	2nd	F-4	F-8
Holbrook, Eddie—1980	1	0	1	0	0	0	0
Williams, Joe—1971, 1973, 1974, 1975, 1978	5	1	6	0	0	0	0
TOTAL	6	1	7	0	0	0	0

GA. SOUTHERN

	Yrs	W	L	Ch.	2nd	F-4	F-8
Kerns, Frank—1983, 1987	2	0	2	0	0	0	0
TOTAL	2	0	2	0	0	0	0

GEO. WASH.

	Yrs	W	L	Ch.	2nd	F-4	F-8
Reinhart, Bill—1954, 1961	2	0	2	0	0	0	0
TOTAL	2	0	2	0	0	0	0

GEORGE MASON

	Yrs	W	L	Ch.	2nd	F-4	F-8
Nestor, Ernie—1989	1	0	1	0	0	0	0
TOTAL	1	0	1	0	0	0	0

GEORGETOWN

	Yrs	W	L	Ch.	2nd	F-4	F-8
Ripley, Elmer—43 (2)	1	2	1	0	1	0	1
Thompson, John—1975, 1976, 1979, 80 (F-8), 1981, 82 (2), 1983, 84 (Ch.), 85 (2), 1986, 87 (F-8), 1988, 89 (F-8), 1990, 1991	15	27	14	1	2	0	6
TOTAL	16	29	15	1	3	0	7

GEORGIA

	Yrs	W	L	Ch.	2nd	F-4	F-8
Durham, Hugh—83 (F-4), 1985, 1987, 1990, 1991	5	4	5	0	0	1	1
TOTAL	5	4	5	0	0	1	1

GEORGIA STATE

	Yrs	W	L	Ch.	2nd	F-4	F-8
Reinhart, Bob—1991	1	0	1	0	0	0	0
TOTAL	1	0	1	0	0	0	0

GEORGIA TECH

	Yrs	W	L	Ch.	2nd	F-4	F-8
Cremins, Bobby—85 (F-8), 1986, 1987, 1988, 1989, 90 (F-4), 1991	7	11	7	0	0	1	2
Hyder, Whack—60 (F-8)	1	1	1	0	0	0	1
TOTAL	8	12	8	0	0	1	3

HARDIN-SIMMONS

	Yrs	W	L	Ch.	2nd	F-4	F-8
Scott, Bill—1953, 1957	2	0	2	0	0	0	0
TOTAL	2	0	2	0	0	0	0

HARVARD

	Yrs	W	L	Ch.	2nd	F-4	F-8
Stahl, Floyd—46 (F-8)	1	0	2	0	0	0	1
TOTAL	1	0	2	0	0	0	1

HAWAII

	Yrs	W	L	Ch.	2nd	F-4	F-8
Rocha, Red—1972	1	0	1	0	0	0	0
TOTAL	1	0	1	0	0	0	0

HOFSTRA

	Yrs	W	L	Ch.	2nd	F-4	F-8
Gaeckler, Roger—1976, 1977	2	0	2	0	0	0	0
TOTAL	2	0	2	0	0	0	0

HOLY CROSS

	Yrs	W	L	Ch.	2nd	F-4	F-8
Blaney, George—1977, 1980	2	0	2	0	0	0	0
Julian, Doggie—47 (Ch.), 48 (F-4)	2	5	1	1	0	1	2
Leening, Roy—1956	1	0	1	0	0	0	0
Sheary, Buster—50 (F-8), 53 (F-8)	2	2	3	0	0	0	2
TOTAL	7	7	7	1	0	1	4

HOUSTON

	Yrs	W	L	Ch.	2nd	F-4	F-8
Foster, Pat—1987, 1990	2	0	2	0	0	0	0
Lewis, Guy—1961, 1965, 1966, 67 (F-4), 68 (F-4), 1970, 1971, 1972, 1973, 1978, 1981, 82 (F-4), 83 (2), 84 (2)	14	26	18	0	2	3	5
Pasche, Alden—1956	1	0	2	0	0	0	0
TOTAL	17	26	22	0	2	3	5

HOUSTON BAPTIST

	Yrs	W	L	Ch.	2nd	F-4	F-8
Iba, Gene—1984	1	0	1	0	0	0	0
TOTAL	1	0	1	0	0	0	0

HOWARD

	Yrs	W	L	Ch.	2nd	F-4	F-8
Williamson, A. B.—1981	1	0	1	0	0	0	0
TOTAL	1	0	1	0	0	0	0

IDAHO

	Yrs	W	L	Ch.	2nd	F-4	F-8
Davis Jr., Kermit—1989, 1990	2	0	2	0	0	0	0
Monson, Don—1981, 1982	2	1	2	0	0	0	0
TOTAL	4	1	4	0	0	0	0

IDAHO STATE

	Yrs	W	L	Ch.	2nd	F-4	F-8
Belko, Steve—1953, 1954, 1955, 1956	4	2	4	0	0	0	0
Boutin, Jim—1987	1	0	1	0	0	0	0
Evans, John—1960	1	0	1	0	0	0	0
Grayson, John—1957, 1958, 1959	3	4	5	0	0	0	0
Killingsworth, Jim—1974, 77 (F-8)	2	2	2	0	0	0	1
TOTAL	11	8	13	0	0	0	1

ILLINOIS

	Yrs	W	L	Ch.	2nd	F-4	F-8
Combes, Harry—49 (F-4), 51 (F-4), 52 (F-4), 63 (F-8)	4	9	4	0	0	3	4
Henson, Lou—1981, 1983, 84 (F-8), 1985, 1986, 1987, 1988, 89 (F-4), 1990	9	11	9	0	0	1	2
Mills, Doug—42 (F-8)	1	0	2	0	0	0	1
TOTAL	14	20	15	0	0	4	7

ILLINOIS STATE

	Yrs	W	L	Ch.	2nd	F-4	F-8
Bender, Bob—1990	1	0	1	0	0	0	0
Donewald, Bob—1983, 1984, 1985	3	2	3	0	0	0	0
TOTAL	4	2	4	0	0	0	0

INDIANA

	Yrs	W	L	Ch.	2nd	F-4	F-8
Knight, Bob—73 (F-4), 75 (F-8), 76 (Ch.), 1978, 1980, 81 (Ch.), 1982, 1983, 84 (F-8), 1986, 87 (Ch.), 1988, 1989, 1990, 1991	15	31	12	3	0	1	6
McCracken, Branch—40 (Ch.), 53 (Ch.), 1954, 1958	4	9	2	2	0	0	2
Watson, Lou—1967	1	1	1	0	0	0	0
TOTAL	20	41	15	5	0	1	8

INDIANA STATE

	Yrs	W	L	Ch.	2nd	F-4	F-8
Hodges, Bill—79 (2)	1	4	1	0	1	0	1
TOTAL	1	4	1	0	1	0	1

IONA

	Yrs	W	L	Ch.	2nd	F-4	F-8
Kennedy, Pat—1984, 1985	2	0	2	0	0	0	0
Valvano, Jim—1979, 1980	2	1	2	0	0	0	0
TOTAL	4	1	4	0	0	0	0

IOWA

	Yrs	W	L	Ch.	2nd	F-4	F-8
Davis, Tom—87 (F-8), 1988, 1989, 1991	4	7	4	0	0	0	1
Miller, Ralph—1970	1	1	1	0	0	0	0
O'Connor, Bucky—55 (F-4), 56 (2)	2	5	3	0	1	1	2
Olson, Lute—1979, 80 (F-4), 1981, 1982, 1983	5	7	6	0	0	1	1
Raveling, George—1985, 1986	2	0	2	0	0	0	0
TOTAL	14	20	16	0	1	2	4

IOWA STATE

	Yrs	W	L	Ch.	2nd	F-4	F-8
Menze, Louis—44 (F-4)	1	1	1	0	0	1	1
Orr, Johnny—1985, 1986, 1988, 1989	4	2	4	0	0	0	0
TOTAL	5	3	5	0	0	1	1

JACKSONVILLE

	Yrs	W	L	Ch.	2nd	F-4	F-8
Locke, Tates—1979	1	0	1	0	0	0	0
Wasdin, Tom—1971, 1973	2	0	2	0	0	0	0
Wenzel, Bob—1986	1	0	1	0	0	0	0
Williams, Joe—70 (2)	1	4	1	0	1	0	1
TOTAL	5	4	5	0	1	0	1

JAMES MADISON

	Yrs	W	L	Ch.	2nd	F-4	F-8
Campanelli, Lou—1981, 1982, 1983	3	3	3	0	0	0	0
TOTAL	3	3	3	0	0	0	0

KANSAS

	Yrs	W	L	Ch.	2nd	F-4	F-8
Allen, Phog—40 (2), 42 (F-8), 52 (Ch.), 53 (2)	4	10	3	1	2	0	4
Brown, Larry—1984, 1985, 86 (F-4), 1987, 88 (Ch.)	5	14	4	1	0	1	2
Harp, Dick—57 (2), 60 (F-8)	2	4	2	0	1	0	2
Owens, Ted—66 (F-8), 1967, 71 (F-4), 74 (F-4), 1975, 1978, 1981	7	8	9	0	0	2	3
Williams, Roy—1990, 91 (2)	2	6	2	0	1	0	1
TOTAL	20	42	20	2	4	3	12

KANSAS STATE

	Yrs	W	L	Ch.	2nd	F-4	F-8
Fitzsimmons, Cotton—1970	1	1	1	0	0	0	0
Gardner, Jack—48 (F-4), 51 (2)	2	4	3	0	1	1	2
Hartman, Jack—72 (F-8), 73 (F-8), 75 (F-8), 1977, 1980, 81 (F-8), 1982	7	11	7	0	0	0	4
Kruger, Lon—1987, 88 (F-8), 1989, 1990	4	4	4	0	0	0	1
Winter, Tex—1956, 58 (F-4), 59 (F-8), 61 (F-8), 64 (F-4), 1968	6	7	9	0	0	2	4
TOTAL	20	27	24	0	1	3	11

KENTUCKY

	Yrs	W	L	Ch.	2nd	F-4	F-8
Hall, Joe—73 (F-8), 75 (2), 77 (F-8), 78 (Ch.), 1980, 1981, 1982, 83 (F-8), 84 (F-4), 1985	10	20	9	1	1	1	6
Rupp, Adolph—42 (F-4), 45 (F-8), 48 (Ch.), 49 (Ch.), 51 (Ch.), 52 (F-8), 1955, 56 (F-8), 57 (F-8), 58 (Ch.), 1959, 61 (F-8), 62 (F-8), 1964, 66 (2), 68 (F-8), 1969, 70 (F-8), 1971, 72 (F-8)	20	30	18	4	1	1	15
Sutton, Eddie—86 (F-8), 1987, 1988	3	5	3	0	0	0	1
TOTAL	33	55	30	5	2	2	22

LA SALLE

	Yrs	W	L	Ch.	2nd	F-4	F-8
Ervin, Lefty—1980, 1983	2	1	2	0	0	0	0
Harding, Jim—1968	1	0	1	0	0	0	0
Loeffler, Ken—54 (Ch.), 55 (2)	2	9	1	1	1	0	2
Morris, Bill—1988, 1989, 1990	3	1	3	0	0	0	0
Westhead, Paul—1975, 1978	2	0	2	0	0	0	0
TOTAL	10	11	9	1	1	0	2

LAFAYETTE

	Yrs	W	L	Ch.	2nd	F-4	F-8
Davidson, George—1957	1	0	2	0	0	0	0
TOTAL	1	0	2	0	0	0	0

LAMAR

	Yrs	W	L	Ch.	2nd	F-4	F-8
Foster, Pat—1981, 1983	2	2	2	0	0	0	0
Tubbs, Billy—1979, 1980	2	3	2	0	0	0	0
TOTAL	4	5	4	0	0	0	0

LEBANON VALLEY

	Yrs	W	L	Ch.	2nd	F-4	F-8
Marquette, Rinso—1953	1	1	2	0	0	0	0
TOTAL	1	1	2	0	0	0	0

LEHIGH

	Yrs	W	L	Ch.	2nd	F-4	F-8
McCaffery, Fran—1988	1	0	1	0	0	0	0
Schneider, Tom—1985	1	0	1	0	0	0	0
TOTAL	2	0	2	0	0	0	0

LIU-BROOKLYN

	Yrs	W	L	Ch.	2nd	F-4	F-8
Lizzo, Paul—1981, 1984	2	0	2	0	0	0	0
TOTAL	2	0	2	0	0	0	0

LONG BEACH STATE

	Yrs	W	L	Ch.	2nd	F-4	F-8
Jones, Dwight—1977	1	0	1	0	0	0	0
Tarkanian, Jerry—1970, 71 (F-8), 72 (F-8), 1973	4	7	5	0	0	0	2
TOTAL	5	7	6	0	0	0	2

LOUISIANA STATE

	Yrs	W	L	Ch.	2nd	F-4	F-8
Brown, Dale—1979, 80 (F-8), 81 (F-4), 1984, 1985, 86 (F-4), 87 (F-8), 1988, 1989, 1990, 1991	11	14	12	0	0	2	4
Rabenhorst, Harry—53 (F-4), 1954	2	2	4	0	0	1	1
TOTAL	13	16	16	0	0	3	5

LOUISIANA TECH

	Yrs	W	L	Ch.	2nd	F-4	F-8
Eagles, Tommy—1987, 1989	2	1	2	0	0	0	0
Lloyd, Jerry—1991	1	0	1	0	0	0	0
Russo, Andy—1984, 1985	2	3	2	0	0	0	0
TOTAL	5	4	5	0	0	0	0

LOUISVILLE

	Yrs	W	L	Ch.	2nd	F-4	F-8
Crum, Denny—72 (F-4), 1974, 75 (F-4), 1977, 1978, 1979, 80 (Ch.), 1981, 82 (F-4), 83 (F-4), 1984, 86 (Ch.), 1988, 1989, 1990	15	32	15	2	0	4	6
Dromo, John—1968	1	1	1	0	0	0	0
Hickman, Peck—1951, 59 (F-4), 1961, 1964, 1967	5	5	7	0	0	1	1
TOTAL	21	38	23	2	0	5	7

LOYOLA MYMT.

	Yrs	W	L	Ch.	2nd	F-4	F-8
Arndt, John—1961	1	1	1	0	0	0	0
Jacobs, Ron—1980	1	0	1	0	0	0	0
Westhead, Paul—1988, 1989, 90 (F-8)	3	4	3	0	0	0	1
TOTAL	5	5	5	0	0	0	1

LOYOLA N.O.

	Yrs	W	L	Ch.	2nd	F-4	F-8
Harding, Jim—1958	1	0	1	0	0	0	0
McCafferty, Jim—1954, 1957	2	0	2	0	0	0	0
TOTAL	3	0	3	0	0	0	0

LOYOLA-CHICAGO

	Yrs	W	L	Ch.	2nd	F-4	F-8
Ireland, George—63 (Ch.), 1964, 1966, 1968	4	7	3	1	0	1	1
Sullivan, Gene—1985	1	2	1	0	0	0	0
TOTAL	5	9	4	1	0	0	1

MANHATTAN

	Yrs	W	L	Ch.	2nd	F-4	F-8
Norton, Ken—1956, 1958	2	1	3	0	0	0	0
TOTAL	2	1	3	0	0	0	0

MARIST

	Yrs	W	L	Ch.	2nd	F-4	F-8
Furjanic, Matt—1986	1	0	1	0	0	0	0
Magarity, Dave—1987	1	0	1	0	0	0	0
TOTAL	2	0	2	0	0	0	0

MARQUETTE

	Yrs	W	L	Ch.	2nd	F-4	F-8
Hickey, Eddie—1959, 1961	2	1	3	0	0	0	0
McGuire, Al—1968, 69 (F-8), 1971, 1972, 1973, 74 (2), 1975, 76 (F-8), 77 (Ch.)	9	20	9	1	1	0	4
Nagel, Jack—55 (F-8)	1	2	1	0	0	0	1
Raymonds, Hank—1978, 1979, 1980, 1982, 1983	5	2	5	0	0	0	0
TOTAL	17	25	18	1	1	0	5

MARSHALL

	Yrs	W	L	Ch.	2nd	F-4	F-8
Huckabay, Ricky—1984, 1985, 1987	3	0	3	0	0	0	0
Rivlin, Jule—1956	1	0	1	0	0	0	0
Tacy, Carl—1972	1	0	1	0	0	0	0
TOTAL	5	0	5	0	0	0	0

MARYLAND

	Yrs	W	L	Ch.	2nd	F-4	F-8
Driesell, Lefty—73 (F-8), 75 (F-8), 1980, 1981, 1983, 1984, 1985, 1986	8	10	8	0	0	0	2
Millikan, Bud—1958	1	2	1	0	0	0	0
Wade, Bob—1988	1	1	1	0	0	0	0
TOTAL	10	13	10	0	0	0	2

MCNEESE STATE

	Yrs	W	L	Ch.	2nd	F-4	F-8
Welch, Steve—1989	1	0	1	0	0	0	0
TOTAL	1	0	1	0	0	0	0

MEMPHIS STATE

	Yrs	W	L	Ch.	2nd	F-4	F-8
Bartow, Gene—73 (2)	1	3	1	0	1	0	1
Finch, Larry—1988, 1989	2	1	2	0	0	0	0
Kirk, Dana—1982, 1983, 1984, 85 (F-4), 1986	5	9	5	0	0	1	1
Lambert, Eugene—1955, 1956	2	0	2	0	0	0	0
Vanatta, Bob—1962	1	0	1	0	0	0	0
Yates, Wayne—1976	1	0	1	0	0	0	0
TOTAL	12	13	12	0	1	1	2

MERCER

	Yrs	W	L	Ch.	2nd	F-4	F-8
Bibb, Bill—1981, 1985	2	0	2	0	0	0	0
TOTAL	2	0	2	0	0	0	0

MIAMI (FLA.)

	Yrs	W	L	Ch.	2nd	F-4	F-8
Hale, Bruce—1960	1	0	1	0	0	0	0
TOTAL	1	0	1	0	0	0	0

MIAMI (OHIO)

	Yrs	W	L	Ch.	2nd	F-4	F-8
Hedric, Darrell—1971, 1973, 1978, 1984	4	1	4	0	0	0	0
Irson, Jerry—1985, 1986	2	0	2	0	0	0	0
Locke, Tates—1969	1	1	2	0	0	0	0
Rohr, Bill—1953, 1955, 1957	3	0	3	0	0	0	0
Shrider, Dick—1958, 1966	2	1	3	0	0	0	0
TOTAL	12	3	14	0	0	0	0

MICHIGAN

	Yrs	W	L	Ch.	2nd	F-4	F-8
Cowles, Ozzie—48 (F-8)	1	1	1	0	0	0	1
Fisher, Steve—89 (Ch.), 1990	2	7	1	1	0	0	1
Frieder, Bill—1985, 1986, 1987, 1988	4	5	4	0	0	0	0
Orr, Johnny—74 (F-8), 1975, 76 (2), 77 (F-8)	4	7	4	0	1	0	3
Strack, Dave—64 (F-4), 65 (2), 66 (F-8)	3	7	3	0	1	1	3
TOTAL	14	27	13	1	2	1	8

MICHIGAN STATE

	Yrs	W	L	Ch.	2nd	F-4	F-8
Anderson, Forddy—57 (F-4), 59 (F-8)	2	3	3	0	0	1	2
Heathcote, Jud—78 (F-8), 79 (Ch.), 1985, 1986, 1990, 1991	6	12	5	1	0	0	2
TOTAL	8	15	8	1	0	1	4

MIDDLE TENN. STATE

	Yrs	W	L	Ch.	2nd	F-4	F-8
Earle, Jimmy—1975, 1977	2	0	2	0	0	0	0
Simpson, Stan—1982	1	1	1	0	0	0	0
Stewart, Bruce—1985, 1987, 1989	3	1	3	0	0	0	0
TOTAL	6	2	6	0	0	0	0

MINNESOTA

	Yrs	W	L	Ch.	2nd	F-4	F-8
Dutcher, Jim—1982	1	1	1	0	0	0	0
Haskins, Clem—1989, 90 (F-8)	2	5	2	0	0	0	1
Musselman, Bill—1972	1	1	1	0	0	0	0
TOTAL	4	7	4	0	0	0	1

MISS. VALLEY STATE

	Yrs	W	L	Ch.	2nd	F-4	F-8
Stribling, Lafayette—1986	1	0	1	0	0	0	0
TOTAL	1	0	1	0	0	0	0

MISSISSIPPI

	Yrs	W	L	Ch.	2nd	F-4	F-8
Weltlich, Bob—1981	1	0	1	0	0	0	0
TOTAL	1	0	1	0	0	0	0

MISSISSIPPI STATE

	Yrs	W	L	Ch.	2nd	F-4	F-8
McCarthy, Babe—1963	1	1	1	0	0	0	0
Williams, Richard—1991	1	0	1	0	0	0	0
TOTAL	2	1	2	0	0	0	0

MISSOURI

	Yrs	W	L	Ch.	2nd	F-4	F-8
Edwards, George—44 (F-8)	1	1	1	0	0	0	1
Stewart, Norm—76 (F-8), 1978, 1980, 1981, 1982, 1983, 1986, 1987, 1988, 1989, 1990	11	7	11	0	0	0	1
TOTAL	12	8	12	0	0	0	2

MONTANA

	Yrs	W	L	Ch.	2nd	F-4	F-8
Heathcote, Jud—1975	1	1	2	0	0	0	0
Morrill, Stew—1991	1	0	1	0	0	0	0
TOTAL	2	1	3	0	0	0	0

MONTANA STATE

	Yrs	W	L	Ch.	2nd	F-4	F-8
Breeden, John—1951	1	0	1	0	0	0	0
Starner, Stu—1986	1	0	1	0	0	0	0
TOTAL	2	0	2	0	0	0	0

MOREHEAD STATE

	Yrs	W	L	Ch.	2nd	F-4	F-8
Laughlin, Robert—1956, 1957, 1961	3	3	4	0	0	0	0
Martin, Wayne—1983, 1984	2	1	2	0	0	0	0
TOTAL	5	4	6	0	0	0	0

MURRAY STATE

	Yrs	W	L	Ch.	2nd	F-4	F-8
Luther, Cal—1964, 1969	2	0	2	0	0	0	0
Newton, Steve—1988, 1990, 1991	3	1	3	0	0	0	0

N. CAROLINA

	Yrs	W	L	Ch.	2nd	F-4	F-8
Carnevale, Ben—46 (2)	1	2	1	0	1	0	1
Lange, Bill—41 (F-8)	1	0	2	0	0	0	1
McGuire, Frank—57 (Ch.), 1959	2	5	1	1	0	0	1
Smith, Dean—67 (F-4), 68 (2), 69 (F-4), 72 (F-4), 1975, 1976, 77 (2), 1978, 1979, 1980, 81 (2), 82 (Ch.), 83 (F-8), 1984, 85 (F-8), 1986, 87 (F-8), 88 (F-8), 1989, 1990, 91 (F-4)	21	47	22	1	3	4	12
TOTAL	25	54	26	2	4	4	15

N.C. AT&T

	Yrs	W	L	Ch.	2nd	F-4	F-8
Corbett, Don—1982, 1983, 1984, 1985, 1986, 1987, 1988	7	0	7	0	0	0	0
TOTAL	7	0	7	0	0	0	0

N.C. STATE

	Yrs	W	L	Ch.	2nd	F-4	F-8
Case, Everett—50 (F-4), 51 (F-8), 1952, 1954, 1956	5	6	6	0	0	1	2
Maravich, Press—1965	1	1	1	0	0	0	0
Robinson, Les—1991	1	1	1	0	0	0	0
Sloan, Norm—1970, 74 (Ch.), 1980	3	5	2	1	0	0	1
Valvano, Jim—1982, 83 (Ch.), 85 (F-8), 86 (F-8), 1987, 1988, 1989	7	14	6	1	0	0	3
TOTAL	17	27	16	2	0	1	6

N.C.-CHARLOTTE

	Yrs	W	L	Ch.	2nd	F-4	F-8
Mullins, Jeff—1988	1	0	1	0	0	0	0
Rose, Lee—77 (F-4)	1	3	2	0	0	1	1
TOTAL	2	3	3	0	0	1	1

NAVY

	Yrs	W	L	Ch.	2nd	F-4	F-8
Carnevale, Ben—47 (F-8), 1953, 54 (F-8), 1959, 1960	5	4	6	0	0	0	2
Evans, Paul—1985, 86 (F-8)	2	4	2	0	0	0	1
Herrmann, Pete—1987	1	0	1	0	0	0	0
TOTAL	8	8	9	0	0	0	3

NEBRASKA

	Yrs	W	L	Ch.	2nd	F-4	F-8
Iba, Moe—1986	1	0	1	0	0	0	0
Nee, Danny—1991	1	0	1	0	0	0	0
TOTAL	2	0	2	0	0	0	0

NEVADA-RENO

	Yrs	W	L	Ch.	2nd	F-4	F-8
Allen, Sonny—1984, 1985	2	0	2	0	0	0	0
TOTAL	2	0	2	0	0	0	0

NEW MEXICO

	Yrs	W	L	Ch.	2nd	F-4	F-8
Bliss, Dave—1991	1	0	1	0	0	0	0
Ellenberger, Norm—1974, 1978	2	2	2	0	0	0	0
King, Bob—1968	1	0	2	0	0	0	0
TOTAL	4	2	5	0	0	0	0

NEW MEXICO STATE

	Yrs	W	L	Ch.	2nd	F-4	F-8
Askew, Presley—1959, 1960	2	0	2	0	0	0	0
Hayes, Ken—1979	1	0	1	0	0	0	0
Henson, Lou—1967, 1968, 1969, 70 (F-4), 1971, 1975	6	7	7	0	0	1	1
McCarthy, George—1952	1	0	2	0	0	0	0
McCarthy, Neil—1990, 1991	2	0	2	0	0	0	0
TOTAL	12	7	14	0	0	1	1

NEW ORLEANS

	Yrs	W	L	Ch.	2nd	F-4	F-8
Dees, Benny—1987	1	1	1	0	0	0	0
Floyd, Tim—1991	1	0	1	0	0	0	0
TOTAL	2	1	2	0	0	0	0

NIAGARA

	Yrs	W	L	Ch.	2nd	F-4	F-8
Layden, Frank—1970	1	1	2	0	0	0	0
TOTAL	1	1	2	0	0	0	0

NORTH TEXAS

	Yrs	W	L	Ch.	2nd	F-4	F-8
Gales, Jimmy—1988	1	0	1	0	0	0	0
TOTAL	1	0	1	0	0	0	0

NORTHEAST LA.

	Yrs	W	L	Ch.	2nd	F-4	F-8
Vining, Mike—1982, 1986, 1990, 1991	4	0	4	0	0	0	0
TOTAL	4	0	4	0	0	0	0

NORTHEASTERN

	Yrs	W	L	Ch.	2nd	F-4	F-8
Calhoun, Jim—1981, 1982, 1984, 1985, 1986	5	3	5	0	0	0	0
Fogel, Karl—1987, 1991	2	0	2	0	0	0	0
TOTAL	7	3	7	0	0	0	0

NORTHERN ILL.

	Yrs	W	L	Ch.	2nd	F-4	F-8
McDougal, John—1982	1	0	1	0	0	0	0
Molinari, Jim—1991	1	0	1	0	0	0	0
TOTAL	2	0	2	0	0	0	0

NORTHERN IOWA

	Yrs	W	L	Ch.	2nd	F-4	F-8
Miller, Eldon—1990	1	1	1	0	0	0	0
TOTAL	1	1	1	0	0	0	0

NOTRE DAME

	Yrs	W	L	Ch.	2nd	F-4	F-8
Dee, Johnny—1965, 1969, 1970, 1971	4	2	6	0	0	0	0
Jordan, John—53 (F-8), 54 (F-8), 1957, 58 (F-8), 1960, 1963	6	8	6	0	0	0	3
Phelps, Digger—1974, 1975, 1976, 1977, 78 (F-4), 79 (F-8), 1980, 1981, 1985, 1986, 1987, 1988, 1989, 1990	14	15	16	0	0	1	2
TOTAL	24	25	28	0	0	1	5

NYU

	Yrs	W	L	Ch.	2nd	F-4	F-8
Cann, Howard—43 (F-8), 45 (2), 46 (F-8)	3	3	4	0	1	0	3
Rossini, Lou—60 (F-4), 1962, 1963	3	6	5	0	0	1	1
TOTAL	6	9	9	0	1	1	4

OHIO

	Yrs	W	L	Ch.	2nd	F-4	F-8
Nee, Danny—1983, 1985	2	1	2	0	0	0	0
Snyder, James—1960, 1961, 64 (F-8), 1965, 1970, 1972, 1974	7	3	8	0	0	0	1
TOTAL	9	4	10	0	0	0	1

OHIO STATE

	Yrs	W	L	Ch.	2nd	F-4	F-8
Ayers, Randy—1990, 1991	2	3	2	0	0	0	0
Dye, Tippy—50 (F-8)	1	1	1	0	0	0	1
Miller, Eldon—1980, 1982, 1983, 1985	4	3	4	0	0	0	0
Olsen, Harold—39(2), 44 (F-4), 45 (F-4), 46 (F-4)	4	6	4	0	1	3	4
Taylor, Fred—60 (Ch.), 61 (2), 62 (2), 68 (F-4), 71 (F-8)	5	14	4	1	2	1	5
Williams, Gary—1987	1	1	1	0	0	0	0
TOTAL	17	28	16	1	3	4	10

OKLAHOMA

	Yrs	W	L	Ch.	2nd	F-4	F-8
Bliss, Dave—1979	1	1	1	0	0	0	0
Drake, Bruce—39 (F-4), 43 (F-8), 47 (2)	3	4	3	0	1	1	3
Tubbs, Billy—1983, 1984, 85 (F-8), 1986, 1987, 88 (2), 1989, 1990	8	15	8	0	1	0	2
TOTAL	12	20	12	0	2	1	5

OKLAHOMA CITY

	Yrs	W	L	Ch.	2nd	F-4	F-8
Lemons, Abe—56 (F-8), 57 (F-8), 1963, 1964, 1965, 1966, 1973	7	7	8	0	0	0	2
Parrack, Doyle—1952, 1953, 1954, 1955	4	1	5	0	0	0	0
TOTAL	11	8	13	0	0	0	2

OKLAHOMA STATE

	Yrs	W	L	Ch.	2nd	F-4	F-8
Hansen, Paul—1983	1	0	1	0	0	0	0
Iba, Henry—45 (Ch.), 46, (Ch.), 49 (2), 51 (F-4), 53 (F-8), 54, (F-8), 58 (F-8), 65 (F-8)	8	15	7	2	1	1	8
Sutton, Eddie—1991	1	2	1	0	0	0	0
TOTAL	10	17	9	2	1	1	8

OLD DOMINION

	Yrs	W	L	Ch.	2nd	F-4	F-8
Webb, Paul—1980, 1982, 1985	3	0	3	0	0	0	0
Young, Tom—1986	1	1	1	0	0	0	0
TOTAL	4	1	4	0	0	0	0

ORAL ROBERTS

	Yrs	W	L	Ch.	2nd	F-4	F-8
Acres, Dick—1984	1	0	1	0	0	0	0
Trickey, Ken—74 (F-8)	1	2	1	0	0	0	1
TOTAL	2	2	2	0	0	0	1

OREGON

	Yrs	W	L	Ch.	2nd	F-4	F-8
Belko, Steve—60 (F-8), 1961	2	2	2	0	0	0	1
Hobson, Howard—39 (Ch.), 45 (F-8)	2	4	1	1	0	0	2
TOTAL	4	6	3	1	0	0	3

OREGON STATE

	Yrs	W	L	Ch.	2nd	F-4	F-8
Anderson, Jim—1990	1	0	1	0	0	0	0
Gill, Amory "Slats"—47 (F-8), 49 (F-4), 55 (F-8), 62 (F-8), 63 (F-4), 1964	6	8	8	0	0	2	5
Miller, Ralph—1975, 1980, 1981, 82 (F-8), 1984, 1985, 1988, 1989	8	3	9	0	0	0	1
Valenti, Paul—66 (F-8)	1	1	1	0	0	0	1
TOTAL	16	12	19	0	0	2	7

PACIFIC

	Yrs	W	L	Ch.	2nd	F-4	F-8
Edwards, Dick—1966, 67 (F-8), 1971	3	2	4	0	0	0	1
Morrison, Stan—1979	1	0	1	0	0	0	0
TOTAL	4	2	5	0	0	0	1

PENN STATE

	Yrs	W	L	Ch.	2nd	F-4	F-8
Egli, John—1955, 1965	2	1	3	0	0	0	0
Gross, Elmer—1952, 54 (F-4)	2	4	3	0	0	1	1
Lawther, John—42 (F-8)	1	1	1	0	0	0	1
Parkhill, Bruce—1991	1	1	1	0	0	0	0
TOTAL	6	7	8	0	0	1	2

PENNSYLVANIA

	Yrs	W	L	Ch.	2nd	F-4	F-8
Dallmar, Howie—1953	1	1	1	0	0	0	0
Daly, Chuck—72 (F-8), 1973, 1974, 1975	4	3	5	0	0	0	1
Harter, Dick—1970, 71 (F-8)	2	2	2	0	0	0	1
Littlepage, Craig—1985	1	0	1	0	0	0	0
Schneider, Tom—1987	1	0	1	0	0	0	0
Weinhauer, Bob—1978, 79 (F-4), 1980, 1982	4	6	5	0	0	1	1
TOTAL	13	12	15	0	0	1	3

PEPPERDINE

	Yrs	W	L	Ch.	2nd	F-4	F-8
Asbury Tom—1991	1	0	1	0	0	0	0
Colson, Gary—1976, 1979	2	2	2	0	0	0	0
Dowell, Duck—1962	1	1	1	0	0	0	0
Duer, Al—44 (F-8)	1	0	2	0	0	0	1
Harrick, Jim—1982, 1983, 1985, 1986	4	1	4	0	0	0	0
TOTAL	9	4	10	0	0	0	1

PITTSBURGH

	Yrs	W	L	Ch.	2nd	F-4	F-8
Carlson, Harold—41 (F-4)	1	1	1	0	0	1	1
Chipman, Roy—1981, 1982, 1985	3	1	3	0	0	0	0
Evans, Paul—1987, 1988, 1989, 1991	4	3	4	0	0	0	0
Ridl, Buzz—74 (F-8)	1	2	1	0	0	0	1
Timmons, Bob—1957, 1958, 1963	3	1	4	0	0	0	0
TOTAL	12	8	13	0	0	1	2

PORTLAND

	Yrs	W	L	Ch.	2nd	F-4	F-8
Negratti, Al—1959	1	0	1	0	0	0	0
TOTAL	1	0	1	0	0	0	0

PRINCETON

	Yrs	W	L	Ch.	2nd	F-4	F-8
Cappon, Franklin—1952, 1955, 1960	3	0	5	0	0	0	0
Carril, Pete—1969, 1976, 1977, 1981, 1983, 1984, 1989, 1990, 1991	9	3	9	0	0	0	0
McCandless, Jake—1961	1	1	2	0	0	0	0
Van Breda Kolff, B.—1963, 1964, 65 (F-4), 1967	4	7	5	0	0	1	1
TOTAL	17	11	21	0	0	1	1

PROVIDENCE

	Yrs	W	L	Ch.	2nd	F-4	F-8
Barnes, Rick—1989, 1990	2	0	2	0	0	0	0
Gavitt, Dave—1972, 73 (F-4), 1974, 1977, 1978	5	5	6	0	0	1	1
Mullaney, Joe—1964, 65 (F-8), 1966	3	2	3	0	0	0	1
Pitino, Rick—87 (F-4)	1	4	1	0	0	1	1
TOTAL	11	11	12	0	0	2	3

PURDUE

	Yrs	W	L	Ch.	2nd	F-4	F-8
Keady, Gene—1983, 1984, 1985, 1986, 1987, 1988, 1990, 1991	8	5	8	0	0	0	0
King, George—69 (2)	1	3	1	0	1	0	1
Rose, Lee—80 (F-4)	1	5	1	0	0	1	1
Schaus, Fred—1977	1	0	1	0	0	0	0
TOTAL	11	13	11	0	1	1	2

RHODE ISLAND

	Yrs	W	L	Ch.	2nd	F-4	F-8
Calverley, Ernie—1961, 1966	2	0	2	0	0	0	0
Kraft, Jack—1978	1	0	1	0	0	0	0
Penders, Tom—1988	1	2	1	0	0	0	0
TOTAL	4	2	4	0	0	0	0

RICE

	Yrs	W	L	Ch.	2nd	F-4	F-8
Brannon, Buster—40 (F-8), 42 (F-8)	2	1	3	0	0	0	2
Knodel, Don—1970	1	0	1	0	0	0	0
Suman, Don—1954	1	1	1	0	0	0	0
TOTAL	4	2	5	0	0	0	2

RICHMOND

	Yrs	W	L	Ch.	2nd	F-4	F-8
Tarrant, Dick—1984, 1986, 1988, 1990, 1991	5	5	5	0	0	0	0
TOTAL	5	5	5	0	0	0	0

RIDER

	Yrs	W	L	Ch.	2nd	F-4	F-8
Carpenter, John—1984	1	0	1	0	0	0	0
TOTAL	1	0	1	0	0	0	0

ROBERT MORRIS

	Yrs	W	L	Ch.	2nd	F-4	F-8
Durham, Jarret—1989, 1990	2	0	2	0	0	0	0
Furjanic, Matt—1982, 1983	2	1	2	0	0	0	0
TOTAL	4	1	4	0	0	0	0

RUTGERS

	Yrs	W	L	Ch.	2nd	F-4	F-8
Wenzel, Bob—1989, 1991	2	0	2	0	0	0	0
Young, Tom—1975, 76 (F-4), 1979, 1983	4	5	5	0	0	1	1
TOTAL	6	5	7	0	0	1	1

S'WESTERN LA.

	Yrs	W	L	Ch.	2nd	F-4	F-8
Paschal, Bobby—1982, 1983	2	0	2	0	0	0	0
Shipley, Beryl—1972, 1973	2	3	3	0	0	0	0
TOTAL	4	3	5	0	0	0	0

S. CAROLINA

	Yrs	W	L	Ch.	2nd	F-4	F-8
Felton, George—1989	1	0	1	0	0	0	0
McGuire, Frank—1971, 1972, 1973, 1974	4	4	5	0	0	0	0
TOTAL	5	4	6	0	0	0	0

S. CAROLINA STATE

	Yrs	W	L	Ch.	2nd	F-4	F-8
Alexander, Cy—1989	1	0	1	0	0	0	0
TOTAL	1	0	1	0	0	0	0

SAN DIEGO

	Yrs	W	L	Ch.	2nd	F-4	F-8
Brovelli, Jim—1984	1	0	1	0	0	0	0
Egan, Hank—1987	1	0	1	0	0	0	0
TOTAL	2	0	2	0	0	0	0

SAN DIEGO STATE

	Yrs	W	L	Ch.	2nd	F-4	F-8
Gaines, Dave Smokey—1985	1	0	1	0	0	0	0
Vezie, Tim—1975, 1976	2	0	2	0	0	0	0
TOTAL	3	0	3	0	0	0	0

SAN FRANCISCO

	Yrs	W	L	Ch.	2nd	F-4	F-8
Barry, Peter—1981, 1982	2	0	2	0	0	0	0
Belluomini, Dan—1979	1	1	1	0	0	0	0
Gaillard, Bob—1972, 73 (F-8), 74 (F-8), 1977, 1978	5	4	5	0	0	0	2
Peletta, Peter—1963, 64 (F-8), 65 (F-8)	3	3	3	0	0	0	2
Woolpert, Phil—55 (Ch.), 56 (Ch.), 57 (F-4), 1958	4	13	2	2	0	1	3
TOTAL	15	21	13	2	0	1	7

SAN JOSE STATE

	Yrs	W	L	Ch.	2nd	F-4	F-8
Berry, Bill—1980	1	0	1	0	0	0	0
McPherson, Walter—1951	1	0	1	0	0	0	0
TOTAL	2	0	2	0	0	0	0

SANTA CLARA

	Yrs	W	L	Ch.	2nd	F-4	F-8
Feerick, Bob—52 (F-4), 53 (F-8), 54 (F-8), 1960	4	6	6	0	0	1	3
Garibaldi, Dick—68 (F-8), 69 (F-8), 1970	3	3	3	0	0	0	2
Williams, Carroll—1987	1	0	1	0	0	0	0
TOTAL	8	9	10	0	0	1	5

SEATTLE

	Yrs	W	L	Ch.	2nd	F-4	F-8
Boyd, Bob—1964	1	2	1	0	0	0	0
Brightman, Al—1953, 1954, 1955, 1956	4	4	6	0	0	0	0
Buckwalter, Morris—1969	1	0	1	0	0	0	0
Castellani, John—58 (2)	1	4	1	0	1	0	1
Cazzetta, Vince—1961, 1962	2	0	2	0	0	0	0
Markey, Clair—1963	1	0	1	0	0	0	0
Purcell, Lionel—1967	1	0	1	0	0	0	0
TOTAL	11	10	13	0	1	0	1

SETON HALL

	Yrs	W	L	Ch.	2nd	F-4	F-8
Carlesimo, P. J.—1988, 89 (2), 91 (F-8)	3	9	3	0	1	0	2
TOTAL	3	9	3	0	1	0	2

SIENA

	Yrs	W	L	Ch.	2nd	F-4	F-8
Deane, Mike—1989	1	1	1	0	0	0	0
TOTAL	1	1	1	0	0	0	0

SMU

	Yrs	W	L	Ch.	2nd	F-4	F-8
Bliss, Dave—1984 1985, 1988	3	3	3	0	0	0	0
Hayes, E. O. "Doc"—1955, 56 (F-4), 1957, 1965, 1966, 67 (F-8)	6	7	8	0	0	1	2
TOTAL	9	10	11	0	0	1	2

SOUTH ALABAMA

	Yrs	W	L	Ch.	2nd	F-4	F-8
Arrow, Ronnie—1989, 1991	2	1	2	0	0	0	0
Ellis, Cliff—1979, 1980	2	0	2	0	0	0	0
TOTAL	4	1	4	0	0	0	0

SOUTH FLORIDA

	Yrs	W	L	Ch.	2nd	F-4	F-8
Paschal, Bobby—1990	1	0	1	0	0	0	0
TOTAL	1	0	1	0	0	0	0

SOUTHERN ILL.

	Yrs	W	L	Ch.	2nd	F-4	F-8
Lambert, Paul—1977	1	1	1	0	0	0	0
TOTAL	1	1	1	0	0	0	0

SOUTHERN MISS.

	Yrs	W	L	Ch.	2nd	F-4	F-8
Turk, M. K.—1990, 1991	2	0	2	0	0	0	0
TOTAL	2	0	2	0	0	0	0

SOUTHERN-B.R.

	Yrs	W	L	Ch.	2nd	F-4	F-8
Hopkins, Robert—1985	1	0	1	0	0	0	0
Jobe, Ben—1987, 1988, 1989	3	0	3	0	0	0	0
Stewart, Carl—1981	1	0	1	0	0	0	0
TOTAL	5	0	5	0	0	0	0

SPRINGFIELD

	Yrs	W	L	Ch.	2nd	F-4	F-8
Hickox, Ed—40 (F-8)	1	0	1	0	0	0	1
TOTAL	1	0	1	0	0	0	1

ST. BONAVENTURE

	Yrs	W	L	Ch.	2nd	F-4	F-8
Donovan, Eddie—1961	1	2	1	0	0	0	0
Statlin, Jim—1978	1	0	1	0	0	0	0
Weise, Larry—1968, 70 (F4)	2	4	4	0	0	1	1
TOTAL	4	6	6	0	0	1	1

ST. FRANCIS-PA.

	Yrs	W	L	Ch.	2nd	F-4	F-8
Baron, Jim—1991	1	0	1	0	0	0	0
TOTAL	1	0	1	0	0	0	0

ST. JOHN'S

	Yrs	W	L	Ch.	2nd	F-4	F-8
Carnesecca, Lou—1967, 1968, 1969, 1976, 1977, 1978, 79 (F-8), 1980, 1982, 1983, 1984, 85 (F-4), 1986, 1987, 1988, 1990, 91 (F-8)	17	17	19	0	0	1	3
Lapchick, Joe—1961	1	0	1	0	0	0	0
McGuire, Frank—51 (F-8), 52 (2)	2	5	2	0	1	0	2
Mulzoff, Frank—1973	1	0	1	0	0	0	0
TOTAL	21	22	23	0	1	1	5

ST. JOSEPH'S

	Yrs	W	L	Ch.	2nd	F-4	F-8
Boyle, Jim—1982, 1986	2	1	2	0	0	0	0
Lynam, Jim—81 (F-8)	1	3	1	0	0	0	1
McKinney, Jack—1969, 1971, 1973, 1974	4	0	4	0	0	0	0
Ramsay, Jack—1959, 1960, 61 (F-4), 1962, 63 (F-8), 1965, 1966	7	8	11	0	0	1	2
TOTAL	14	12	18	0	0	1	3

ST. LOUIS

	Yrs	W	L	Ch.	2nd	F-4	F-8
Hickey, Eddie—52 (F-8), 1957	2	1	3	0	0	0	1
TOTAL	2	1	3	0	0	0	1

ST. MARY'S

	Yrs	W	L	Ch.	2nd	F-4	F-8
Nance, Lynn—1989	1	0	1	0	0	0	0
Weaver, James—59 (F-8)	1	1	1	0	0	0	1
TOTAL	2	1	2	0	0	0	1

ST. PETER'S

	Yrs	W	L	Ch.	2nd	F-4	F-8
Fiore, Ted—1991	1	0	1	0	0	0	0
TOTAL	1	0	1	0	0	0	0

STANFORD

	Yrs	W	L	Ch.	2nd	F-4	F-8
Dean, Everett—42 (Ch.)	1	3	0	1	0	0	1
Montgomery, Mike—1989	1	0	1	0	0	0	0
TOTAL	2	3	1	1	0	0	1

SW MISSOURI STATE

	Yrs	W	L	Ch.	2nd	F-4	F-8
Spoonhour, Charles—1987, 1988, 1989, 1990	4	1	4	0	0	0	0
TOTAL	4	1	4	0	0	0	0

SYRACUSE

	Yrs	W	L	Ch.	2nd	F-4	F-8
Boeheim, Jim—1977, 1978, 1979, 1980, 1983, 1984, 1985, 1986, 87 (2), 1988, 89 (F-8), 1990, 1991	13	18	13	0	1	0	2
Danforth, Roy—1973, 1974, 75 (F-4), 1976	4	5	5	0	0	1	1
Guley, Marc—57 (F-8)	1	2	1	0	0	0	1
Lewis, Fred—66 (F-8)	1	1	1	0	0	0	1
TOTAL	19	26	20	0	1	1	5

TCU

	Yrs	W	L	Ch.	2nd	F-4	F-8
Brannon, Buster—1952, 1953, 1959	3	3	3	0	0	0	0
Killingsworth, Jim—1987	1	1	1	0	0	0	0
Swaim, Johnny—68 (F-8), 1971	2	1	2	0	0	0	1
TOTAL	6	5	6	0	0	0	1

TEMPLE

	Yrs	W	L	Ch.	2nd	F-4	F-8
Casey, Don—1979	1	0	1	0	0	0	0
Chaney, John—1984, 1985, 1986, 1987, 88 (F-8), 1990, 91 (F-8)	7	10	7	0	0	0	2
Cody, Josh—44 (F-8)	1	1	1	0	0	0	1
Litwack, Harry—56 (F-4), 58 (F-4), 1964, 1967, 1970, 1972	6	7	6	0	0	2	2
TOTAL	15	18	15	0	0	2	5

TENN.-CHATT.

	Yrs	W	L	Ch.	2nd	F-4	F-8
Arnold, Murray—1981, 1982, 1983	3	1	3	0	0	0	0
McCarthy, Mack—1988	1	0	1	0	0	0	0
TOTAL	4	1	4	0	0	0	0

TENNESSEE

	Yrs	W	L	Ch.	2nd	F-4	F-8
Devoe, Don—1979, 1980, 1981, 1982, 1983, 1989	6	5	6	0	0	0	0
Mears, Ray—1967, 1976, 1977	3	0	4	0	0	0	0
TOTAL	9	5	10	0	0	0	0

TENNESSEE TECH

	Yrs	W	L	Ch.	2nd	F-4	F-8
Oldham, Johnny—1958, 1963	2	0	2	0	0	0	0
TOTAL	2	0	2	0	0	0	0

TEXAS

	Yrs	W	L	Ch.	2nd	F-4	F-8
Black, Leon—1972, 1974	2	1	3	0	0	0	0
Bradley, Harold—1960, 1963	2	2	3	0	0	0	0
Gilstrap, H. C. Bully—43 (F-4)	1	1	1	0	0	1	1
Gray, Jack—39 (F-8), 47 (F-4)	2	2	3	0	0	1	2
Lemons, Abe—1979	1	0	1	0	0	0	0
Penders, Tom—1989, 90 (F-8), 1991	3	5	3	0	0	0	1
TOTAL	11	11	14	0	0	2	4

TEXAS A&M

	Yrs	W	L	Ch.	2nd	F-4	F-8
Floyd, John—1951	1	0	1	0	0	0	0
Metcalf, Shelby—1964, 1969, 1975, 1980, 1987	5	3	6	0	0	0	0
TOTAL	6	3	7	0	0	0	0

TEXAS SOUTHERN

	Yrs	W	L	Ch.	2nd	F-4	F-8
Moreland, Bob—1990	1	0	1	0	0	0	0
TOTAL	1	0	1	0	0	0	0

TEXAS TECH

	Yrs	W	L	Ch.	2nd	F-4	F-8
Gibson, Gene—1962	1	1	2	0	0	0	0
Myers, Gerald—1973, 1976, 1985, 1986	4	1	4	0	0	0	0
Robinson, Polk—1954, 1956, 1961	3	1	3	0	0	0	0
TOTAL	8	3	9	0	0	0	0

TEXAS-SAN ANT.

	Yrs	W	L	Ch.	2nd	F-4	F-8
Burmeister, Ken—1988	1	0	1	0	0	0	0
TOTAL	1	0	1	0	0	0	0

TOLEDO

	Yrs	W	L	Ch.	2nd	F-4	F-8
Bush, Jerry—1954	1	0	1	0	0	0	0
Nichols, Bob—1967, 1979, 1980	3	1	3	0	0	0	0
TOTAL	4	1	4	0	0	0	0

TOWSON STATE

	Yrs	W	L	Ch.	2nd	F-4	F-8
Truax, Terry—1990, 1991	2	0	2	0	0	0	0
TOTAL	2	0	2	0	0	0	0

TRINITY

	Yrs	W	L	Ch.	2nd	F-4	F-8
Polk, Bob—1969	1	0	1	0	0	0	0
TOTAL	1	0	1	0	0	0	0

TUFTS

	Yrs	W	L	Ch.	2nd	F-4	F-8
Cochran, Richard—45 (F-8)	1	0	2	0	0	0	1
TOTAL	1	0	2	0	0	0	1

TULSA

	Yrs	W	L	Ch.	2nd	F-4	F-8
Barnett, J. D.—1986, 1987	2	0	2	0	0	0	0
Iba, Clarence—1955	1	1	1	0	0	0	0
Richardson, Nolan—1982, 1984, 1985	3	0	3	0	0	0	0
TOTAL	6	1	6	0	0	0	0

UC SANTA BARB.

	Yrs	W	L	Ch.	2nd	F-4	F-8
Pimm, Jerry—1988, 1990	2	1	2	0	0	0	0
TOTAL	2	1	2	0	0	0	0

UCLA

	Yrs	W	L	Ch.	2nd	F-4	F-8
Bartow, Gene—76 (F-4), 1977	2	5	2	0	0	1	1
Brown, Larry—80 (2), 1981	2	5	2	0	1	0	1
Cunningham, Gary—1978, 79 (F-8)	2	3	2	0	0	0	1
Farmer, Larry—1983	1	0	1	0	0	0	0
Harrick, Jim—1989, 1990, 1991	3	3	3	0	0	0	0
Hazzard, Walt—1987	1	1	1	0	0	0	0
Wooden, John—50 (F-8), 1952, 1956, 62 (F-4), 1963, 64 (Ch.), 65 (Ch.), 67 (Ch.), 68 (Ch.), 69 (Ch.), 70 (Ch.), 71 (Ch.), 72 (Ch.), 73 (Ch.), 74 (F-4), 75 (Ch.)	16	47	10	10	0	2	13
TOTAL	27	64	21	10	1	3	16

U. CONN.

	Yrs	W	L	Ch.	2nd	F-4	F-8
Calhoun, Jim—90 (F-8), 1991	2	5	2	0	0	0	1
Greer, Hugh—1951, 1954, 1956, 1957, 1958, 1959, 1960	7	1	8	0	0	0	0
Perno, Dom—1979	1	0	1	0	0	0	0
Rowe, Dee—1976	1	1	1	0	0	0	0
Shabel, Fred—64 (F-8), 1965, 1967	3	2	3	0	0	0	1
Wigton, George—1963	1	0	1	0	0	0	0
TOTAL	15	9	16	0	0	0	2

U. MASS.

	Yrs	W	L	Ch.	2nd	F-4	F-8
Zunic, Matt—1962	1	0	1	0	0	0	0
TOTAL	1	0	1	0	0	0	0

UNLV

	Yrs	W	L	Ch.	2nd	F-4	F-8
Tarkanian, Jerry—1975, 1976, 77 (F-4), 1983, 1984, 1985, 1986, 87 (F-4), 1988, 89 (F-8), 90 (Ch.), 91 (F-4)	12	30	11	1	0	3	5
TOTAL	12	30	11	1	0	3	5

USC

	Yrs	W	L	Ch.	2nd	F-4	F-8
Barry, Sam—40 (F-4)	1	1	1	0	0	1	1
Boyd, Bob—1979	1	1	1	0	0	0	0
Morrison, Stan—1982, 1985	2	0	2	0	0	0	0
Raveling, George—1991	1	0	1	0	0	0	0
Twogood, Forrest—54 (F-4), 1960, 1961	3	3	5	0	0	1	1
TOTAL	8	5	10	0	0	2	2

UTAH

	Yrs	W	L	Ch.	2nd	F-4	F-8
Archibald, Lynn—1986	1	0	1	0	0	0	0
Gardner, Jack—1955, 56 (F-8), 1959, 1960, 61 (F-4), 66 (F-4)	6	8	9	0	0	2	3
Majerus, Rick—1991	1	2	1	0	0	0	0
Peterson, Vadal—44 (Ch.), 45 (F-8)	2	3	2	1	0	0	2
Pimm, Jerry—1977, 1978, 1979, 1981, 1983	5	5	5	0	0	0	0
TOTAL	15	18	18	1	0	2	5

UTAH STATE

	Yrs	W	L	Ch.	2nd	F-4	F-8
Anderson, Ladell—1962, 1963, 1964, 70 (F-8), 1971	5	4	7	0	0	0	1
Belnap, Dutch—1975, 1979	2	0	2	0	0	0	0
Romney, Dick—39 (F-8)	1	1	1	0	0	0	1
Tueller, Rod—1980, 1983, 1988	3	0	3	0	0	0	0
TOTAL	11	5	13	0	0	0	2

UTEP

	Yrs	W	L	Ch.	2nd	F-4	F-8
Haskins, Don—1963, 1964, 66 (Ch.), 1967, 1970, 1975, 1984, 1985, 1986, 1987, 1988, 1989, 1990	13	12	12	1	0	0	1
TOTAL	13	12	12	1	0	0	1

VA. COMMONWEALTH

	Yrs	W	L	Ch.	2nd	F-4	F-8
Barnett, J. D.—1980, 1981, 1983, 1984, 1985	5	4	5	0	0	0	0
TOTAL	5	4	5	0	0	0	0

VANDERBILT

	Yrs	W	L	Ch.	2nd	F-4	F-8
Fogler, Eddie—1991	1	0	1	0	0	0	0
Newton, C. M.—1988, 1989	2	2	2	0	0	0	0
Skinner, Roy—65 (F-8), 1974	2	1	3	0	0	0	1
TOTAL	5	3	6	0	0	0	1

VILLANOVA

	Yrs	W	L	Ch.	2nd	F-4	F-8
Kraft, Jack—62 (F-8), 1964, 1969, 70 (F-8), 71 (2), 1972	6	11	7	0	1	0	3
Massimino, Rollie—78 (F-8), 1980, 1981, 82 (F-8), 83 (F-8), 1984, 85 (Ch.), 1986, 88 (F-8), 1990, 1991	11	20	10	1	0	0	5
Severance, Alex—39 (F-4), 49 (F-8), 1951, 1955	4	4	4	0	0	1	2
TOTAL	21	35	21	1	1	1	10

VIRGINIA

	Yrs	W	L	Ch.	2nd	F-4	F-8
Holland, Terry—1976, 81 (F-4), 1982, 83 (F-8), 84 (F-4), 1986, 1987, 89 (F-8), 1990	9	15	9	0	0	2	4
Jones, Jeff—1991	1	0	1	0	0	0	0
TOTAL	10	15	10	0	0	2	4

VIRGINIA TECH

	Yrs	W	L	Ch.	2nd	F-4	F-8
Devoe, Don—1976	1	0	1	0	0	0	0
Moir, Charles—1979, 1980, 1985, 1986	4	2	4	0	0	0	0
Shannon, Howard—67 (F-8)	1	2	1	0	0	0	1
TOTAL	6	4	6	0	0	0	1

VMI

	Yrs	W	L	Ch.	2nd	F-4	F-8
Blair, Bill—76 (F-8)	1	2	1	0	0	0	1
Miller, Weenie—1964	1	0	1	0	0	0	0
Schmaus, Charlie—1977	1	1	1	0	0	0	0
TOTAL	3	3	3	0	0	0	1

WAKE FOREST

	Yrs	W	L	Ch.	2nd	F-4	F-8
Greason, Murray—39 (F-8), 1953	2	1	2	0	0	0	1
McKinney, Bones—61 (F-8), 62 (F-4)	2	6	2	0	0	1	2
Odom, Dave—1991	1	1	1	0	0	0	0
Tacy, Carl—77 (F-8), 1981, 1982, 84 (F-8)	4	5	4	0	0	0	2
TOTAL	9	13	9	0	0	1	5

WASHINGTON

	Yrs	W	L	Ch.	2nd	F-4	F-8
Dye, Tippy—51 (F-8), 53 (F-4)	2	5	2	0	0	1	2
Edmunson, Hec—43 (F-8)	1	0	2	0	0	0	1
Harshman, Marv—1976, 1984, 1985	3	2	3	0	0	0	0
McLarney, Art—48 (F-8)	1	1	1	0	0	0	1
Russo, Andy—1986	1	0	1	0	0	0	0
TOTAL	8	8	9	0	0	1	4

WASHINGTON STATE

	Yrs	W	L	Ch.	2nd	F-4	F-8
Friel, Jack—41 (2)	1	2	1	0	1	0	1
Raveling, George—1980, 1983	2	1	2	0	0	0	0
TOTAL	3	3	3	0	1	0	1

WAYNE STATE

	Yrs	W	L	Ch.	2nd	F-4	F-8
Mason, Joel—1956	1	1	2	0	0	0	0
TOTAL	1	1	2	0	0	0	0

WEBER STATE

	Yrs	W	L	Ch.	2nd	F-4	F-8
Johnson, Phil—1969, 1970, 1971	3	2	3	0	0	0	0
McCarthy, Neil—1978, 1979, 1980, 1983	4	1	4	0	0	0	0
Motta, Dick—1968	1	0	1	0	0	0	0
Visscher, Gene—1972, 1973	2	1	3	0	0	0	0
TOTAL	10	4	11	0	0	0	0

WEST TEXAS STATE

	Yrs	W	L	Ch.	2nd	F-4	F-8
Mill, Gus—1955	1	0	1	0	0	0	0
TOTAL	1	0	1	0	0	0	0

WEST VIRGINIA

	Yrs	W	L	Ch.	2nd	F-4	F-8
Catlett, Gale—1982, 1983, 1984, 1986, 1987, 1989	6	3	6	0	0	0	0
King, George—1962, 1963, 1965	3	2	3	0	0	0	0
Schaus, Fred—1955, 1956, 1957, 1958, 59 (2), 1960	6	6	6	0	1	0	1
Waters, Bucky—1967	1	0	1	0	0	0	0
TOTAL	16	11	16	0	1	0	1

WESTERN KY.

	Yrs	W	L	Ch.	2nd	F-4	F-8
Arnold, Murray—1987	1	1	1	0	0	0	0
Diddle, Ed—40 (F-8), 1960, 1962	3	3	4	0	0	0	1
Haskins, Clem—1981, 1986	2	1	2	0	0	0	0
Keady, Gene—1980	1	0	1	0	0	0	0
Oldham, Johnny—1966, 1967, 1970, 71 (F-4)	4	6	4	0	0	1	1
Richards, Jim—1976, 1978	2	1	2	0	0	0	0
TOTAL	13	12	14	0	0	1	2

WESTERN MICH.

	Yrs	W	L	Ch.	2nd	F-4	F-8
Miller, Eldon—1976	1	1	1	0	0	0	0
TOTAL	1	1	1	0	0	0	0

WICHITA STATE

	Yrs	W	L	Ch.	2nd	F-4	F-8
Fogler, Eddie—1987, 1988	2	0	2	0	0	0	0
Miller, Harry—1976	1	0	1	0	0	0	0
Miller, Ralph—64 (F-8)	1	1	1	0	0	0	1
Smithson, Gene—81 (F-8), 1985	2	3	2	0	0	0	1
Thompson, Gary—65 (F-4)	1	2	2	0	0	1	1
TOTAL	7	6	8	0	0	1	3

WILLIAMS

	Yrs	W	L	Ch.	2nd	F-4	F-8
Shaw, Alex—1955	1	0	1	0	0	0	0
TOTAL	1	0	1	0	0	0	0

WIS.-GREEN BAY

	Yrs	W	L	Ch.	2nd	F-4	F-8
Bennett, Dick—1991	1	0	1	0	0	0	0
TOTAL	1	0	1	0	0	0	0

WISCONSIN

	Yrs	W	L	Ch.	2nd	F-4	F-8
Foster, Bud—41 (Ch.), 47 (F-8)	2	4	1	1	0	0	2
TOTAL	2	4	1	1	0	0	2

WYOMING

	Yrs	W	L	Ch.	2nd	F-4	F-8
Brandenburg, Jim—1981, 1982, 1987	3	4	3	0	0	0	0
Dees, Benny—1988	1	0	1	0	0	0	0
Shelton, Everett—41 (F-8), 43 (Ch.), 47 (F-8), 48 (F-8), 49 (F-8), 52 (F-8), 1953, 1958	8	4	12	1	0	0	6
Strannigan, Bill—1967	1	0	2	0	0	0	0
TOTAL	13	8	18	1	0	0	6

XAVIER (OHIO)

	Yrs	W	L	Ch.	2nd	F-4	F-8
Gillen, Pete—1986, 1987, 1988, 1989, 1990, 1991	6	4	6	0	0	0	0
McCafferty, Jim—1961	1	0	1	0	0	0	0
Staak, Bob—1983	1	0	1	0	0	0	0
TOTAL	8	4	8	0	0	0	0

YALE

	Yrs	W	L	Ch.	2nd	F-4	F-8
Hobson, Howard—49 (F-8)	1	0	2	0	0	0	1
Vancisin, Joe—1957, 1962	2	0	2	0	0	0	0
TOTAL	3	0	4	0	0	0	1

This section is divided into two parts, the first covering players' records and the second concerning team records. These records have been derived from the box score data found in **The Encyclopedia of the NCAA Basketball Tournament** as well as this book, except for team won-lost and appearance records, which are based on the Complete School-by-School Records found in the first section of Part 3 of this book. The all-time records found here have been compiled to be as accurate and complete as possible. However, since they are based on *available* information, they do not include, for example: Bill Russell's rebounds per game, Oscar Robertson's assists, Lew Alcindor's blocked shots, and other performances of individuals and teams that would, in all likelihood, be among all-time leading performances *if statistics were available.*

ALL-TIME TOURNAMENT RECORDS

INDIVIDUAL PERFORMANCES

SCORING

Most points in a game

1	AUSTIN CARR, NOTRE DAME (vs. OHIO, 1970)	61
2	BILL BRADLEY, PRINCETON (vs. WICHITA STATE, 1965)	58
3	OSCAR ROBERTSON, CINCINNATI (vs. ARKANSAS, 1958)	56
4	AUSTIN CARR, NOTRE DAME (vs. KENTUCKY, 1970)	52
4	AUSTIN CARR, NOTRE DAME (vs. TCU, 1971)	52

Most points in a Final Four game

1	BILL WALTON, UCLA (vs. MEMPHIS STATE, 1973)	44
2	GAIL GOODRICH, UCLA (vs. MICHIGAN, 1965)	42
3	JACK GIVENS, KENTUCKY (vs. DUKE, 1978)	41
4	AL WOOD, N. CAROLINA (vs. VIRGINIA, 1981)	39
5	3 tied for fifth place.	38

Most points in a championship game

1	BILL WALTON, UCLA (vs. MEMPHIS STATE, 1973)	44
2	GAIL GOODRICH, UCLA (vs. MICHIGAN, 1965)	42
3	JACK GIVENS, KENTUCKY (vs. DUKE, 1978)	41
4	LEW ALCINDOR, UCLA (vs. PURDUE, 1969)	37
5	JOHN MORTON, SETON HALL (vs. MICHIGAN, 1989)	35

Most points in a tournament

1	GLEN RICE, MICHIGAN (1989)	184
2	BILL BRADLEY, PRINCETON (1965)	177
3	ELVIN HAYES, HOUSTON (1968)	167
4	DANNY MANNING, KANSAS (1988)	163
5	2 tied for fifth place.	160

Most points in a career

1	ELVIN HAYES, HOUSTON (1966, 1967, 1968)	358
2	DANNY MANNING, KANSAS (1985, 1986, 1987, 1988)	328
3	OSCAR ROBERTSON, CINCINNATI (1958, 1959, 1960)	324
4	GLEN RICE, MICHIGAN (1986, 1987, 1988, 1989)	308
5	LEW ALCINDOR, UCLA (1967, 1968, 1969)	304

Highest scoring average in a tournament (minimum 3 games)

1	AUSTIN CARR, NOTRE DAME (1970) (158-3)	52.67
2	AUSTIN CARR, NOTRE DAME (1971) (125-3)	41.67
3	BO KIMBLE, LOYOLA MYMT. (1990) (143-4)	35.75
3	JERRY CHAMBERS, UTAH (1966) (143-4)	35.75
5	BILL BRADLEY, PRINCETON (1965) (177-5)	35.40

Highest scoring average in a career (minimum 6 games)

1	AUSTIN CARR, NOTRE DAME (1969, 1970, 1971) (289-7)	41.29
2	BILL BRADLEY, PRINCETON (1963, 1964, 1965) (303-9)	33.67
3	OSCAR ROBERTSON, CINCINNATI (1958, 1959, 1960) (324-10)	32.40
4	JERRY WEST, WEST VIRGINIA (1958, 1959, 1960) (275-9)	30.56
5	BOB PETTIT, LOUISIANA ST. (1953, 1954) (183-6)	30.50

FIELD GOALS

Most field goals in a game

1	AUSTIN CARR, NOTRE DAME (vs. OHIO, 1970)	25
2	AUSTIN CARR, NOTRE DAME (vs. KENTUCKY, 1970)	22
2	BILL BRADLEY, PRINCETON (vs. WICHITA STATE, 1965)	22
2	DAVID ROBINSON, NAVY (vs. MICHIGAN, 1987)	22
5	3 tied for fifth place.	21

Most field goals in a Final Four game

1	BILL WALTON, UCLA (vs. MEMPHIS STATE, 1973)	21
2	JACK GIVENS, KENTUCKY (vs. DUKE, 1978)	18
3	DON MAY, DAYTON (vs. N. CAROLINA, 1967)	16
3	LARRY BIRD, INDIANA STATE (vs. DEPAUL, 1979)	16
5	4 tied for fifth place.	15

Most field goals in a championship game

1	BILL WALTON, UCLA (vs. MEMPHIS STATE, 1973)	21
2	JACK GIVENS, KENTUCKY (vs. DUKE, 1978)	18
3	LEW ALCINDOR, UCLA (vs. PURDUE, 1969)	15
3	LEW ALCINDOR, UCLA (vs. N. CAROLINA, 1968)	15
5	4 tied for fifth place.	13

Most field goals in a tournament

1	GLEN RICE, MICHIGAN (1989)	75
2	ELVIN HAYES, HOUSTON (1968)	70
3	DANNY MANNING, KANSAS (1988)	69
4	AUSTIN CARR, NOTRE DAME (1970)	68
5	JOHNNY DAWKINS, DUKE (1986)	66

Most field goals in a career

1	ELVIN HAYES, HOUSTON (1966, 1967, 1968)	152
2	DANNY MANNING, KANSAS (1985, 1986, 1987, 1988)	140
3	GLEN RICE, MICHIGAN (1986, 1987, 1988, 1989)	128
4	OSCAR ROBERTSON, CINCINNATI (1958, 1959, 1960)	117
4	AUSTIN CARR, NOTRE DAME (1969, 1970, 1971)	117

Most field goal attempts in a game

1	AUSTIN CARR, NOTRE DAME (vs. OHIO, 1970)	44
2	DWIGHT LAMAR, S'WESTERN LA. (vs. LOUISVILLE, 1972)	42
2	LENNIE ROSENBLUTH, N. CAROLINA (vs. MICHIGAN ST., 1957)	42
4	AUSTIN CARR, NOTRE DAME (vs. HOUSTON, 1971)	40
5	AUSTIN CARR, NOTRE DAME (vs. IOWA, 1970)	39

Most field goal attempts in a Final Four game

1	LENNIE ROSENBLUTH, N. CAROLINA (vs. MICHIGAN ST., 1957)	42
2	RICK MOUNT, PURDUE (vs. UCLA, 1969)	36
2	ERNIE DIGREGORIO, PROVIDENCE (vs. MEMPHIS STATE, 1973)	36
4	JIM DUNN, WESTERN KY. (vs. VILLANOVA, 1971)	33
5	ELGIN BAYLOR, SEATTLE (vs. KENTUCKY, 1958)	32

Most field goal attempts in a championship game

1	RICK MOUNT, PURDUE (vs. UCLA, 1969)	36
2	ELGIN BAYLOR, SEATTLE (vs. KENTUCKY, 1958)	32
3	KEVIN GREVEY, KENTUCKY (vs. UCLA, 1975)	30
4	ARTIS GILMORE, JACKSONVILLE (vs. UCLA, 1970)	29
4	BILL SPIVEY, KENTUCKY (vs. KANSAS STATE, 1951)	29

Most field goal attempts in a tournament

1	JIM MCDANIELS, WESTERN KY. (1971)	138
2	ELVIN HAYES, HOUSTON (1968)	137
3	GLEN RICE, MICHIGAN (1989)	131
4	DANNY MANNING, KANSAS (1988)	125
5	LENNIE ROSENBLUTH, N. CAROLINA (1957)	124

Most field goal attempts in a career

1	ELVIN HAYES, HOUSTON (1966, 1967, 1968)	310
2	DANNY MANNING, KANSAS (1985, 1986, 1987, 1988)	257
3	OSCAR ROBERTSON, CINCINNATI (1958, 1959, 1960)	235
4	AUSTIN CARR, NOTRE DAME (1969, 1970, 1971)	225
5	GLEN RICE, MICHIGAN (1986, 1987, 1988, 1989)	224

Highest field goal percentage in a game (minimum 10 attempts)

1	KENNY WALKER, KENTUCKY (vs. WESTERN KY., 1986) (11-11)	1.000
2	MARVIN BARNES, PROVIDENCE (vs. PENNSYLVANIA, 1973) (10-10)	1.000
3	BILL WALTON, UCLA (vs. MEMPHIS STATE, 1973) (21-22)	.955
4	DENNY HOLMAN, SMU (vs. CINCINNATI, 1966) (12-13)	.923
5	PEMBROOK BURROWS, JACKSONVILLE (vs. IOWA, 1970) (11-12)	.917

Highest field goal percentage in a Final Four game (minimum 10 attempts)

1	BILL WALTON, UCLA (vs. MEMPHIS STATE, 1973) (21-22)	.955
2	JERRY LUCAS, OHIO STATE (vs. ST. JOSEPH'S, 1961) (10-11)	.909
2	BILLY THOMPSON, LOUISVILLE (vs. LOUISIANA ST., 1986) (10-11)	.909
4	EARVIN JOHNSON, MICHIGAN ST. (vs. PENNSYLVANIA, 1979) (9-10)	.900
5	BILL WALTON, UCLA (vs. LOUISVILLE, 1972) (11-13)	.846

Highest field goal percentage in a championship game (minimum 10 attempts)

1	BILL WALTON, UCLA (vs. MEMPHIS STATE, 1973) (21-22)	.955
2	OLIVER DARDEN, MICHIGAN (vs. UCLA, 1965) (8-10)	.800
3	JAMES WORTHY, N. CAROLINA (vs. GEORGETOWN, 1982) (13-17)	.765
4	LEW ALCINDOR, UCLA (vs. PURDUE, 1969) (15-20)	.750
5	ANDERSON HUNT, UNLV (vs. DUKE, 1990) (12-16)	.750

Highest field goal percentage in a tournament (min. 25 attempts)

1	CHRISTIAN LAETTNER, DUKE (1989) (26-33)	.788
2	HEYWARD DOTSON, COLUMBIA (1968) (22-28)	.786
3	KEVIN GAMBLE, IOWA (1987) (32-41)	.781
4	MARK DRESSLER, MISSOURI (1980) (27-35)	.771
5	ROBERT WERDANN, ST. JOHN'S (1991) (20-26)	.769

Highest field goal percentage in a career (min. 50 attempts)

1	STEVE SCHALL, ARKANSAS (1977, 1978, 1979) (41-58)	.707
2	JOHN SHUMATE, NOTRE DAME (1974) (35-50)	.700
3	BILL WALTON, UCLA (1972, 1973, 1974) (109-159)	.686
4	STEPHEN THOMPSON, SYRACUSE (1987, 1988, 1989, 1990) (78-114)	.684
5	ROBERT MILLER, CINCINNATI (1975, 1976, 1977) (34-50)	.680

3-PT. FIELD GOALS

Most 3-pt. field goals in a game

1	JEFF FRYER, LOYOLA MYMT. (vs. MICHIGAN, 1990)	11
2	FREDDIE BANKS, UNLV (vs. INDIANA, 1987)	10
3	GARDE THOMPSON, MICHIGAN (vs. NAVY, 1987)	9
4	4 tied for fourth place.	8

Most 3-pt. field goals in a Final Four game

1	FREDDIE BANKS, UNLV (vs. INDIANA, 1987)	10
2	3 tied for second place.	7

Most 3-pt. field goals in a championship game

1	DAVE SIEGER, OKLAHOMA (vs. KANSAS, 1988)	7
1	STEVE ALFORD, INDIANA (vs. SYRACUSE, 1987)	7
3	GLEN RICE, MICHIGAN (vs. SETON HALL, 1989)	5

Most 3-pt. field goals in a tournament

1	GLEN RICE, MICHIGAN (1989)	27
2	FREDDIE BANKS, UNLV (1987)	26
3	DENNIS SCOTT, GEORGIA TECH (1990)	24
4	JEFF FRYER, LOYOLA MYMT. (1990)	23
5	2 tied for fifth place.	21

Most 3-pt. field goals in a career

1	JEFF FRYER, LOYOLA MYMT. (1988, 1989, 1990)	38
2	GLEN RICE, MICHIGAN (1986, 1987, 1988, 1989)	35
3	ANDERSON HUNT, UNLV (1989, 1990, 1991)	34
4	DENNIS SCOTT, GEORGIA TECH (1988, 1989, 1990)	33
5	2 tied for fifth place.	26

Most 3-pt. field goal attempts in a game

1	JEFF FRYER, LOYOLA MYMT. (vs. ARKANSAS, 1989)	22
2	CHRIS WALKER, VILLANOVA (vs. LOUISIANA ST., 1990)	20
3	GERALD PADDIO, UNLV (vs. IOWA, 1988)	19
3	FREDDIE BANKS, UNLV (vs. INDIANA, 1987)	19
5	2 tied for fifth place.	16

Most 3-pt. field goal attempts in a Final Four game.

1	FREDDIE BANKS, UNLV (vs. INDIANA, 1987)	19
2	DENNIS SCOTT, GEORGIA TECH (vs. UNLV, 1990)	14
3	DAVE SIEGER, OKLAHOMA (vs. KANSAS, 1988)	13

Most 3-pt. field goal attempts in a championship game

1	DAVE SIEGER, OKLAHOMA (vs. KANSAS, 1988)	13
2	JOHN MORTON, SETON HALL (vs. MICHIGAN, 1989)	12
2	GLEN RICE, MICHIGAN (vs. SETON HALL, 1989)	12

Most 3-pt. field goal attempts in a tournament

1	FREDDIE BANKS, UNLV (1987)	65
2	JEFF FRYER, LOYOLA MYMT. (1990)	55
3	DENNIS SCOTT, GEORGIA TECH (1990)	54
4	GLEN RICE, MICHIGAN (1989)	49
5	DAVE SIEGER, OKLAHOMA (1988)	46

Most 3-pt. field goal attempts in a career

1	ANDERSON HUNT, UNLV (1989, 1990, 1991)	103
2	JEFF FRYER, LOYOLA MYMT. (1988, 1989, 1990)	97
3	DENNIS SCOTT, GEORGIA TECH (1988, 1989, 1990)	76
4	PHIL HENDERSON, DUKE (1988, 1989, 1990)	65
4	FREDDIE BANKS, UNLV (1984, 1985, 1986, 1987)	65

Highest 3-pt. field goal percentage in a game (minimum 6 attempts)

1	MIGJEN BAKALLI, N.C. STATE (vs. SOUTHERN MISS., 1991) (6-6)	1.000
1	MIKE BUCK, MIDDLE TENN. ST (vs. FLORIDA STATE, 1989) (6-6)	1.000
3	WILLIAM SCOTT, KANSAS STATE (vs. DEPAUL, 1988) (7-8)	.875
4	8 tied for fourth place.	.833

Highest 3-pt. field goal percentage in a Final Four game (min. 6 attempts)

1	STEVE ALFORD, INDIANA (vs. SYRACUSE, 1987) (7-10)	.700
2	ANDERSON HUNT, UNLV (vs. DUKE, 1990) (4-7)	.571
3	ANDERSON HUNT, UNLV (vs. GEORGIA TECH, 1990) (5-9)	.556

Highest 3-pt. field goal percentage in a championship game (min. 6 attempts)

1	STEVE ALFORD, INDIANA (vs. SYRACUSE, 1987) (7-10)	.700
2	ANDERSON HUNT, UNLV (vs. DUKE, 1990) (4-7)	.571
3	DAVE SIEGER, OKLAHOMA (vs. KANSAS, 1988) (7-13)	.538

Highest 3-pt. field goal percentage in a tournament (minimum 12 attempts)

1	GARDE THOMPSON, MICHIGAN (1987) (12-16)	.750
2	CHRIS FLEMING, RICHMOND (1991) (9-13)	.692
3	BILLY DONOVAN, PROVIDENCE (1987) (14-22)	.636
4	WILLIAM SCOTT, KANSAS STATE (1988) (21-34)	.618
4	STEVE ALFORD, INDIANA (1987) (21-34)	.618

Highest 3-pt. field goal percentage in a career (minimum 20 attempts)

1 WILLIAM SCOTT, KANSAS STATE
(1987, 1988) (26-40) .650
2 BILLY DONOVAN, PROVIDENCE
(1987) (14-22) .636
3 STEVE ALFORD, INDIANA
(1984, 1986, 1987) (21-34) .618
4 JASON BUCHANAN, ST. JOHN'S
(1990, 1991) (12-20) .600
5 TIM MCCALISTER, OKLAHOMA
(1984, 1985, 1986, 1987) (13-22) .591

FREE THROWS

Most free throws in a game

1 BOB CARNEY, BRADLEY
(vs. COLORADO, 1954) 23
1 TRAVIS MAYS, TEXAS (vs. GEORGIA, 1990) 23
3 DAVID ROBINSON, NAVY
(vs. SYRACUSE, 1986) 21
4 TOM HAMMONDS, GEORGIA TECH
(vs. IOWA STATE, 1988) 19
5 3 tied for fifth place. 18

Most free throws in a Final Four game

1 GAIL GOODRICH, UCLA
(vs. MICHIGAN, 1965) 18
2 JERRY WEST, WEST VIRGINIA
(vs. LOUISVILLE, 1959) 14
3 DON SCHLUNDT, INDIANA
(vs. LOUISIANA ST., 1953) 13
4 4 tied for fourth place. 12

Most free throws in a championship game

1 GAIL GOODRICH, UCLA
(vs. MICHIGAN, 1965) 18
2 CHRISTIAN LAETTNER, DUKE
(vs. KANSAS, 1991) 12
2 VERNON HATTON, KENTUCKY
(vs. SEATTLE, 1958) 12
4 4 tied for fourth place. 11

Most free throws in a tournament

1 BOB CARNEY, BRADLEY (1954) 55
2 DON SCHLUNDT, INDIANA (1953) 49
2 CHRISTIAN LAETTNER, DUKE (1991) 49
4 BILL BRADLEY, PRINCETON (1965) 47
5 JERRY WEST, WEST VIRGINIA (1959) 46

Most free throws in a career

1 CHRISTIAN LAETTNER, DUKE
(1989, 1990, 1991) 112
2 OSCAR ROBERTSON, CINCINNATI
(1958, 1959, 1960) 90
3 BILL BRADLEY, PRINCETON
(1963, 1964, 1965) 87
4 ED PINCKNEY, VILLANOVA
(1982, 1983, 1984, 1985) 83
5 JERRY WEST, WEST VIRGINIA
(1958, 1959, 1960) 81

Most free throw attempts in a game

1 TRAVIS MAYS, TEXAS (vs. GEORGIA, 1990) 27
1 DAVID ROBINSON, NAVY
(vs. SYRACUSE, 1986) 27
3 BOB CARNEY, BRADLEY
(vs. COLORADO, 1954) 26
4 DONNIE GAUNCE, MOREHEAD STATE
(vs. IOWA, 1956) 24
5 3 tied for fifth place. 22

Most free throw attempts in a Final Four game

1 JERRY WEST, WEST VIRGINIA
(vs. LOUISVILLE, 1959) 20
1 GAIL GOODRICH, UCLA
(vs. MICHIGAN, 1965) 20
3 BOB PETTIT, LOUISIANA ST.
(vs. INDIANA, 1953) 18
4 3 tied for fourth place. 17

Most free throw attempts in a championship game

1 GAIL GOODRICH, UCLA
(vs. MICHIGAN, 1965) 20
2 BOB CARNEY, BRADLEY
(vs. LA SALLE, 1954) 17
3 WILT CHAMBERLAIN, KANSAS
(vs. N. CAROLINA, 1957) 16
4 VERNON HATTON, KENTUCKY
(vs. SEATTLE, 1958) 15
5 ED WARNER, CCNY (vs. BRADLEY, 1950) 14

Most free throw attempts in a tournament

1 JERRY WEST, WEST VIRGINIA (1959) 71
2 BOB CARNEY, BRADLEY (1954) 70
3 DON SCHLUNDT, INDIANA (1953) 63
4 LEN CHAPPELL, WAKE FOREST (1962) 62
4 WILT CHAMBERLAIN, KANSAS (1957) 62

Most free throw attempts in a career
1	CHRISTIAN LAETTNER, DUKE (1989, 1990, 1991)	132
2	LEW ALCINDOR, UCLA (1967, 1968, 1969)	119
3	OSCAR ROBERTSON, CINCINNATI (1958, 1959, 1960)	116
4	ED PINCKNEY, VILLANOVA (1982, 1983, 1984, 1985)	115
5	JERRY WEST, WEST VIRGINIA (1958, 1959, 1960)	114

Highest free throw percentage in a game (minimum 10 attempts)
1	BILL BRADLEY, PRINCETON (vs. ST. JOSEPH'S, 1963) (16-16)	1.000
1	FENNIS DEMBO, WYOMING (vs. UCLA, 1987) (16-16)	1.000
3	MIKE MALOY, DAVIDSON (vs. ST. JOHN'S, 1969) (13-13)	1.000
3	BILL BRADLEY, PRINCETON (vs. PROVIDENCE, 1965) (13-13)	1.000
3	AL GOODEN, BALL ST. (vs. BOSTON COLLEGE, 1981) (13-13)	1.000

Highest free throw percentage in a Final Four game (minimum 10 attempts)
1	CHRISTIAN LAETTNER, DUKE (vs. KANSAS, 1991) (12-12)	1.000
1	JIM SPANARKEL, DUKE (vs. NOTRE DAME, 1978) (12-12)	1.000
3	RON KING, FLORIDA STATE (vs. N. CAROLINA, 1972) (10-10)	1.000
4	3 tied for fourth place.	.917

Highest free throw percentage in a championship game (minimum 10 attempts)
1	CHRISTIAN LAETTNER, DUKE (vs. KANSAS, 1991) (12-12)	1.000
2	DICK ESTERGARD, BRADLEY (vs. LA SALLE, 1954) (11-12)	.917
3	GAIL GOODRICH, UCLA (vs. MICHIGAN, 1965) (18-20)	.900
4	JOHN MORTON, SETON HALL (vs. MICHIGAN, 1989) (9-10)	.900
4	RUMEAL ROBINSON, MICHIGAN (vs. SETON HALL, 1989) (9-10)	.900

Highest free throw percentage in a tournament (min. 20 att.)
1	RICHARD MORGAN, VIRGINIA (1989) (23-23)	1.000
2	SIDNEY MONCRIEF, ARKANSAS (1979) (26-27)	.963
3	JEFF LAMP, VIRGINIA (1981) (25-26)	.962
4	DWAYNE MCCLAIN, VILLANOVA (1985) (24-25)	.960
5	STEVE ALFORD, INDIANA (1984) (21-22)	.955

Highest free throw percentage in a career (min. 30 attempts)
1	OLIVER ROBINSON, ALA.-BIRMINGHAM (1981, 1982) (29-30)	.967
2	LABRADFORD SMITH, LOUISVILLE (1988, 1989, 1990) (45-47)	.957
3	PHIL FORD, N. CAROLINA (1975, 1976, 1977, 1978) (37-39)	.949
4	JOHN MCCARTHY, NOTRE DAME (1957, 1958) (46-49)	.939
5	WAYNE ESTES, UTAH STATE (1963, 1964) (29-31)	.936

REBOUNDING

Most rebounds in a game
1	FRED COHEN, TEMPLE (vs. U. CONN., 1956)	34
2	NATE THURMOND, BOWLING GREEN (vs. MISSISSIPPI ST., 1963)	31
3	JERRY LUCAS, OHIO STATE (vs. KENTUCKY, 1961)	30
4	THOMAS KIMBALL, U. CONN. (vs. ST. JOSEPH'S, 1965)	29
5	ELVIN HAYES, HOUSTON (vs. PACIFIC, 1966)	28

Most rebounds in a Final Four game
1	BILL RUSSELL, SAN FRANCISCO (vs. IOWA, 1956)	27
2	ELVIN HAYES, HOUSTON (vs. UCLA, 1967)	24
3	BILL RUSSELL, SAN FRANCISCO (vs. SMU, 1956)	23
4	4 tied for fourth place.	22

Most rebounds in a championship game
1	BILL RUSSELL, SAN FRANCISCO (vs. IOWA, 1956)	27
2	BILL SPIVEY, KENTUCKY (vs. KANSAS STATE, 1951)	21
3	BILL WALTON, UCLA (vs. FLORIDA STATE, 1972)	20
3	LEW ALCINDOR, UCLA (vs. PURDUE, 1969)	20
5	3 tied for fifth place.	19

Most rebounds in a tournament
1	ELVIN HAYES, HOUSTON (1968)	97
2	ARTIS GILMORE, JACKSONVILLE (1970)	93
3	SAM LACEY, NEW MEXICO ST. (1970)	90
4	CLARENCE GLOVER, WESTERN KY. (1971)	89
5	LEN CHAPPELL, WAKE FOREST (1962)	86

Most rebounds in a career
1	ELVIN HAYES, HOUSTON (1966, 1967, 1968)	226
2	LEW ALCINDOR, UCLA (1967, 1968, 1969)	201
3	JERRY LUCAS, OHIO STATE (1960, 1961, 1962)	197
4	BILL WALTON, UCLA (1972, 1973, 1974)	176
5	PAUL HOGUE, CINCINNATI (1960, 1961, 1962)	160

Most rebounds per game in a tournament (minimum 3 games)

1 NATE THURMOND, BOWLING GREEN
(1963) (70-3) — 23.33
2 HOWARD JOLLIFF, OHIO (1960) (65-3) — 21.67
3 ELVIN HAYES, HOUSTON (1968) (97-5) — 19.40
4 JOHN GREEN, MICHIGAN ST.
(1957) (77-4) — 19.25
5 PAUL SILAS, CREIGHTON (1964) (57-3) — 19.00

Most rebounds per game in a career (minimum 6 games)

1 JOHN GREEN, MICHIGAN ST.
(1957, 1959) (118-6) — 19.67
2 ARTIS GILMORE, JACKSONVILLE
(1970, 1971) (115-6) — 19.17
3 ELVIN HAYES, HOUSTON
(1966, 1967, 1968) (226-13) — 17.39
4 LEN CHAPPELL, WAKE FOREST
(1961, 1962) (137-8) — 17.13
5 LEW ALCINDOR, UCLA
(1967, 1968, 1969) (201-12) — 16.75

ASSISTS

Most assists in a game

1 MARK WADE, UNLV (vs. INDIANA, 1987) — 18
2 JACKIE MEEHAN, NOTRE DAME
(vs. OHIO, 1970) — 17
3 BERT BERTELKAMP, TENNESSEE
(vs. MARYLAND, 1980) — 16
4 4 tied for fourth place. — 15

Most assists in a Final Four game

1 MARK WADE, UNLV (vs. INDIANA, 1987) — 18
2 GREG LEE, UCLA
(vs. MEMPHIS STATE, 1973) — 14
2 ANDRE MCCARTER, UCLA
(vs. KENTUCKY, 1975) — 14
4 LUCIUS ALLEN, UCLA (vs. HOUSTON, 1968) — 12
4 RUMEAL ROBINSON, MICHIGAN
(vs. ILLINOIS, 1989) — 12

Most assists in a championship game

1 GREG LEE, UCLA
(vs. MEMPHIS STATE, 1973) — 14
1 ANDRE MCCARTER, UCLA
(vs. KENTUCKY, 1975) — 14
3 REX MORGAN, JACKSONVILLE
(vs. UCLA, 1970) — 11
3 RUMEAL ROBINSON, MICHIGAN
(vs. SETON HALL, 1989) — 11
5 CHRIS FORD, VILLANOVA (vs. UCLA, 1971) — 10

Most assists in a tournament

1 MARK WADE, UNLV (1987) — 61
2 RUMEAL ROBINSON, MICHIGAN (1989) — 56
3 EARVIN JOHNSON, MICHIGAN ST. (1979) — 50
4 SHERMAN DOUGLAS, SYRACUSE (1987) — 49
5 3 tied for fifth place. — 45

Most assists in a career

1 SHERMAN DOUGLAS, SYRACUSE
(1986, 1987, 1988, 1989) — 106
2 GREG ANTHONY, UNLV (1989, 1990, 1991) — 100
3 MARK WADE, UNLV (1986, 1987) — 93
3 RUMEAL ROBINSON, MICHIGAN
(1988, 1989, 1990) — 93
5 ANDRE TURNER, MEMPHIS STATE
(1983, 1984, 1985, 1986) — 87

Most assists per game in a tournament (minimum 3 games)

1 MARK WADE, UNLV (1987) (61-5) — 12.20
2 MARK WADE, UNLV (1986) (32-3) — 10.67
3 EARVIN JOHNSON, MICHIGAN ST.
(1979) (50-5) — 10.00
4 OSCAR ROBERTSON, CINCINNATI
(1959) (39-4) — 9.75
4 JOHN CROTTY, VIRGINIA (1989) (39-4) — 9.75

Most assists per game in a career (minimum 6 games)

1 MARK WADE, UNLV (1986, 1987) (93-8) — 11.63
2 EARVIN JOHNSON, MICHIGAN ST.
(1978, 1979) (76-8) — 9.50
3 JOHN CROTTY, VIRGINIA
(1989, 1990, 1991) (60-7) — 8.57
4 RUMEAL ROBINSON, MICHIGAN
(1988, 1989, 1990) (93-11) — 8.46
5 PHILIP BOND, LOUISVILLE
(1975, 1977) (49-6) — 8.17

BLOCKED SHOTS

Most blocked shots in a game

1 SHAWN BRADLEY, BRIGHAM YOUNG
(vs. VIRGINIA, 1991) — 10
2 DAVID ROBINSON, NAVY
(vs. CLEVELAND ST., 1986) — 9
3 5 tied for third place. — 8

Most blocked shots in a Final Four game

1 AKEEM OLAJUWON, HOUSTON
(vs. LOUISVILLE, 1983) — 8
2 TOM BURLESON, N.C. STATE
(vs. MARQUETTE, 1974) — 7
2 AKEEM OLAJUWON, HOUSTON
(vs. N.C. STATE, 1983) — 7

Most blocked shots in a championship game

1	TOM BURLESON, N.C. STATE (vs. MARQUETTE, 1974)	7
1	AKEEM OLAJUWON, HOUSTON (vs. N.C. STATE, 1983)	7
3	PAT EWING, GEORGETOWN (vs. HOUSTON, 1984)	4

Most blocked shots in a tournament

1	AKEEM OLAJUWON, HOUSTON (1983)	28
2	DAVID ROBINSON, NAVY (1986)	23
3	TIM PERRY, TEMPLE (1988)	20
4	ALONZO MOURNING, GEORGETOWN (1989)	19
5	AKEEM OLAJUWON, HOUSTON (1984)	18

Most blocked shots in a career

1	AKEEM OLAJUWON, HOUSTON (1982, 1983, 1984)	56
2	PAT EWING, GEORGETOWN (1982, 1983, 1984, 1985)	37
3	TIM PERRY, TEMPLE (1985, 1986, 1987, 1988)	34
4	RONY SEIKALY, SYRACUSE (1985, 1986, 1987, 1988)	33
5	PERVIS ELLISON, LOUISVILLE (1986, 1988, 1989)	32

STEALS

Most steals in a game

1	GARY GARLAND, DEPAUL (vs. USC, 1979)	10
2	ALVIN ROBERTSON, ARKANSAS (vs. PURDUE, 1983)	8
2	ALVIN ROBERTSON, ARKANSAS (vs. VIRGINIA, 1984)	8
4	9 tied for fourth place.	7

Most steals in a Final Four game

1	MOOKIE BLAYLOCK, OKLAHOMA (vs. KANSAS, 1988)	7
1	TOMMY AMAKER, DUKE (vs. LOUISVILLE, 1986)	7
3	2 tied for third place.	6

Most steals in a championship game

1	MOOKIE BLAYLOCK, OKLAHOMA (vs. KANSAS, 1988)	7
1	TOMMY AMAKER, DUKE (vs. LOUISVILLE, 1986)	7
3	ROD FOSTER, UCLA (vs. LOUISVILLE, 1980)	6

Most steals in a tournament

1	MOOKIE BLAYLOCK, OKLAHOMA (1988)	23
2	GARY GARLAND, DEPAUL (1979)	22
3	MARK WADE, UNLV (1987)	18
3	LEE MAYBERRY, ARKANSAS (1990)	18
5	KENDALL GILL, ILLINOIS (1989)	17

Most steals in a career

1	MOOKIE BLAYLOCK, OKLAHOMA (1988, 1989)	32
2	STACEY AUGMON, UNLV (1988, 1989, 1990, 1991)	30
2	GREG ANTHONY, UNLV (1989, 1990, 1991)	30
4	CLYDE DREXLER, HOUSTON (1981, 1982, 1983)	29
5	RICKY GRACE, OKLAHOMA (1987, 1988)	28

TURNOVERS

Most turnovers in a game

1	MAURICE WILLIAMSON, LOUISIANA ST. (vs. VILLANOVA, 1990)	13
2	ED FOGLER, N. CAROLINA (vs. DRAKE, 1969)	11
2	LARRY BIRD, INDIANA STATE (vs. DEPAUL, 1979)	11
2	GARY GARLAND, DEPAUL (vs. UCLA, 1979)	11
5	5 tied for fifth place.	10

Most turnovers in a Final Four game

1	LARRY BIRD, INDIANA STATE (vs. DEPAUL, 1979)	11
2	HERBERT CROOK, LOUISVILLE (vs. DUKE, 1986)	9
3	REX MORGAN, JACKSONVILLE (vs. UCLA, 1970)	8
3	AKEEM OLAJUWON, HOUSTON (vs. VIRGINIA, 1984)	8
3	SIDNEY LOWE, N.C. STATE (vs. GEORGIA, 1983)	8

Most turnovers in a championship game

1	HERBERT CROOK, LOUISVILLE (vs. DUKE, 1986)	9
2	REX MORGAN, JACKSONVILLE (vs. UCLA, 1970)	8
3	5 tied for third place.	7

Most turnovers in a tournament

1	RUMEAL ROBINSON, MICHIGAN (1989)	26
1	BOBBY HURLEY, DUKE (1990)	26
1	LARRY BIRD, INDIANA STATE (1979)	26
4	SHERMAN DOUGLAS, SYRACUSE (1987)	25
5	4 tied for fifth place.	24

Most turnovers in a career

1	SHERMAN DOUGLAS, SYRACUSE (1986, 1987, 1988, 1989)	54
2	DANNY MANNING, KANSAS (1985, 1986, 1987, 1988)	51
3	KENNY SMITH, N. CAROLINA (1984, 1985, 1986, 1987)	45
4	OTHELL WILSON, VIRGINIA (1981, 1982, 1983, 1984)	44
4	MILT WAGNER, LOUISVILLE (1982, 1983, 1984, 1986)	44

TEAM PERFORMANCES

SCORING

Most points in a game—one team

1	LOYOLA MYMT. (vs. MICHIGAN, 1990)	149
2	UNLV (vs. LOYOLA MYMT., 1990)	131
3	ST. JOSEPH'S (vs. UTAH, 1961)	127
4	OKLAHOMA (vs. LOUISIANA TECH, 1989)	124
5	N. CAROLINA (vs. LOYOLA MYMT., 1988)	123

Most points in a game—both teams

1	LOYOLA MYMT. (vs. MICHIGAN, 1990)	264
2	ST. JOSEPH'S (vs. UTAH, 1961)	247
3	LOYOLA MYMT. (vs. WYOMING, 1988)	234
4	UNLV (vs. LOYOLA MYMT., 1990)	232
5	IOWA (vs. NOTRE DAME, 1970)	227

Most points in a half—one team

1	LOYOLA MYMT. (vs. MICHIGAN, 1990)	84
2	IOWA (vs. NOTRE DAME, 1970)	75
3	OKLAHOMA (vs. LOUISIANA TECH, 1989)	69
4	ARKANSAS (vs. LOYOLA MYMT., 1989)	68
5	UNLV (vs. LOYOLA MYMT., 1990)	67

Most points in a half—both teams

1	LOYOLA MYMT. (vs. MICHIGAN, 1990)	141
2	ARKANSAS (vs. LOYOLA MYMT., 1989)	121
3	LOYOLA MYMT. (vs. WYOMING, 1988)	119
3	NAVY (vs. SYRACUSE, 1986)	119
3	OKLAHOMA (vs. LOUISIANA TECH, 1989)	119

Largest winning margin in a game

1	LOYOLA-CHICAGO (vs. TENNESSEE TECH, 1963)	69
2	UCLA (vs. WYOMING, 1967)	49
2	SYRACUSE (vs. BROWN, 1986)	49
4	DUKE (vs. U. CONN., 1964)	47
4	DEPAUL (vs. EASTERN KY., 1965)	47

Largest point differential—one half

1	LOYOLA-CHICAGO (vs. TENNESSEE TECH, 1963)	41
2	DEPAUL (vs. EASTERN KY., 1965)	37
2	UCLA (vs. WYOMING, 1967)	37
4	DUKE (vs. U. CONN., 1964)	35
5	4 tied for fifth place.	33

Most points in a game by a losing team

1	UTAH (vs. ST. JOSEPH'S, 1961)	120
2	WYOMING (vs. LOYOLA MYMT., 1988)	115
2	MICHIGAN (vs. LOYOLA MYMT., 1990)	115
4	UNLV (vs. ARIZONA, 1976)	109
5	2 tied for fifth place.	106

Fewest points in a game—one team

1	N. CAROLINA (vs. PITTSBURGH, 1941)	20
2	SPRINGFIELD (vs. INDIANA, 1940)	24
3	PITTSBURGH (vs. N. CAROLINA, 1941)	26
4	KENTUCKY (vs. DARTMOUTH, 1942)	28
5	2 tied for fifth place.	29

Fewest points in a game—both teams

1	PITTSBURGH (vs. N. CAROLINA, 1941)	46
2	DUQUESNE (vs. WESTERN KY., 1940)	59
3	WISCONSIN (vs. PITTSBURGH, 1941)	66
4	INDIANA (vs. DUQUESNE, 1940)	69
5	USC (vs. COLORADO, 1940)	70

Fewest points in a half—one team

1	BROWN (vs. VILLANOVA, 1939)	7
2	PITTSBURGH (vs. N. CAROLINA, 1941)	8
2	N. CAROLINA (vs. PITTSBURGH, 1941)	8

Fewest points in a half—both teams

1	PITTSBURGH (vs. N. CAROLINA, 1941)	20
2	VILLANOVA (vs. BROWN, 1939)	24
3	DUQUESNE (vs. WESTERN KY., 1940)	26
4	BOSTON COLLEGE (vs. U. CONN., 1967)	27
5	PENN STATE (vs. ILLINOIS, 1942)	28

Most points in a Final Four game—one team

1	UCLA (vs. WICHITA STATE, 1965)	108
2	UNLV (vs. DUKE, 1990)	103
3	UCLA (vs. HOUSTON, 1968)	101
3	MICHIGAN ST. (vs. PENNSYLVANIA, 1979)	101
5	2 tied for fifth place.	98

Most points in a Final Four game—both teams

1	UCLA (vs. WICHITA STATE, 1965)	197
2	INDIANA (vs. UNLV, 1987)	190
3	MEMPHIS STATE (vs. PROVIDENCE, 1973)	183
4	KENTUCKY (vs. DUKE, 1978)	182
5	2 tied for fifth place.	181

Largest winning margin in a Final Four game

1	CINCINNATI (vs. OREGON STATE, 1963)	34
1	MICHIGAN ST. (vs. PENNSYLVANIA, 1979)	34
3	UCLA (vs. HOUSTON, 1968)	32
4	UNLV (vs. DUKE, 1990)	30
5	KENTUCKY (vs. ILLINOIS, 1949)	29

Most points in a Final Four game by a losing team

1	UNLV (vs. INDIANA, 1987)	93
2	WICHITA STATE (vs. UCLA, 1965)	89
2	WESTERN KY. (vs. VILLANOVA, 1971)	89
4	DUKE (vs. KENTUCKY, 1978)	88
5	NOTRE DAME (vs. DUKE, 1978)	86

Fewest points in a Final Four game—one team

1	KENTUCKY (vs. DARTMOUTH, 1942)	28
2	PITTSBURGH (vs. WISCONSIN, 1941)	30
2	OREGON STATE (vs. OKLAHOMA STATE, 1949)	30
2	DUQUESNE (vs. INDIANA, 1940)	30
5	IOWA STATE (vs. UTAH, 1944)	31

Fewest points in a Final Four game—both teams

1	WISCONSIN (vs. PITTSBURGH, 1941)	66
2	INDIANA (vs. DUQUESNE, 1940)	69
3	UTAH (vs. IOWA STATE, 1944)	71
4	WISCONSIN (vs. WASHINGTON ST., 1941)	73
5	DARTMOUTH (vs. KENTUCKY, 1942)	76

Most points in a championship game—one team

1	UNLV (vs. DUKE, 1990)	103
2	UCLA (vs. DUKE, 1964)	98
3	KENTUCKY (vs. DUKE, 1978)	94

Most points in a championship game—both teams

1	KENTUCKY (vs. DUKE, 1978)	182
2	UCLA (vs. DUKE, 1964)	181
3	UCLA (vs. KENTUCKY, 1975)	177

Largest winning margin in a championship game

1	UNLV (vs. DUKE, 1990)	30
2	UCLA (vs. N. CAROLINA, 1968)	23
3	UCLA (vs. MEMPHIS STATE, 1973)	21

Fewest points in a championship game—one team

1	OHIO STATE (vs. OREGON, 1939)	33
2	GEORGETOWN (vs. WYOMING, 1943)	34
2	WASHINGTON ST. (vs. WISCONSIN, 1941)	34

Fewest points in a championship game—both teams

1	WISCONSIN (vs. WASHINGTON ST., 1941)	73
2	OREGON (vs. OHIO STATE, 1939)	79
3	WYOMING (vs. GEORGETOWN, 1943)	80

Most total points in a tournament—one team

1	UNLV (1990)	571
2	OKLAHOMA (1988)	552
3	MICHIGAN (1989)	540
4	INDIANA (1987)	535
5	LOUISVILLE (1986)	513

Most points per game in a tournament (minimum 3 games)

1	LOYOLA MYMT. (1990) (423-4)	105.75
2	NOTRE DAME (1970) (317-3)	105.67
3	UNLV (1977) (505-5)	101.00
4	UCLA (1965) (400-4)	100.00
5	S'WESTERN LA. (1972) (296-3)	98.67

Largest average winning margin in a tournament (minimum 3 games)

1	UCLA (1967) (95-4)	23.75
2	LOYOLA-CHICAGO (1963) (115-5)	23.00
3	INDIANA (1981) (113-5)	22.60
4	UCLA (1968) (85-4)	21.25
5	NOTRE DAME (1974) (63-3)	21.00

Fewest points per game in a tournament (minimum 3 games)

1	WISCONSIN (1941) (126-3)	42.00
2	UTAH (1944) (127-3)	42.33
3	CALIFORNIA (1946) (130-3)	43.33
3	DARTMOUTH (1942) (130-3)	43.33
5	OKLAHOMA STATE (1949) (131-3)	43.67

Most opponents' points per game in a tournament (minimum 3 games)

1	NOTRE DAME (1970) (312-3)	104.00
2	LOYOLA MYMT. (1990) (398-4)	99.50
3	NOTRE DAME (1971) (292-3)	97.33
4	IOWA (1988) (283-3)	94.33
5	ST. BONAVENTURE (1968) (279-3)	93.00

Fewest opponents' points per game in a tournament (minimum 3 games)

1	INDIANA (1940) (96-3)	32.00
2	OKLAHOMA STATE (1946) (104-3)	34.67
3	UTAH (1944) (106-3)	35.33
4	OREGON (1939) (111-3)	37.00
5	WISCONSIN (1941) (114-3)	38.00

FIELD GOALS

Most field goals in a game—one team

1	IOWA (vs. NOTRE DAME, 1970)	52
2	UCLA (vs. DAYTON, 1974)	51
2	UNLV (vs. LOYOLA MYMT., 1990)	51
4	3 tied for fourth place.	50

Most field goal attempts in a game—one team

1	MARSHALL (vs. S'WESTERN LA., 1972)	112
2	INDIANA (vs. MIAMI OHIO), 1958)	106
3	WESTERN KY. (vs. VILLANOVA, 1971)	105
4	3 tied for fourth place.	103

Highest field goal percentage in a game—one team

1 N. CAROLINA (vs. LOYOLA MYMT., 1988)
   (49-62) .790
2 VILLANOVA (vs. GEORGETOWN, 1985)
   (22-28) .786
3 NORTHEASTERN
   (vs. VA. COMMONWEALTH, 1984) (33-44) .750
4 GEORGETOWN (vs. OREGON STATE, 1982)
   (29-39) .744
5 N.C. STATE (vs. UTEP, 1985) (30-41) .732

Fewest field goals in a game—one team

1 SPRINGFIELD (vs. INDIANA, 1940) 8
2 PITTSBURGH (vs. N. CAROLINA, 1941) 9
2 N. CAROLINA (vs. PITTSBURGH, 1941) 9
2 OKLAHOMA STATE (vs. KENTUCKY, 1949) 9
5 3 tied for fifth place. 10

Fewest field goal attempts in a game—one team

1 BOSTON COLLEGE (vs. U. CONN., 1967) 26
2 KANSAS (vs. OHIO, 1985) 28
2 VILLANOVA (vs. GEORGETOWN, 1985) 28
4 3 tied for fourth place. 29

Lowest field goal percentage in a game—one team

1 SPRINGFIELD (vs. INDIANA, 1940) (8-63) .127
2 HARVARD (vs. OHIO STATE, 1946) (10-72).139
3 CREIGHTON (vs. CINCINNATI, 1962)
   (14-72) .195
4 N.C. STATE (vs. BAYLOR, 1950) (15-77) .195
5 ARKANSAS (vs. OREGON STATE, 1949)
   (13-63) .206

Most field goals in a game—two teams

1 IOWA (vs. NOTRE DAME, 1970) 97
2 KENTUCKY (vs. AUSTIN PEAY, 1973) 96
3 ST. JOSEPH'S (vs. UTAH, 1961) 95
4 LOYOLA MYMT. (vs. MICHIGAN, 1990) 94
5 UCLA (vs. DAYTON, 1974) 91

Most field goal attempts in a game—two teams

1 ST. JOSEPH'S (vs. UTAH, 1961) 204
2 KENTUCKY (vs. AUSTIN PEAY, 1973) 196
3 IOWA (vs. NOTRE DAME, 1970) 195
4 INDIANA (vs. MIAMI (OHIO), 1958) 194
4 HOUSTON (vs. PACIFIC, 1966) 194

Highest field goal percentage in a game—two teams

1 VA. COMMONWEALTH
   (vs. NORTHEASTERN, 1984) (66-97) .681
2 WASHINGTON (vs. DUKE, 1984) (57-90) .633
3 VILLANOVA (vs. GEORGETOWN, 1985)
   (51-81) .630
4 SYRACUSE (vs. N. CAROLINA, 1975)
   (67-109) .615
5 ARKANSAS (vs. PURDUE, 1983) (58-96) .604

Fewest field goals in a game—two teams

1 PITTSBURGH (vs. N. CAROLINA, 1941) 18
2 WISCONSIN (vs. PITTSBURGH, 1941) 22
3 DUQUESNE (vs. WESTERN KY., 1940) 24
3 INDIANA (vs. DUQUESNE, 1940) 24
5 KENTUCKY (vs. OKLAHOMA STATE, 1949) 25

Fewest field goal attempts in a game—two teams

1 BOSTON COLLEGE (vs. U. CONN., 1967) 59
2 VILLANOVA (vs. PRINCETON, 1991) 66
3 GEORGETOWN (vs. WYOMING, 1982) 69
3 FRESNO STATE (vs. WEST VIRGINIA, 1982) 69
5 KANSAS (vs. OHIO, 1985) 70

Lowest field goal percentage in a game—two teams

1 OHIO STATE (vs. HARVARD, 1946)
   (27-135) .200
2 INDIANA (vs. SPRINGFIELD, 1940)
   (27-132) .205
3 N.C. STATE (vs. BAYLOR, 1950) (31-137) .226
4 INDIANA (vs. DUQUESNE, 1940) (24-103) .233
5 N. CAROLINA (vs. OHIO STATE, 1946)
   (42-180) .234

Most field goals in a Final Four game—one team

1 UCLA (vs. WICHITA STATE, 1965) 44
2 UCLA (vs. HOUSTON, 1968) 43
3 4 tied for third place. 41

Most field goal attempts in a Final Four game

1 WESTERN KY. (vs. VILLANOVA, 1971) 105
2 PURDUE (vs. UCLA, 1969) 92
3 N. CAROLINA (vs. OHIO STATE, 1946) 91
3 KENTUCKY (vs. ILLINOIS, 1951) 91
5 2 tied for fifth place. 89

Highest field goal percentage in a Final Four game

1 VILLANOVA (vs. GEORGETOWN, 1985)
   (22-28) .786
2 OHIO STATE (vs. CALIFORNIA, 1960)
   (31-46) .674
3 UCLA (vs. MEMPHIS STATE, 1973)
   (40-62) .645
4 KANSAS (vs. OKLAHOMA, 1988) (35-55) .636
5 2 tied for fifth place. .633

Fewest field goals in a Final Four game—one team

1 OKLAHOMA STATE (vs. KENTUCKY, 1949) 9
2 WISCONSIN (vs. PITTSBURGH, 1941) 10
2 KENTUCKY (vs. DARTMOUTH, 1942) 10
4 OREGON STATE
   (vs. OKLAHOMA STATE, 1949) 11
4 DUQUESNE (vs. INDIANA, 1940) 11

Fewest field goal attempts in a Final Four game

1	VILLANOVA (vs. GEORGETOWN, 1985)	28
2	VILLANOVA (vs. MEMPHIS STATE, 1985)	38
2	OKLAHOMA STATE (vs. OREGON STATE, 1949)	38
4	GEORGETOWN (vs. LOUISVILLE, 1982)	41
4	DUKE (vs. KANSAS, 1991)	41

Lowest field goal percentage in a Final Four game

1	OHIO STATE (vs. N. CAROLINA, 1946) (19-89)	.214
2	WASHINGTON ST. (vs. WISCONSIN, 1941) (14-65)	.215
3	INDIANA (vs. DUQUESNE, 1940) (13-56)	.232
4	DUQUESNE (vs. INDIANA, 1940) (11-47)	.234
5	BAYLOR (vs. KENTUCKY, 1948) (15-64)	.234

Most field goals in a Final Four game—two teams

1	UCLA (vs. WICHITA STATE, 1965)	80
2	MEMPHIS STATE (vs. PROVIDENCE, 1973)	79
3	VILLANOVA (vs. WESTERN KY., 1971)	75

Most field goal attempts in a Final Four game—two teams

1	N. CAROLINA (vs. OHIO STATE, 1946)	180
2	VILLANOVA (vs. WESTERN KY., 1971)	178
3	N. CAROLINA (vs. MICHIGAN ST., 1957)	168

Highest field goal percentage in a Final Four game—two teams

1	VILLANOVA (vs. GEORGETOWN, 1985) (51-81)	.630
2	INDIANA STATE (vs. DEPAUL, 1979) (71-122)	.582
3	GEORGETOWN (vs. HOUSTON, 1984) (65-116)	.560

Fewest field goals in a Final Four game—two teams

1	WISCONSIN (vs. PITTSBURGH, 1941)	22
2	INDIANA (vs. DUQUESNE, 1940)	24
3	KENTUCKY (vs. OKLAHOMA STATE, 1949)	25

Fewest field goal attempts in a Final Four game—two teams

1	VILLANOVA (vs. GEORGETOWN, 1985)	81
2	VILLANOVA (vs. MEMPHIS STATE, 1985)	88
3	GEORGETOWN (vs. LOUISVILLE, 1982)	89

Lowest field goal percentage in a Final Four game—two teams

1	INDIANA (vs. DUQUESNE, 1940) (24-103)	.233
2	N. CAROLINA (vs. OHIO STATE, 1946) (42-180)	.234
3	WISCONSIN (vs. WASHINGTON ST., 1941) (30-128)	.235

Most field goals in a championship game—one team

1	UNLV (vs. DUKE, 1990)	41
2	UCLA (vs. MEMPHIS STATE, 1973)	40
3	KENTUCKY (vs. DUKE, 1978)	39

Most field goal attempts in a championship game—one team

1	PURDUE (vs. UCLA, 1969)	92
2	SAN FRANCISCO (vs. IOWA, 1956)	87
3	KENTUCKY (vs. UCLA, 1975)	86
4	LOYOLA-CHICAGO (vs. CINCINNATI, 1963)	84
5	2 tied for fifth place.	83

Highest field goal percentage in a championship game—one team

1	VILLANOVA (vs. GEORGETOWN, 1985) (22-28)	.786
2	OHIO STATE (vs. CALIFORNIA, 1960) (31-46)	.674
3	UCLA (vs. MEMPHIS STATE, 1973) (40-62)	.645

Fewest field goals in a championship game—one team

1	OKLAHOMA STATE (vs. KENTUCKY, 1949)	9
2	N. CAROLINA (vs. OKLAHOMA STATE, 1946)	13
3	OHIO STATE (vs. OREGON, 1939)	14
3	GEORGETOWN (vs. WYOMING, 1943)	14
3	WASHINGTON ST. (vs. WISCONSIN, 1941)	14

Fewest field goal attempts in a championship game—one team

1	VILLANOVA (vs. GEORGETOWN, 1985)	28
2	DUKE (vs. KANSAS, 1991)	41
3	MICHIGAN ST. (vs. INDIANA STATE, 1979)	43

Lowest field goal percentage in a championship game—one team

1	WASHINGTON ST. (vs. WISCONSIN, 1941) (14-65)	.215
2	BAYLOR (vs. KENTUCKY, 1948) (15-64)	.234
3	WISCONSIN (vs. WASHINGTON ST., 1941) (16-63)	.254

Most field goals in a championship game—two teams
1	UCLA (vs. KENTUCKY, 1975)	71
2	UCLA (vs. DUKE, 1964)	68
2	KENTUCKY (vs. DUKE, 1978)	68

Most field goal attempts in a championship game—two teams
1	SAN FRANCISCO (vs. IOWA, 1956)	167
2	UCLA (vs. KENTUCKY, 1975)	164
3	SAN FRANCISCO (vs. LA SALLE, 1955)	151

Highest field goal percentage in a championship game—two teams
1	VILLANOVA (vs. GEORGETOWN, 1985) (51-81)	.630
2	GEORGETOWN (vs. HOUSTON, 1984) (65-116)	.560
3	UCLA (vs. MICHIGAN, 1965) (66-122)	.541

Fewest field goals in a championship game—two teams
1	KENTUCKY (vs. OKLAHOMA STATE, 1949)	25
2	OKLAHOMA STATE (vs. N. CAROLINA, 1946)	29
3	WISCONSIN (vs. WASHINGTON ST., 1941)	30

Fewest field goal attempts in a championship game—two teams
1	VILLANOVA (vs. GEORGETOWN, 1985)	81
2	N. CAROLINA (vs. KANSAS, 1957)	92
3	INDIANA (vs. N. CAROLINA, 1981)	95

Lowest field goal percentage in a championship game—two teams
1	WISCONSIN (vs. WASHINGTON ST., 1941) (30-128)	.235
2	KENTUCKY (vs. BAYLOR, 1948) (38-147)	.259
3	KENTUCKY (vs. KANSAS STATE, 1951) (51-149)	.342

Most field goals in a tournament
1	UNLV (1977)	218
2	UNLV (1990)	217
2	MICHIGAN (1989)	217
4	OKLAHOMA (1988)	206
5	LOUISVILLE (1986)	203

Most field goal attempts in a tournament
1	WESTERN KY. (1971)	442
2	UNLV (1977)	441
3	HOUSTON (1968)	418
4	OKLAHOMA (1988)	412
5	UNLV (1990)	410

Highest field goal percentage in a tournament (min. 3 games) (since 1963)
1	N. CAROLINA (1975) (113-187)	.604
2	MICHIGAN (1988) (96-161)	.596
3	MICHIGAN ST. (1978) (92-156)	.590
4	ALABAMA (1987) (99-169)	.586
5	ARKANSAS (1979) (83-143)	.581

Most field goals per game (minimum 3 games)
1	UNLV (1977) (218-5)	43.60
2	NOTRE DAME (1970) (130-3)	43.33
3	NOTRE DAME (1974) (128-3)	42.67
4	UCLA (1965) (162-4)	40.50
5	S'WESTERN LA. (1972) (119-3)	39.67

Lowest field goal percentage in a tournament (minimum 3 games)
1	CREIGHTON (1962) (71-235)	.302
2	N.C. STATE (1951) (74-230)	.322
3	BOWLING GREEN (1963) (73-222)	.329
4	OKLAHOMA STATE (1951) (76-228)	.334
5	N.C. STATE (1950) (73-218)	.335

Fewest field goals per game (minimum 3 games)
1	OKLAHOMA STATE (1949) (41-3)	13.67
2	WISCONSIN (1941) (43-3)	14.33
3	OREGON STATE (1949) (48-3)	16.00
4	OKLAHOMA STATE (1946) (51-3)	17.00
5	2 tied for fifth place.	17.33

Highest opponents' field goal percentage in a tournament (minimum 3 games)
1	WAKE FOREST (1977) (101-174)	.581
2	GEORGETOWN (1980) (91-159)	.572
3	VILLANOVA (1978) (105-187)	.562
4	OREGON STATE (1982) (67-121)	.554
5	ST. BONAVENTURE (1968) (112-204)	.549

Most opponents' field goals per game (minimum 3 games)
1	NOTRE DAME (1970) (131-3)	43.67
2	NOTRE DAME (1971) (120-3)	40.00
3	LOYOLA MYMT. (1990) (158-4)	39.50
4	BOSTON COLLEGE (1975) (116-3)	38.67
5	3 tied for fifth place.	38.33

Lowest opponents' field goal percentage in a tournament (minimum 3 games)
1	BAYLOR (1950) (63-227)	.278
2	TEMPLE (1958) (79-268)	.295
3	ST. JOHN'S (1951) (63-202)	.312
4	KENTUCKY (1951) (96-305)	.315
5	N.C. STATE (1950) (77-242)	.318

Fewest opponents' field goals per game (minimum 3 games)

1	INDIANA (1940) (34-3)	11.33
2	OKLAHOMA STATE (1946) (38-3)	12.67
3	OKLAHOMA STATE (1949) (42-3)	14.00
3	OREGON (1939) (42-3)	14.00
5	OKLAHOMA STATE (1945) (46-3)	15.33

FREE THROWS

Most free throws in a game—one team

1	UTAH (vs. SANTA CLARA, 1960)	41
1	NAVY (vs. SYRACUSE, 1986)	41
3	SEATTLE (vs. UTAH, 1955)	39
3	UTEP (vs. TULSA, 1985)	39
5	2 tied for fifth place.	38

Most free throw attempts in a game—one team

1	UTEP (vs. TULSA, 1985)	55
2	MOREHEAD STATE (vs. PITTSBURGH, 1957)	54
3	MOREHEAD STATE (vs. IOWA, 1956)	53
4	4 tied for fourth place.	52

Highest free throw percentage in a game—one team

1	FORDHAM (vs. S. CAROLINA, 1971) (22-22)	1.000
2	DAYTON (vs. VILLANOVA, 1985) (17-17)	1.000
2	VILLANOVA (vs. KENTUCKY, 1988) (17-17)	1.000
4	VILLANOVA (vs. N. CAROLINA, 1991) (12-12)	1.000
4	TCU (vs. NOTRE DAME, 1987) (12-12)	1.000

Fewest free throws in a game—one team

1	ILLINOIS (vs. ALABAMA, 1986)	0
1	FURMAN (vs. BOSTON COLLEGE, 1975)	0
3	4 tied for third place.	1

Fewest free throw attempts in a game—one team

1	ILLINOIS (vs. ALABAMA, 1986)	0
2	JACKSONVILLE (vs. VIRGINIA TECH, 1979)	1
3	5 tied for third place.	2

Lowest free throw percentage in a game—one team (min. 5 attempts)

1	UNLV (vs. N. CAROLINA, 1977) (1-5)	.200
2	UCLA (vs. ARKANSAS, 1978) (2-8)	.250
2	N. CAROLINA (vs. PITTSBURGH, 1941) (2-8)	.250
4	LOUISIANA ST. (vs. DEPAUL, 1987) (2-7)	.286
5	WASHINGTON ST. (vs. CREIGHTON, 1941) (4-14)	.286

Most free throws in a game—two teams

1	PITTSBURGH (vs. MOREHEAD STATE, 1957)	69
2	OKLAHOMA CITY (vs. KANSAS STATE, 1956)	68
2	IOWA (vs. MOREHEAD STATE, 1956)	68
4	BRADLEY (vs. COLORADO, 1954)	64
5	3 tied for fifth place.	63

Most free throw attempts in a game—two teams

1	IOWA (vs. MOREHEAD STATE, 1956)	105
2	PITTSBURGH (vs. MOREHEAD STATE, 1957)	97
3	UCLA (vs. SEATTLE, 1956)	92
3	OKLAHOMA CITY (vs. KANSAS STATE, 1956)	92
5	MANHATTAN (vs. WEST VIRGINIA, 1958)	91

Fewest free throws in a game—two teams

1	ILLINOIS STATE (vs. ALABAMA, 1984)	3
2	ALABAMA (vs. ILLINOIS, 1986)	6
3	GEORGETOWN (vs. SMU, 1984)	7
3	VA. COMMONWEALTH (vs. NORTHEASTERN, 1984)	7
3	UCLA (vs. SAN FRANCISCO, 1973)	7

Fewest free throw attempts in a game—two teams

1	ILLINOIS STATE (vs. ALABAMA, 1984)	4
2	ALABAMA (vs. ILLINOIS, 1986)	9
2	UCLA (vs. SAN FRANCISCO, 1973)	9
4	ST. JOSEPH'S (vs. DEPAUL, 1981)	12
5	3 tied for fifth place.	14

Most free throws in a Final Four game—one team

1	JACKSONVILLE (vs. ST. BONAVENTURE, 1970)	37
2	BRADLEY (vs. LA SALLE, 1954)	32
2	DUKE (vs. NOTRE DAME, 1978)	32

Most free throw attempts in a Final Four game—one team

1	JACKSONVILLE (vs. ST. BONAVENTURE, 1970)	45
2	BRADLEY (vs. LA SALLE, 1954)	44
2	UCLA (vs. DRAKE, 1969)	44
2	LOUISIANA ST. (vs. INDIANA, 1953)	44
2	SYRACUSE (vs. PROVIDENCE, 1987)	44

Highest free throw percentage in a Final Four game—one team

1	OHIO STATE (vs. CINCINNATI, 1961) (15-16)	.938
2	IOWA (vs. LOUISVILLE, 1980) (14-15)	.933
3	MARQUETTE (vs. N. CAROLINA, 1977) (23-25)	.920

Fewest free throws in a Final Four game—one team
1	UNLV (vs. N. CAROLINA, 1977)	1
2	DEPAUL (vs. INDIANA STATE, 1979)	2
2	DARTMOUTH (vs. UTAH, 1944)	2

Fewest free throw attempts in a Final Four game—one team
1	DEPAUL (vs. INDIANA STATE, 1979)	5
1	UNLV (vs. N. CAROLINA, 1977)	5
1	DARTMOUTH (vs. UTAH, 1944)	5

Lowest free throw percentage in a Final Four game—one team
1	UNLV (vs. N. CAROLINA, 1977) (1-5)	.200
2	OKLAHOMA STATE (vs. NYU, 1945) (5-15)	.333
3	TEMPLE (vs. IOWA, 1956) (6-17)	.353

Most free throws in a Final Four game—two teams
1	INDIANA (vs. LOUISIANA ST., 1953)	53
2	JACKSONVILLE (vs. ST. BONAVENTURE, 1970)	52
3	LA SALLE (vs. BRADLEY, 1954)	50

Most free throw attempts in a Final Four game—two teams
1	INDIANA (vs. LOUISIANA ST., 1953)	86
2	KENTUCKY (vs. SYRACUSE, 1975)	70
3	LA SALLE (vs. BRADLEY, 1954)	68
3	FLORIDA STATE (vs. N. CAROLINA, 1972)	68
3	UCLA (vs. DRAKE, 1969)	68

Fewest free throws in a Final Four game—two teams
1	INDIANA STATE (vs. DEPAUL, 1979)	8
2	STANFORD (vs. DARTMOUTH, 1942)	9
3	2 tied for third place.	11

Fewest free throw attempts in a Final Four game—two teams
1	INDIANA STATE (vs. DEPAUL, 1979)	14
1	STANFORD (vs. DARTMOUTH, 1942)	14
3	HOUSTON (vs. VIRGINIA, 1984)	19
3	UCLA (vs. INDIANA, 1973)	19
3	UTAH (vs. DARTMOUTH, 1944)	19

Most free throws in a championship game—one team
1	BRADLEY (vs. LA SALLE, 1954)	32
2	DUKE (vs. KENTUCKY, 1978)	30
3	2 tied for third place.	28

Most free throw attempts in a championship game—one team
1	BRADLEY (vs. LA SALLE, 1954)	44
2	UCLA (vs. PURDUE, 1969)	41
3	KENTUCKY (vs. SEATTLE, 1958)	36

Highest free throw percentage in a championship game—one team
1	OHIO STATE (vs. CINCINNATI, 1961) (15-16)	.938
2	MARQUETTE (vs. N. CAROLINA, 1977) (23-25)	.920
3	DUKE (vs. LOUISVILLE, 1986) (19-21)	.905

Fewest free throws in a championship game—one team
1	DARTMOUTH (vs. UTAH, 1944)	2
2	DARTMOUTH (vs. STANFORD, 1942)	4
2	KANSAS (vs. DUKE, 1991)	4

Fewest free throw attempts in a championship game—one team
1	DARTMOUTH (vs. UTAH, 1944)	5
2	DARTMOUTH (vs. STANFORD, 1942)	6
3	4 tied for third place.	8

Lowest free throw percentage in a championship game—one team
1	OKLAHOMA STATE (vs. NYU, 1945) (5-15)	.333
2	DARTMOUTH (vs. UTAH, 1944) (2-5)	.400
3	GEORGETOWN (vs. WYOMING, 1943) (6-14)	.429

Most free throws in a championship game—two teams
1	LA SALLE (vs. BRADLEY, 1954)	50
2	3 tied for second place.	46

Most free throw attempts in a championship game—two teams
1	LA SALLE (vs. BRADLEY, 1954)	68
2	KENTUCKY (vs. SEATTLE, 1958)	66
3	UCLA (vs. PURDUE, 1969)	65

Fewest free throws in a championship game—two teams
1	STANFORD (vs. DARTMOUTH, 1942)	9
2	UTAH (vs. DARTMOUTH, 1944)	12
3	WISCONSIN (vs. WASHINGTON ST., 1941)	13

Fewest free throw attempts in a championship game—two teams
1	STANFORD (vs. DARTMOUTH, 1942)	14
2	UTAH (vs. DARTMOUTH, 1944)	19
3	WISCONSIN (vs. WASHINGTON ST., 1941)	22

Most free throws in a tournament

1	BRADLEY (1954)	146
2	UCLA (1980)	136
2	DUKE (1990)	136
4	SMU (1956)	130
5	WEST VIRGINIA (1959)	129

Most free throw attempts in a tournament

1	BRADLEY (1954)	194
2	WEST VIRGINIA (1959)	192
3	DUKE (1990)	183
4	PURDUE (1980)	178
5	SYRACUSE (1987)	175

Highest free throw percentage in a tournament (min. 3 games)

1	ST. JOHN'S (1969) (47-54)	.870
2	NOTRE DAME (1987) (47-55)	.855
3	OKLAHOMA STATE (1958) (69-81)	.852
4	ALABAMA (1987) (50-59)	.848
5	TEMPLE (1988) (76-90)	.845

Most free throws per game (minimum 3 games)

1	MOREHEAD STATE (1956) (91-3)	30.33
2	BRADLEY (1954) (146-5)	29.20
3	UTAH (1960) (85-3)	28.33
4	ALA.-BIRMINGHAM (1981) (84-3)	28.00
5	SEATTLE (1964) (83-3)	27.67

Lowest free throw percentage in a tournament (minimum 3 games)

1	DARTMOUTH (1944) (11-25)	.440
2	WASHINGTON ST. (1941) (22-45)	.489
3	CALIFORNIA (1946) (24-46)	.522
4	WYOMING (1943) (23-44)	.523
5	TEMPLE (1958) (49-93)	.527

Fewest free throws per game (minimum 3 games)

1	DARTMOUTH (1944) (11-3)	3.67
2	MARQUETTE (1976) (17-3)	5.67
3	DARTMOUTH (1942) (20-3)	6.67
4	WASHINGTON ST. (1941) (22-3)	7.33
5	3 tied for fifth place.	7.67

Most opponents' free throws per game (minimum 3 games)

1	PITTSBURGH (1957) (99-3)	33.00
2	OKLAHOMA CITY (1956) (88-3)	29.33
3	CANISIUS (1955) (86-3)	28.67
4	BRADLEY (1955) (81-3)	27.00
5	LOUISIANA ST. (1953) (103-4)	25.75

Fewest opponents' free throws per game (minimum 3 games)

1	UTAH (1944) (12-3)	4.00
2	ARIZONA (1989) (18-3)	6.00
2	KANSAS (1940) (18-3)	6.00
2	WISCONSIN (1941) (18-3)	6.00
5	4 tied for fifth place.	6.67

3-PT. FIELD GOALS (Since 1987)

Most 3-pt. field goals in a game—one team

1	LOYOLA MYMT. (vs. MICHIGAN, 1990)	21
2	LOYOLA MYMT. (vs. UNLV, 1990)	17
3	PROVIDENCE (vs. ALABAMA, 1987)	14
4	4 tied for fourth place.	13

Most 3-pt. field goal attempts in a game—one team

1	LOYOLA MYMT. (vs. UNLV, 1990)	41
2	LOYOLA MYMT. (vs. MICHIGAN, 1990)	40
3	LOYOLA MYMT. (vs. N. CAROLINA, 1988)	39
3	LOYOLA MYMT. (vs. ARKANSAS, 1989)	39
5	2 tied for fifth place.	35

Highest 3-pt. field goal percentage in a game—one team (min. 10 attempts)

1	ALABAMA (vs. N.C. A&T, 1987) (9-11)	.818
2	KANSAS STATE (vs. PURDUE, 1988) (8-10)	.800
3	KANSAS STATE (vs. DEPAUL, 1988) (10-13)	.769
4	DUKE (vs. INDIANA, 1987) (8-11)	.727
4	ALABAMA (vs. COLORADO STATE, 1990) (8-11)	.727

Most 3-pt. field goals in a game—two teams

1	LOYOLA MYMT. (vs. MICHIGAN, 1990)	25
2	UNLV (vs. LOYOLA MYMT., 1990)	24
3	ARIZONA (vs. ST. FRANCIS-PA., 1991)	21
3	PROVIDENCE (vs. ALABAMA, 1987)	21
5	2 tied for fifth place.	20

Most 3-pt. field goal attempts in a game—two teams

1	UNLV (vs. LOYOLA MYMT., 1990)	59
2	LA SALLE (vs. SOUTHERN MISS., 1990)	56
3	LOYOLA MYMT. (vs. MICHIGAN, 1990)	53
4	N. CAROLINA (vs. LOYOLA MYMT., 1988)	48
4	ARKANSAS (vs. LOYOLA MYMT., 1989)	48

Highest 3-pt. field goal percentage in a game—two teams (min. 15 attempts)
1 SYRACUSE (vs. GA. SOUTHERN, 1987) (11-16) .688
1 KANSAS STATE (vs. GEORGIA, 1987) (11-16) .688
3 KANSAS STATE (vs. PURDUE, 1988) (17-26) .654
4 GEORGETOWN (vs. NOTRE DAME, 1989) (9-15) .600
5 UCLA (vs. CENTRAL MICH., 1987) (12-21) .571

Most 3-pt. field goals in a Final Four game—one team
1 UNLV (vs. INDIANA, 1987) 13
2 OKLAHOMA (vs. KANSAS, 1988) 10
2 UNLV (vs. GEORGIA TECH, 1990) 10

Most 3-pt. field goal attempts in a Final Four Game—one team
1 UNLV (vs. INDIANA, 1987) 35
2 OKLAHOMA (vs. KANSAS, 1988) 24
3 2 tied for third place. 23

Highest 3-pt. field goal pct. in a Final Four game—one team (min. 10 att.)
1 UNLV (vs. GEORGIA TECH, 1990) (10-15) .667
2 INDIANA (vs. SYRACUSE, 1987) (7-11) .636
3 DUKE (vs. KANSAS, 1991) (6-10) .600

Most 3-pt. field goals in a Final Four game—two teams
1 UNLV (vs. GEORGIA TECH, 1990) 18
2 INDIANA (vs. UNLV, 1987) 15
3 KANSAS (vs. OKLAHOMA, 1988) 14

Most 3-pt. field goal attempts in a Final Four game—two teams
1 INDIANA (vs. UNLV, 1987) 39
1 MICHIGAN (vs. SETON HALL, 1989) 39
3 OKLAHOMA (vs. ARIZONA, 1988) 37

Highest 3-pt. field goal pct. in a Final Four game—two teams (min. 15 att.)
1 INDIANA (vs. SYRACUSE, 1987) (11-21) .524
2 UNLV (vs. GEORGIA TECH, 1990) (18-36) .500
3 KANSAS (vs. OKLAHOMA, 1988) (14-30) .467

Most 3-pt. field goals in a championship game—one team
1 OKLAHOMA (vs. KANSAS, 1988) 10
2 UNLV (vs. DUKE, 1990) 8
3 KANSAS (vs. DUKE, 1991) 7
3 INDIANA (vs. SYRACUSE, 1987) 7
5 SETON HALL (vs. MICHIGAN, 1989) 7

Most 3-pt. field goal attempts in a championship game—one team
1 OKLAHOMA (vs. KANSAS, 1988) 24
2 SETON HALL (vs. MICHIGAN, 1989) 23
3 KANSAS (vs. DUKE, 1991) 18

Highest 3-pt. field goal pct. in a championship game—one team (min. 10 att.)
1 INDIANA (vs. SYRACUSE, 1987) (7-11) .636
2 DUKE (vs. KANSAS, 1991) (6-10) .600
3 UNLV (vs. DUKE, 1990) (8-14) .571

Most 3-pt. field goals in a tournament
1 LOYOLA MYMT. (1990) 56
2 PROVIDENCE (1987) 45
3 UNLV (1987) 43
3 MICHIGAN (1989) 43
5 OKLAHOMA (1988) 41

Most 3-pt. field goal attempts in a tournament
1 LOYOLA MYMT. (1990) 137
2 UNLV (1987) 132
3 OKLAHOMA (1988) 105
4 UNLV (1990) 102
5 GEORGIA TECH (1990) 98

Highest 3-pt. field goal percentage in a tournament (min. 20 attempts)
1 INDIANA (1989) (14-23) .609
2 ST. JOHN'S (1991) (16-27) .593
3 WIS.-GREEN BAY (1991) (11-20) .550
3 UC SANTA BARB. (1988) (11-20) .550
5 EASTERN MICH. (1988) (12-22) .545

Most 3-pt. field goals per game in a tournament (minimum 3 games)
1 LOYOLA MYMT. (1990) (56-4) 14.00
2 PROVIDENCE (1987) (45-5) 9.00
3 UNLV (1987) (43-5) 8.60
4 KANSAS STATE (1988) (33-4) 8.25
5 GEORGIA TECH (1990) (39-5) 7.80

REBOUNDING

Most rebounds in a game—one team
1 NOTRE DAME (vs. TENNESSEE TECH, 1958) 83
2 TEMPLE (vs. U. CONN., 1956) 76
3 UCLA (vs. SEATTLE, 1956) 72
3 HOUSTON (vs. N. CAROLINA, 1967) 72
5 HOUSTON (vs. TCU, 1968) 67

Largest rebound differential in a game
1 NOTRE DAME (vs. TENNESSEE TECH, 1958) 44
2 ST. JOHN'S (vs. U. CONN., 1951) 35
3 TEMPLE (vs. U. CONN., 1956) 30
4 UCLA (vs. WEBER ST., 1972) 29
4 CINCINNATI (vs. TEXAS TECH, 1961) 29

Fewest rebounds in a game—one team
1	PRINCETON (vs. VILLANOVA, 1991)	9
2	U. CONN. (vs. BOSTON COLLEGE, 1967)	11
3	WEST VIRGINIA (vs. FRESNO STATE, 1982)	12
3	FRESNO STATE (vs. GEORGETOWN, 1982)	12
5	2 tied for fifth place.	13

Most rebounds in a game—two teams
1	UCLA (vs. SEATTLE, 1956)	128
2	S'WESTERN LA. (vs. MARSHALL, 1972)	126
3	HOUSTON (vs. PACIFIC, 1966)	124
4	3 tied for fourth place.	122

Fewest rebounds in a game—two teams
1	BOSTON COLLEGE (vs. U. CONN., 1967)	24
2	FRESNO STATE (vs. WEST VIRGINIA, 1982)	28
3	NORTHEASTERN (vs. FRESNO STATE, 1981)	30
4	VILLANOVA (vs. GEORGETOWN, 1985)	31
5	MEMPHIS STATE (vs. WAKE FOREST, 1982)	33

Most rebounds in a Final Four game—one team
1	WESTERN KY. (vs. VILLANOVA, 1971)	61
2	SAN FRANCISCO (vs. IOWA, 1956)	60
3	MICHIGAN ST. (vs. N. CAROLINA, 1957)	58

Largest rebound differential in a Final Four game
1	UCLA (vs. WICHITA STATE, 1965)	21
1	SYRACUSE (vs. PROVIDENCE, 1987)	21
3	2 tied for third place.	20

Fewest rebounds in a Final Four game—one team
1	VILLANOVA (vs. GEORGETOWN, 1985)	14
2	OKLAHOMA STATE (vs. KANSAS STATE, 1951)	15
3	GEORGETOWN (vs. VILLANOVA, 1985)	17

Most rebounds in a Final Four game—two teams
1	VILLANOVA (vs. WESTERN KY., 1971)	111
2	SAN FRANCISCO (vs. IOWA, 1956)	108
3	N. CAROLINA (vs. MICHIGAN ST., 1957)	107

Fewest rebounds in a Final Four game—two teams
1	VILLANOVA (vs. GEORGETOWN, 1985)	31
2	KANSAS STATE (vs. OKLAHOMA STATE, 1951)	43
3	N. CAROLINA (vs. GEORGETOWN, 1982)	48

Most rebounds in a championship game—one team
1	SAN FRANCISCO (vs. IOWA, 1956)	60
2	UCLA (vs. PURDUE, 1969)	56
3	2 tied for third place.	50

Largest rebound differential in a championship game
1	UCLA (vs. MEMPHIS STATE, 1973)	19
2	KENTUCKY (vs. KANSAS STATE, 1951)	15
2	LOUISVILLE (vs. DUKE, 1986)	15

Fewest rebounds in a championship game—one team
1	VILLANOVA (vs. GEORGETOWN, 1985)	14
2	GEORGETOWN (vs. VILLANOVA, 1985)	17
3	MEMPHIS STATE (vs. UCLA, 1973)	19

Most rebounds in a championship game—two teams
1	SAN FRANCISCO (vs. IOWA, 1956)	108
2	UCLA (vs. PURDUE, 1969)	99
3	UCLA (vs. KENTUCKY, 1975)	95

Fewest rebounds in a championship game—two teams
1	VILLANOVA (vs. GEORGETOWN, 1985)	31
2	N. CAROLINA (vs. GEORGETOWN, 1982)	48
3	CINCINNATI (vs. OHIO STATE, 1961)	54
3	MARQUETTE (vs. N. CAROLINA, 1977)	54
3	UCLA (vs. MICHIGAN, 1965)	54

Most total rebounds in a tournament
1	HOUSTON (1968)	265
2	WESTERN KY. (1971)	260
3	UNLV (1990)	251
4	NEW MEXICO ST. (1970)	243
5	2 tied for fifth place.	241

Most rebounds per game in a tournament (minimum 3 games)
1	NOTRE DAME (1958) (174-3)	58.00
2	MICHIGAN ST. (1957) (222-4)	55.50
3	S'WESTERN LA. (1972) (165-3)	55.00
4	IOWA (1956) (214-4)	53.50
5	HOUSTON (1968) (265-5)	53.00

Fewest rebounds in a tournament (minimum 3 games)
1	DUKE (1980)	63
2	KENTUCKY (1983)	66
3	GEORGETOWN (1980)	68
4	3 tied for fourth place.	70

Fewest rebounds per game in a tournament (minimum 3 games)
1	DUKE (1980) (63-3)	21.00
2	KENTUCKY (1983) (66-3)	22.00
3	N. CAROLINA (1982) (112-5)	22.40
4	GEORGETOWN (1980) (68-3)	22.67
5	3 tied for fifth place.	23.33

Fewest opponents' rebounds per game in a tournament (minimum 3 games)

1	GEORGETOWN (1982) (96-5)	19.20
2	GEORGETOWN (1985) (124-6)	20.67
3	MARQUETTE (1971) (65-3)	21.67
3	OREGON STATE (1982) (65-3)	21.67
5	N. CAROLINA (1982) (111-5)	22.20

Largest average rebound differential in a tournament (minimum 3 games)

1	MARQUETTE (1971) (52-3)	17.33
2	CINCINNATI (1960) (61-4)	15.25
3	UCLA (1972) (59-4)	14.75
4	CLEMSON (1990) (44-3)	14.67
5	CINCINNATI (1961) (57-4)	14.25

ASSISTS

Most assists in a game—one team

1	N. CAROLINA (vs. LOYOLA MYMT., 1988)	36
2	UNLV (vs. LOYOLA MYMT., 1990)	35
3	LOYOLA MYMT. (vs. MICHIGAN, 1990)	33
4	ARKANSAS (vs. GEORGIA STATE, 1991)	32
4	LOUISVILLE (vs. SYRACUSE, 1975)	32

Most assists in a game—two teams

1	LOUISVILLE (vs. SYRACUSE, 1975)	59
2	UNLV (vs. LOYOLA MYMT., 1990)	58
3	MICHIGAN (vs. FLORIDA, 1988)	55
4	LOYOLA MYMT. (vs. MICHIGAN, 1990)	54
5	2 tied for fifth place.	53

Most assists in a Final Four game—one team

1	UCLA (vs. HOUSTON, 1968)	26
1	UCLA (vs. MEMPHIS STATE, 1973)	26
1	LOUISVILLE (vs. LOUISIANA ST., 1986)	26

Most assists in a Final Four game—two teams

1	KENTUCKY (vs. SYRACUSE, 1975)	41
2	KENTUCKY (vs. ILLINOIS, 1951)	40
3	5 tied for third place.	39

Most assists in a championship game—one team

1	UCLA (vs. MEMPHIS STATE, 1973)	26
2	UNLV (vs. DUKE, 1990)	24
3	UCLA (vs. KENTUCKY, 1975)	23

Most assists in a championship game—two teams

1	UCLA (vs. KENTUCKY, 1975)	39
1	GEORGETOWN (vs. HOUSTON, 1984)	39
3	UCLA (vs. VILLANOVA, 1971)	38

Most assists in a tournament

1	UNLV (1990)	140
2	OKLAHOMA (1988)	136
3	MICHIGAN (1989)	125
4	LOUISVILLE (1986)	120
5	KANSAS (1988)	115

Most assists per game in a tournament (minimum 3 games)

1	PURDUE (1988) (72-3)	24.00
2	N. CAROLINA (1989) (71-3)	23.67
3	UNLV (1990) (140-6)	23.33
4	OKLAHOMA (1988) (136-6)	22.67
5	LOUISVILLE (1988) (68-3)	22.67

BLOCKED SHOTS

Most blocked shots in a game—one team

1	BRIGHAM YOUNG (vs. VIRGINIA, 1991)	13
1	HOUSTON (vs. VILLANOVA, 1983)	13
1	LOUISVILLE (vs. ILLINOIS, 1989)	13
4	CLEMSON (vs. ST. MARY'S, 1989)	12
5	5 tied for fifth place.	11

Most blocked shots in a Final Four game—one team

1	HOUSTON (vs. LOUISVILLE, 1983)	10
2	KANSAS (vs. DUKE, 1988)	9
3	2 tied for third place.	8

Most blocked shots in a championship game—one team

1	N.C. STATE (vs. MARQUETTE, 1974)	8
1	HOUSTON (vs. N.C. STATE, 1983)	8
3	UCLA (vs. KENTUCKY, 1975)	7
3	SYRACUSE (vs. INDIANA, 1987)	7
3	LOUISVILLE (vs. DUKE, 1986)	7

Most blocked shots in a tournament

1	HOUSTON (1983)	43
2	UNLV (1990)	33
3	UNLV (1991)	32
4	SYRACUSE (1987)	30
5	SETON HALL (1989)	29

Most blocked shots per game in a tournament (minimum 3 games)

1	HOUSTON (1983) (43-5)	8.60
2	LOUISVILLE (1989) (25-3)	8.33
3	S. CAROLINA (1973) (23-3)	7.67
4	MEMPHIS STATE (1984) (20-3)	6.67
5	UNLV (1991) (32-5)	6.40

STEALS

Most steals in a game—one team

1	OREGON STATE (vs. MIDDLE TENN. ST, 1975)	19
1	PROVIDENCE (vs. AUSTIN PEAY, 1987)	19
1	U. CONN. (vs. BOSTON UNIV., 1990)	19
4	3 tied for fourth place.	17

Most steals in a Final Four game—one team

1	UNLV (vs. DUKE, 1990)	16
2	OKLAHOMA (vs. KANSAS, 1988)	13
2	DUKE (vs. LOUISVILLE, 1986)	13

Most steals in a championship game—one team

1	UNLV (vs. DUKE, 1990)	16
2	OKLAHOMA (vs. KANSAS, 1988)	13
2	DUKE (vs. LOUISVILLE, 1986)	13

Most steals in a tournament

1	OKLAHOMA (1988)	72
2	PENNSYLVANIA (1979)	64
3	ARKANSAS (1990)	57
4	DUKE (1991)	55
5	UNLV (1990)	54

Most steals per game in a tournament (minimum 3 games)

1	LOYOLA MYMT. (1990) (51-4)	12.75
2	OKLAHOMA (1988) (72-6)	12.00
3	U. CONN. (1990) (48-4)	12.00
4	ARKANSAS (1990) (57-5)	11.40
5	MICHIGAN (1977) (34-3)	11.33

PERSONAL FOULS

Most personal fouls in a game—one team

1	DAYTON (vs. ILLINOIS, 1952)	41
2	KANSAS (vs. NOTRE DAME, 1975)	39
3	UCLA (vs. SEATTLE, 1956)	36
3	N. CAROLINA (vs. TEXAS A&M, 1980)	36
5	5 tied for fifth place.	35

Most personal fouls in a Final Four game—one team

1	ST. JOHN'S (vs. KANSAS, 1952)	35
2	PROVIDENCE (vs. SYRACUSE, 1987)	33
3	ST. BONAVENTURE (vs. JACKSONVILLE, 1970)	32
3	BRADLEY (vs. CCNY, 1950)	32
5	2 tied for fifth place.	31

Most personal fouls in a championship game—one team

1	ST. JOHN'S (vs. KANSAS, 1952)	35
2	BRADLEY (vs. CCNY, 1950)	32
3	PURDUE (vs. UCLA, 1969)	30

Most personal fouls in a tournament

1	PENNSYLVANIA (1979)	150
2	PROVIDENCE (1987)	135
3	KENTUCKY (1975)	128
4	MICHIGAN (1989)	124
5	UNLV (1977)	123

Most personal fouls per game in a tournament (minimum 3 games)

1	PROVIDENCE (1987) (135-5)	27.00
2	OKLAHOMA STATE (1951) (108-4)	27.00
3	PITTSBURGH (1957) (79-3)	26.33
4	ST. JOHN'S (1952) (105-4)	26.25
5	KENTUCKY (1975) (128-5)	25.60

TURNOVERS

Most turnovers in a game—one team

1	N. CAROLINA (vs. DRAKE, 1969)	36
2	JACKSONVILLE (vs. WESTERN KY., 1971)	33
2	LOUISVILLE (vs. SYRACUSE, 1975)	33
4	GEORGIA STATE (vs. ARKANSAS, 1991)	32
4	SAN FRANCISCO (vs. UNLV, 1977)	32

Fewest turnovers in a game—one team

1	ST. JOHN'S (vs. WICHITA STATE, 1987)	2
2	UNLV (vs. DEPAUL, 1989)	3
2	CINCINNATI (vs. OHIO STATE, 1961)	3
2	LOYOLA-CHICAGO (vs. CINCINNATI, 1963)	3
5	11 tied for fifth place.	4

Most turnovers in a game—two teams

1	DRAKE (vs. N. CAROLINA, 1969)	59
2	OREGON STATE (vs. MIDDLE TENN. ST., 1975)	55
3	ARKANSAS (vs. GEORGIA STATE, 1991)	54
4	FLORIDA STATE (vs. N. CAROLINA, 1972)	53
5	2 tied for fifth place.	52

Fewest turnovers in a game—two teams

1	NEW MEXICO ST. (vs. WEBER ST., 1968)	10
2	GEORGIA TECH (vs. LOUISIANA ST., 1990)	11
2	ST. JOHN'S (vs. WICHITA STATE, 1987)	11
2	CINCINNATI (vs. OHIO STATE, 1961)	11
2	CALIFORNIA (vs. CINCINNATI, 1959)	11

Most turnovers in a Final Four game—one team

1	FLORIDA STATE (vs. N. CAROLINA, 1972)	27
2	N. CAROLINA (vs. FLORIDA STATE, 1972)	26
2	N. CAROLINA (vs. PURDUE, 1969)	26
2	UCLA (vs. N. CAROLINA, 1968)	26
2	SYRACUSE (vs. KENTUCKY, 1975)	26

Fewest turnovers in a Final Four game—one team

1	CINCINNATI (vs. OHIO STATE, 1961)	3
1	LOYOLA-CHICAGO (vs. CINCINNATI, 1963)	3
3	2 tied for third place.	4

Most turnovers in a Final Four game—two teams

1	FLORIDA STATE (vs. N. CAROLINA, 1972)	53
2	UCLA (vs. N. CAROLINA, 1968)	49
2	KENTUCKY (vs. SYRACUSE, 1975)	49

Fewest turnovers in a Final Four game—two teams

1	CINCINNATI (vs. OHIO STATE, 1961)	11
1	CALIFORNIA (vs. CINCINNATI, 1959)	11
3	SEATTLE (vs. KANSAS STATE, 1958)	14

Most turnovers in a championship game—one team

1	UCLA (vs. N. CAROLINA, 1968)	26
2	DUKE (vs. UCLA, 1964)	24
2	LOUISVILLE (vs. DUKE, 1986)	24

Fewest turnovers in a championship game—one team

1	CINCINNATI (vs. OHIO STATE, 1961)	3
1	LOYOLA-CHICAGO (vs. CINCINNATI, 1963)	3
3	PURDUE (vs. UCLA, 1969)	4

Most turnovers in a championship game—two teams

1	UCLA (vs. N. CAROLINA, 1968)	49
2	UCLA (vs. DUKE, 1964)	43
3	2 tied for third place.	41

Fewest turnovers in a championship game—two teams

1	CINCINNATI (vs. OHIO STATE, 1961)	11
2	CINCINNATI (vs. OHIO STATE, 1962)	17
3	2 tied for third place.	19

Most turnovers in a tournament

1	PENNSYLVANIA (1979)	115
2	KANSAS (1988)	111
3	SYRACUSE (1975)	110
4	UCLA (1980)	102
4	PURDUE (1980)	102

Most turnovers per game in a tournament (minimum 3 games)

1	N. CAROLINA (1969) (98-4)	24.50
2	SYRACUSE (1975) (110-5)	22.00
3	N. CAROLINA (1975) (66-3)	22.00
4	HOUSTON (1970) (63-3)	21.00
5	NOTRE DAME (1975) (61-3)	20.33

Fewest turnovers in a tournament (minimum 3 games)

1	LOYOLA-CHICAGO (1985)	22
2	NOTRE DAME (1987)	26
3	AUBURN (1985)	27
3	ILLINOIS (1984)	27
5	2 tied for fifth place.	28

Fewest turnovers per game in a tournament (minimum 3 games)

1	TEMPLE (1991) (28-4)	7.00
2	LOYOLA-CHICAGO (1985) (22-3)	7.33
3	NOTRE DAME (1987) (26-3)	8.67
4	UCLA (1962) (35-4)	8.75
5	2 tied for fifth place.	9.00

Largest turnover differential in a game

1	S. CAROLINA (vs. FORDHAM, 1971)	20
1	N. CAROLINA (vs. LOYOLA MYMT., 1988)	20
3	DAVIDSON (vs. ST. JOSEPH'S, 1966)	17
3	CALIFORNIA (vs. U. CONN., 1990)	17
5	4 tied for fifth place.	16

Largest turnover differential in a Final Four game

1	UCLA (vs. PURDUE, 1969)	15
2	INDIANA STATE (vs. DEPAUL, 1979)	14
3	2 tied for third place.	13

Largest turnover differential in a championship game

1	UCLA (vs. PURDUE, 1969)	15
2	CINCINNATI (vs. LOYOLA-CHICAGO, 1963)	13
3	LOUISVILLE (vs. DUKE, 1986)	10

Largest average turnover differential in a tournament (minimum 3 games)

1	N. CAROLINA (1969) (31-4)	7.75
2	GEORGIA TECH (1986) (23-3)	7.67
3	COLORADO STATE (1969) (18-3)	6.00
4	MICHIGAN ST. (1990) (17-3)	5.67
5	N. CAROLINA (1988) (22-4)	5.50

OVERTIMES

Most overtime periods—one game

1	CANISIUS (vs. N.C. STATE, 1956)	4
1	ST. JOSEPH'S (vs. UTAH, 1961)	4
3	4 tied for third place.	3

Most overtime periods—tournament

1	N. CAROLINA (1957)	6
2	UCLA (1974)	5
3	6 tied for third place.	4

Most overtime games—tournament

1	SYRACUSE (1975)	3
2	15 tied for second place.	2

Most points in overtime—one game/one team

1	ST. JOSEPH'S (vs. UTAH, 1961)	38
2	UTAH (vs. ST. JOSEPH'S, 1961)	31
2	UCLA (vs. DAYTON, 1974)	31
4	N.C. STATE (vs. IOWA, 1989)	27
5	2 tied for fifth place.	25

Most points in overtime—one game/two teams

1	ST. JOSEPH'S (vs. UTAH, 1961)	69
2	UCLA (vs. DAYTON, 1974)	51
3	N.C. STATE (vs. IOWA, 1989)	48
4	LOUISIANA ST. (vs. PURDUE, 1986)	43
5	N.C. STATE (vs. PEPPERDINE, 1983)	42

Most points in one overtime period—one team

1	TEXAS A&M (vs. N. CAROLINA, 1980)	25
2	WAKE FOREST (vs. ST. JOSEPH'S, 1962)	22
3	LOUISIANA ST. (vs. PURDUE, 1986)	21
4	5 tied for fourth place.	19

Most points in one overtime period—two teams

1	LOUISIANA ST. (vs. PURDUE, 1986)	35
2	WAKE FOREST (vs. ST. JOSEPH'S, 1962)	33
2	TEXAS A&M (vs. N. CAROLINA, 1980)	33
4	N.C. STATE (vs. IOWA, 1989)	32
5	UTEP (vs. ARIZONA, 1987)	31

Fewest points in one overtime period—two teams

1	TEXAS A&M (vs. N. CAROLINA, 1980)	0
1	N. CAROLINA (vs. KANSAS, 1957)	0
1	CANISIUS (vs. N.C. STATE, 1956)	0
4	USC (vs. SANTA CLARA, 1954)	1
5	TENNESSEE (vs. VA. COMMONWEALTH, 1981)	2

APPEARANCES/WINS

Most tournament appearances

1	KENTUCKY	33
2	UCLA	27
3	N. CAROLINA	25
4	NOTRE DAME	24
5	3 tied for fifth place.	21

Most consecutive tournament appearances

1	N. CAROLINA	17
2	UCLA	15
3	GEORGETOWN	13
4	MARQUETTE	10
5	4 tied for fifth place.	9

Most tournament games won

1	UCLA	64
2	KENTUCKY	55
3	N. CAROLINA	54
4	DUKE	44
5	KANSAS	42

Most consecutive tournament games won

1	UCLA	38
2	KENTUCKY	12
2	CINCINNATI	12
4	SAN FRANCISCO	11
5	2 tied for fifth place.	10

Highest tournament winning percentage (min. 25 games)

1	UCLA (64-21)	.753
2	DUKE (44-15)	.746
3	INDIANA (41-15)	.732
4	UNLV (30-11)	.732
5	CINCINNATI (20-9)	.690

Most Final Four appearances

1	UCLA	14
2	N. CAROLINA	10
3	KENTUCKY	9
3	KANSAS	9
3	DUKE	9

Most consecutive Final Four appearances

1	UCLA	10
2	CINCINNATI	5
3	DUKE	4
4	4 tied for fourth place.	3

Most championships

1	UCLA	10
2	KENTUCKY	5
2	INDIANA	5
4	7 tied for fourth place.	2

Most consecutive championships

1	UCLA	7
2	SAN FRANCISCO	2
2	OKLAHOMA STATE	2
2	KENTUCKY	2
2	CINCINNATI	2